CAPITALISM AND DEMOCRACY

CAPITALISM

═══ AND ═══

DEMOCRACY

Prosperity, Justice, and the Good Society

THOMAS A. SPRAGENS, JR.

University of Notre Dame
Notre Dame, Indiana

University of Notre Dame Press
Notre Dame, Indiana 46556
undpress.nd.edu
All Rights Reserved

Copyright © 2021 by University of Notre Dame

Published in the United States of America

Library of Congress Control Number: 2020950577

ISBN: 978-0-268-20013-8 (Hardback)
ISBN: 978-0-268-20014-5 (Paperback)
ISBN: 978-0-268-20012-1 (WebPDF)
ISBN: 978-0-268-20015-2 (Epub)

CONTENTS

PREFACE

The central purpose of this book is to provide a synthesis and overview of some of the most important arguments that bear upon the complex and perennially controversial issues regarding the proper role of the capitalist marketplace within a democratic society. I also will try to explain why these controversies are not fully resolvable in some definitive way. And I will in the final chapter offer a few of my own judgments about the questions at hand.

The intended audience for this book is not so much my academic peers, because there is not a great deal of cutting-edge scholarship here. Instead, I have written with two other audiences principally in mind. The first of these is the educated public—those among my fellow citizens who are aware of the importance of the issues in question here and would like to improve their understanding of them but who also are understandably somewhat overwhelmed by the cacophonous political disputation and the sometimes complex arguments that surround them. My other major target audience is those college-level students seeking a reasonably succinct and approachable overview of important issues they know that they will likely confront in courses they might take in the fields of economics, political science, moral philosophy, and public policy. I also had in mind the possibility that a work like this one could serve as a core text for some of these courses, where it could provide a useful framework to pair with and complement other works, both explanatory and normative, that focus more specifically on one or another of the three constituent topics here: prosperity, social justice, and democratic ideals. In fact, both my interest in writing this book and much of its content are the product of several courses I have taught on these topics over the years.

I want to acknowledge and thank a number of people who have played important roles in bringing this project to fruition. These include many of my faculty colleagues at Duke, not only in the Political Science Department but also in other departments and programs, including economics, philosophy, public policy, classics, and the Kenan Ethics Institute. They include the great and noble company of political theorists around the country—and abroad—who through their written work and conversations have informed much of what is found here. I also am indebted to the talented students, both undergraduate and graduate, who have thoughtfully engaged these issues with me in courses and conversations over the years. I owe a particular debt of gratitude to the director of the University of Notre Dame Press, Stephen Wrinn, for his encouragement of and enthusiasm for this project—and to his assistant acquisitions editor, Rachel Kindler, for ably shepherding it to completion. I am also grateful to fellow theorist Terence Ball and to a second unidentified outside reader for both their endorsement of this project and also their useful suggestions for additions and improvements to my original manuscript. Finally, my sincere thanks to staff assistant Steffani Shouse in the Department of Political Science at Duke for her skilled help in converting my words into a finished manuscript, and to Elisabeth Magnus for her able and careful copyediting.

Introduction

On June 10, 1962, in New Haven, Connecticut, President John Fitzgerald Kennedy stepped to the podium to deliver the Yale University Commencement Address. He began with a few ingratiating remarks to his audience of new graduates and their families, friends, and faculty. Alluding to the honorary degree conferred upon him, he said that he now had "the best of both worlds, a Harvard education and a Yale degree." And he added, "I am particularly glad to become a Yale man because as I think about my troubles, I find that of a lot of them come from other Yale men" such as Henry Luce and William F. Buckley.

Kennedy then turned to his chosen topic for the day, which was the relationship between business and government, between the private marketplace and public policy. He lamented that when it came to discussions about the proper way to institutionalize this relationship and the best way to manage our national economy, there was a danger of "meeting present problems with old clichés" and that "some conversations I have heard in our own country sound like old records, long-playing, left over from the middle thirties." Instead of letting ourselves be distracted by "incantations from the forgotten past," he continued, we need to realize that "the problems of fiscal and monetary policies in the sixties as opposed to the kinds of problems we faced in the thirties represent subtle challenges for which technical answers, not political answers, must be provided." "To maintain the kind of vigorous economy upon which our country depends," he said, we have to be "prepared to face technical problems without ideological preconceptions. . . . What is at stake in our economic decisions today is not some grand warfare of rival ideologies which will sweep the country with passion, but the practical management of a modern economy." Success in this management task, he concluded, involves "sophisticated and technical questions" that are "basically an administrative or executive problem in which political labels or clichés do not give us a solution."[1]

Against the backdrop of American political history, this suggestion that questions about fiscal policy and the size and shape of government had become essentially technical issues rather than political and ideological ones had to seem on its face quite remarkable. Ever since the transformation of the American economy in the decades following the Civil War from a rural and agricultural one to an urban and industrial one, the relationship between corporate capitalism and democratic purposes had served as a central fault line in American political conflict. The many major innovations in government policies and institutions that regulated the capitalist marketplace—the creation of the independent regulatory commissions, the Sherman Act, the Fair Labor Practices Act, Social Security, unemployment insurance, minimum-wage and maximum-hours legislation, and so on—had usually emerged out of fierce political battles.

Kennedy's argument that more detailed and focused debates on technical questions of economic management had superseded 1930s-style ideological battles about the New Deal did not seem entirely implausible at the time, however. For when the Republicans had recaptured the White House for the first time in twenty years in 1952, the Eisenhower administration had seemingly accepted the basic contours of the welfare state rather than trying to repeal it. Moreover, Eisenhower was willing to undertake large-scale government investments in the national economic infrastructure, since one of the most notable endeavors of his presidency was the building of our modern interstate highway system. And later, when Eisenhower's vice president, Richard Nixon, became president in 1968, his administration proposed extensions of the welfare state in some respects, including sending to Congress a measure that would have established a national guaranteed minimum income.

Moreover, Kennedy was not alone in his conviction that political and economic developments in the advanced industrial countries had rendered the standard ideological clashes of the previous decades obsolete. Only two years before his Yale speech, for example, the eminent social scientists Seymour Martin Lipset and Daniel Bell had published major books with similar arguments. The great debate between laissez-faire capitalism and Marxist-style socialism was a thing of the past, they wrote, rendered irrelevant by changes and events in countries on the opposing sides of the Cold War. On the one hand, the heady utopian aspirations and expectations voiced by communist societies had lost credibility in the face of the dreary oppression on clear display in the Soviet bloc. On the other hand, what Lipset referred to as "the democratic social revolution in the West" had pragmatically modified and constrained market economies to make them more stable, successful, and beneficial to the larger populace. As Bell wrote: "Such calamities as the Moscow trials, the Nazi-Soviet pact, the concentration camps, the suppression of the Hungarian workers, formed one chain [of events]; such social changes as the modification of capitalism, the rise of the Welfare State, another." The result, he continued, was the displacement of ideological disputation by the emergence of a "rough consensus among intellectuals on political issues: the acceptance of a Welfare State; the desirability of decentralized power; a system of mixed economy and of political pluralism."[2]

Since its articulation around 1960, however, this "end of ideology" thesis has had a bumpy ride. Only a few years down the road, a "New Left" appeared and with it somewhat new and different axes of ideological conflict. With the benefit of hindsight, however, the most consequential components of the late '60s and '70s battles can be seen as turning on manifestly unfinished business within the "democratic social revolution" cited by Lipset. For in 1960, Jim Crow racial oppression and exclusion was still alive and well in this country; and however one might define the content of a twentieth-century democratic social revolution, clearly the dismantling of profoundly anti-democratic practices such as these would have to count as an essential part of it. So with the demise of Soviet-style socialism in 1989 and with the largely successful results of the civil rights movement in this country, the perception that the technocratic management of a broadly consensual welfare state market economy was where the political action of the future resided regained credibility. On the academic side of things, the appearance of Francis Fukuyama's *The End of History and the Last Man* was a prominent example of this renewed perception of ideological decline and the ascendance of a mixed economy run by technocrats. And on the ground, Bill Clinton's and Tony Blair's depiction of the refinement and management of a "third way" political economy as the principal task of their administrations gave concrete expression to a similar sensibility.

It has come as something of a surprise to many political observers and analysts, therefore, that essentially the same spirited ideological battle that JFK derided decades ago as an outmoded and distracting relic of the 1930s has resurfaced with renewed intensity a decade into the next millennium. Voices can now be heard in the public square proclaiming that the regulatory reforms and social insurance protections of the contemporary welfare state are destructive and/or morally illegitimate. Within the social sciences, economists of the public choice school skillfully highlight cases where the displacement of market allocations by governmentally determined distributions of resources seems not only inefficient but inequitable. On the pop culture side, television propagandists like Glenn Beck have resurrected and dramatized the dubious 1950s insistence of Friedrich von Hayek that any institutionalized restrictions on the free market will put a country upon a slippery slope to Nazi-like tyranny.

How, then, are we to account for this return to front and center of the American political arena of the 1930s' set-piece confrontation between the partisans of laissez-faire economics and the minimal state on the one side and the adherents of welfare state regulatory and redistributive policies on the other? I think a number of contributory causes are at work here.

In the first place there is in any society—and certainly in those shaped by a liberal culture and institutions—a perennial antigovernment constituency. Freedom is a great good. Constraints are onerous. Governments perform their functions through the enactment and implementation of laws. Laws, even those providing important benefits, always impose constraints in the form of prohibitions or obligations upon some or all of those under the state's jurisdiction. So at some level of our being, we are all anarchists. Laissez-faire. Leave us alone indeed. We want drunks off the roads, but we chafe at highway checkpoints. We want to reach our destinations as quickly as possible, so we dislike stop signs and are loath to find highway patrol cars along our path. We may want government services, but no one loves the IRS. People who live near public land are frustrated if they are not permitted to hunt there or cut timber there or graze their livestock there. So, even if we know better, we all have a piece of us that sympathizes with the ne'er-do-well who had suffered numerous unpleasant encounters with the law and who came upon the American revolutionary leader, later to be president, John Adams on the road one evening in the fall of 1775. "Oh, Mr. Adams," he reportedly exclaimed. "What great things have you and your colleagues done for us! We can never be grateful enough to you. There are no courts of justice now in this province, and I hope there will never be another!"[3] Adams himself, conservative jurist that he was, was dismayed by this encounter. But the profound natural desire to live without constraints has deep roots in the country whose independence he helped to achieve. Indeed, I think that one thing Alexis de Tocqueville got wrong in his account of American political mores and values was his claim that Americans— as citizens of the most democratic society of his day—had as their ruling political passion a love of equality, something they valued above all other goods including liberty.[4] If anything, in my view, Tocqueville got it backwards. Yes, there is in American political culture a strong and enduring animus against political hierarchy and aristocracy. But the principal source of that animus is not so much some kind of passion for equality per se. Instead it embodies the recognition, born of painful experience and not logic alone, that the corrupt fruit of entrenched political inequality is domination by those on top. Dominion is control, and to be subject to the control of others is to be unfree. As Jefferson's memorable analogy captures this dynamic, those at the top of a political hierarchy often act as if they had been "born booted and spurred, ready to ride others by the grace of God." The ultimate source of the democratic and American animus against entrenched social and political inequality, then, is that such inequality enables the abridgement of liberty. Patrick Henry's famous oration, after all, was "Give me liberty or give me death"; and New Hampshire's state motto is "Live free or die." They didn't say, "Give me equality or give me death" or "Live equal or die."

Second, the scope of welfare state transfer payments and the role of government in the American economy have undergone significant expansion since the day that JFK addressed his audience of Yale graduates. Between the years 1960 and 2010, government-mediated transfers of resources to individuals increased by 700 percent in real dollars. In 1980, approximately 30 percent of Americans were recipients of some form of government entitlement benefits; today that number is almost 50 percent.[5] As a result, even someone who might have found a 1960s-level government safety net reasonable and acceptable could also consider today's more extensive government programs to be problematic in principle and dangerous in their practical consequences. Moreover, in that context the ballooning of the federal budget deficit in the face of curtailed revenues produced by the 2009 financial crisis and tax cuts enacted during the administration of George W. Bush on the one hand and the growth of government outlays for social services—especially for Medicare and Medicaid—on the other only sharpen this understandable worry.

People seem to forget, however, that the most discussed issue in the 2000 presidential election debates between George W. Bush and Al Gore was "what to do with the surplus in the federal budget" that the Clinton administration had been able to create. And most of today's programs were already in place at that time. So, to some very real extent, our assessment of the sustainability of transfer payments for things such as health care, old age support, and education depends upon the trade-offs that we as a society decide to make between these important public goods and consumer goods.

The debate about the sustainability of welfare programs, then, is to a considerable extent a function of competing beliefs about the proper role of the government. The former senator and leading advocate of free-market economics Richard Armey made that clear with his candid acknowledgment that "balancing the budget . . . is the attention-getting device that enables me to reduce the size of government. . . . The national concern over the deficit is larger than life. . . . So I take what I can get and focus it on the job I want. If you're anxious about the deficit, then let me use your anxiety to cut the size of the government."[6] Nonetheless, the deficit numbers today can raise concern even among those not so ideologically motivated. Few can contemplate without flinching the blithe assurance offered by Vice President Dick Cheney, when he was questioned about the prudence of proposed further tax cuts in the aftermath of the 2004 election, that "President Reagan showed us that deficits don't matter." At some point, deficits matter very much. So the debate over the proper and prudent extent of entitlement programs—along with other government disbursements—has understandably achieved renewed salience and urgency.

Third, the 2008 bursting of the housing bubble and the resulting financial crisis caused the American public a notable loss of wealth and purchasing power, at least for the time being. And, for understandable reasons, conflict over the distribution of resources tends to rise in such circumstances. Compromises are always easier to work out when at the end of the day everyone can be a bit better off and the battle is only about how much better off specific groups are going to be. In a declining economy, on the other hand, not only do concrete political battles become more intense, but ideological conflicts tend to sharpen as well. Combatants in the wars of ideology become increasingly insistent upon their "principles" and increasingly loath to concede any points to adversaries when doing so entails absorbing financial loss. The battle of ideas in straitened circumstances ceases to seem essentially academic, for wins and losses carry a price tag. And even during the more recent recovery from the recession, some sectors of the populace have lagged behind.

The past several decades have also seen a conscious and extremely well financed movement on the part of a number of wealthy devotees of free-market economics to create and fund a panoply of institutes and foundations to promote their ideas in the public forum. Prominent examples include the Cato Institute, the Heritage Foundation, the American Enterprise Institute, the Liberty Fund, the Charles Koch Foundation, and the Charles Koch Institute. The mission statement of the last of these could serve for the most part as that of all of them: its goals include "helping people who are passionate about economic freedom develop the skills necessary to advance it," "building the professional skills of tomorrow's economic freedom advocates," and "equipping individuals for careers in advancing economic freedom." Within the academic domain, it is also relevant in this context to mention the rise and influence of the "public choice" school of political analysis. Public choice theory essentially consists in deploying the standard tools and models of economics to explain and to evaluate political behavior, policies, and institutions. This form of analysis can be quite illuminating, as seminal works such as James Buchanan and Gordon Tullock's *The Calculus of Consent* amply demonstrate.[7] At the same time it is important to understand that the construction of political relationships and transactions as a subspecies of economic transactions operates from and gives force to a particular "moral point of view."[8] Specifically, it essentially assumes that the only morally legitimate political relationships (among adults) are those freely consented to by all the individual parties involved, acting in their self-interest as they understand it. To adopt this mode of political analysis not merely as an ideal-type model useful for explaining certain patterns of human behavior but also as the proper standard for normative evaluation of moral and political legitimacy, in other words, implies a commitment to a specific moral and political persuasion—to wit, to a form of libertarian individualism.

The central point here is that the efforts of the various institutes and foundations devoted to the spread of "economic freedom" and laissez-faire politics, in tandem with the importation of economizing explanatory and normative models into academic political theorizing, have given new voice and injected new vitality into what adherents like to refer to as "classical liberalism." In the process, champions of laissez-faire such as Friedrich von Hayek and Ayn Rand have achieved new prominence and a wide following.[9] These developments have therefore contributed to the return to the center of today's public discourse the clash between the public philosophies of free-market liberalism on the one hand and the reform liberalism associated with the New Deal, the welfare state, and the "democratic socialism" endorsed by the followers of Bernie Sanders on the other.

The final, and perhaps the most important, reason for the return to the forefront of today's politics of this long-standing political fault line in the economically advanced liberal democracies is that President Kennedy's claim about the fundamentally technical nature of governmental economic policy is at best only partially true. Technical issues turn upon ascertaining means-ends causal relationships, whereas ideological issues almost invariably also involve contestation over the desirability and propriety of the ends themselves. So for the thesis of Kennedy's Yale commencement address to be vindicated, it would be necessary for decisions about the government's economic role to depend exclusively upon our understanding of the causal factors of wealth creation and not also upon our conceptions of distributive justice and other possibly important features of a good democratic society. And whether we look at either the debates surrounding New Deal policies in the 1930s or our current equally passionate debates over social insurance programs such as Social Security and Medicare, over public investment in education and environmental protection, and over tax policy and levels of public spending, it seems quite clear that Kennedy's characterization of the relevant issues as technical rather than moral and ideological is more a wistful hope than an accurate depiction of what is at stake in these debates.

As a result of these several causes, the ideological battles between advocates of free markets and minimal government on the one hand and partisans of greater democratic equality and some form of the welfare state on the other, rather than withering away as relics from a bygone era, have in recent years returned in full force. Anyone who wants to make sense of contemporary American politics and policy debates, therefore, needs to have some understanding of the divergent beliefs and goals that animate the combatants in this partisan warfare.

The central purpose of this book, then, is to serve as a guide to those intrigued but also somewhat perplexed by the political sound and fury that confronts us at every turn these days; following us into our homes in the newspapers we read, the constant debates on television news, and the inescapable exhortations of political advertising. My principal purpose here is explanatory—to identify the major issues and to clarify the most important arguments of the opposing sides of the free-market-versus-welfare-state debate. Having done that, however, I will also offer toward the end some observations and judgments about these controversies. I do not pretend to have any definitive answers to the issues at hand, something I believe impossible for reasons to be discussed later. But I also believe that it is possible to narrow the geography of debate to a place where reasonable people may differ. And I hope here to make a contribution to that important task.

In the service of these goals, the topics and roles of the chapters to come are as follows. Upon examination, the sharp disagreement encountered these days between advocates of laissez-faire and champions of a more expansive welfare state turns out to be not one disagreement but three. One dispute is about political economy: Do unchecked markets maximize prosperity? Or do they often produce wasteful and economically damaging outcomes that require some form of government intervention? A second dispute takes place on the terrain of moral philosophy: Are the distributions of economic resources produced by the capitalist marketplace morally justified or at least morally acceptable? Or do they instead violate important standards of justice and fairness? The third and broadest dispute is about political philosophy: Is a society of free markets and minimal government the best kind of society possible? Or would that kind of society violate important democratic ideals and not really be all that good a place to live?

The next three chapters examine the central issues and competing arguments in these three areas. Chapter 1 first outlines the logical and evidentiary basis for the claim that a free-market system creates the best economic outcomes we can achieve. Then it will examine some of the main counterarguments that insist upon the need for government intervention and regulation to head off destructive dynamics found in unfettered markets, to create economic stability, to promote economic productivity, and to protect the economic interests of future generations. Chapter 2 looks at the several different arguments offered to defend market outcomes as morally acceptable with respect to their justice and fairness. It will then look at some of the more important lines of argument that depict market distributions as in violation of any defensible conception of social justice. In chapter 3, we will consider the claim that a free-market society with minimal government should be seen as the best society available to us—perhaps even a utopia of sorts. We will then look at why others argue that a purely free-market society would violate democratic norms, subvert the attainment of important democratic ideals and purposes, and not be a very pleasant place to live.

In the final two chapters I will try to step back from the arguments canvassed in the previous three chapters and offer my assessment of these controversies. In chapter 4 I want to explain why there can be no final and definitive judgments about whose argument is right regarding any of the three central issues: prosperity, justice, and the good society. Having there conceded the impossibility of fully settling these controversies about the proper relationship between capitalism and democracy, I will try to explain in chapter 5 why some of the answers given to that question are better and more persuasive than others. My concluding argument will be that any society that values liberal freedoms and wants to foster economic growth and efficiency needs to give a significant role to the capitalist marketplace. But I will also argue that both practical considerations and a dedication to moral and democratic values require us at times to constrain and supplement the workings of the invisible hand through the visible hand of a popularly elected government.

CHAPTER ONE

The Political Economy Debate

What Brings Prosperity?

In this chapter, we shall look at the debate about the right institutional strategy to create the best possible economic outcomes for a society. The laissez-faire or "classical liberal" claim is that leaving all members of a society entirely free to allocate their productive efforts and their economic assets as they choose will produce both the greatest efficiency in the short run and also the greatest advances in economic productivity in the long run. Reform liberals are generally willing to agree that societies wanting to be successful economically need to give a large role to the operation of the free market, but they also believe that unfettered markets are subject to dynamics that create significant problems and suboptimal results. Laissez-faire liberals therefore seek economic arrangements that give maximum play to free-market transactions and minimal scope to government. Governments, in their view, should function simply as "night watchmen"—protecting property and enforcing contracts, but not participating in or interfering with economic transactions themselves. Reform liberals argue in contrast that government constraints upon private economic transactions are at times essential. Part of the need for public regulation and resource redistribution comes about for moral and political reasons, which we shall consider in later chapters. But some of the reasons are prudential and economic, since reform liberals argue that—in the real world—markets can be dysfunctional and destructive.

The Logic of Laissez-Faire: Markets and Their Magic

The central mechanism of a free marketplace is voluntary exchange among individuals (or households). All individuals in the marketplace are entirely free to decide how to deploy their economic assets—both their labor and any capital they may own—in productive enterprise. And they are all simultaneously free to choose what goods they want to consume and what they are willing to pay for them. The fundamental claim of those who advocate leaving the marketplace entirely free is that doing so leads to the best possible economic results for any society. The free marketplace maximizes economic efficiency by directing resources to where they are most productive. Leaving markets free is also optimal in the long run, because they create incentives that maximize innovation and economic growth. What is amazing about the market system, moreover, is that it is entirely self-regulating. No external supervisory institution or authority is required to administer it, govern it, or make it work. It creates its great results automatically, as if—in Adam Smith's famous analogy—led by an "invisible hand."

Adam Smith's account of the magic of the marketplace may be the most well known. Wearing a necktie decorated with profiles of Smith in fact became something of a hallmark of free-market conservatives during the Reagan administration. But Smith was certainly not the only political economist who rhapsodized over the magic of the markets' invisible hand toward the end of the eighteenth century. To cite but one example, consider the classic statement of the dynamics and virtues of the self-regulating market provided by the eminent Enlightenment liberal theorist the Marquis de Condorcet in his *Essay on the Progress of the Human Mind*. "How with all the astonishing multifariousness of labor and production, supply and demand," he wrote, with all the frightening complexity of conflicting interests that link the survival and well-being of one individual to the general organization of societies, it makes his well-being dependent on every accident of nature and every political event, his pain and pleasure on what is happening in the remotest corner of the globe, how, with all this seeming chaos, is it that, by a universal moral law, the efforts made by each individual on his own behalf minister to the welfare of all, and that the interests of society demand that everyone should understand where his own interests lie, and should be able to follow them without hindrance? [People] therefore should be able to use their faculties, dispose of their wealth and provide for their needs in complete freedom. The common interest of any society, far from demanding that they should restrain such activity, on the contrary, forbids any interference with it.[1]

As it happens, a great deal can be said in response to Condorcet's rhetorical query "How is it that the efforts made by each individual on his own behalf minister to the welfare of all?" if we look at the motives and mechanisms through which the market's invisible hand accomplishes its magic. It may seem counterintuitive to say that if everyone selfishly pursues his or her self-interest the result will be the greatest general good; and in some areas of life, this alchemy of turning self-seeking into common good would certainly not work. I would not recommend that anyone employ this strategy in relationships with friends, lovers, or family, for example. But in the case of economic efforts and transactions—and in a context where force and fraud are effectively prohibited and contracts are enforced—the salutary dynamics of free market transactions and allocations are pretty easy to understand.

The starting point and initial impetus for the development of economic markets is what Adam Smith called "the propensity to truck, barter, and exchange one thing for another."[2] The term *propensity* is somewhat ambiguous and potentially misleading here, since propensities can be idiosyncratic or irrational, as in "He has a propensity to become agitated when questioned" or "She has a propensity to judge people by their looks." But the specific propensity cited here by Smith is found almost universally in human societies, because swapping things is a rational strategy motivated by our interest in satisfying our needs and desires. We truck and barter because we make ourselves better off in doing so. The development of markets in goods and services, therefore, can be said to happen "spontaneously" and "naturally"—so long as we are clear about what those adjectives mean in this context. *Spontaneous* does not here mean uncaused, and *naturally* does not mean without human agency: markets are a product of human actions, and those actions are caused by the interplay between human desires and the circumstances of economic production. So to say that economic exchanges occur spontaneously and naturally simply means that no preexisting institutions, overarching plan, or governing authority is involved in the process. You and a classmate open your lunch boxes. You have a candy bar and she has chocolate chip cookies. She casts a covetous eye on your candy bar, which is one of her favorites. You admire her chocolate chip cookies—your favorite dessert! Your eyes meet. "I'll swap you," one says. The deal is done. Both parties are happier—or, as economists are wont to say, their preferences are maximized under the circumstances at hand—even though no additional goods had to be created, no additional costs were incurred, and no outside party had to arrange the transaction.

The creation of a marketplace begins with straightforward exchanges of this sort, but it does not end there. The benefits of such deals lead to a number of other important institutional arrangements that serve to facilitate these exchanges and to maximize their value. To see how this process of evolutionary institutional development comes about, consider how simple exchanges of the sort seen in the lunchroom wind up creating a large-scale marketplace in agriculture. You live in a small farming village. You grow your family's food on your own land. You end up one year having more green beans than your family wants or needs, but you are short on tomatoes. You discover that your neighbor would love to have more beans and has tomatoes to spare. Voila! Just as in the lunchroom, a swap is made and both families eat better—or at least more happily.

Now it is possible that this exchange becomes an annual event. Each year you swap some of your beans for your neighbor's tomatoes. It is also possible, however, that the circumstances that led to this pattern of repeated exchanges may lead to changes in what you and your neighbor do on your farms. Suppose you realize that your land is more suited for growing beans than your neighbor's land, while his land is better for growing tomatoes. That's why you keep winding up making the exchange you do. Or possibly you are just more skilled at cultivating beans than he is, while he has a better knack for producing bumper crops of tomatoes. In that case, if you are smart, you realize that you will both be even better off if you don't simply exchange goods ex post facto but instead change what you grow. The logical thing to do is to become specialists: you grow only beans and he grows only tomatoes! When you do that, you can make your annual exchange as usual. But then you both will have additional produce left over that you can use to swap for something else you want. By specializing in your strong suit, you now not only get all the beans and tomatoes your family wants but also have the wherewithal to make some other swaps for sweet potatoes or corn, and now you're really cooking. To put this in terms of economics, what has happened here is that you and your neighbor have come to recognize the presence of a pattern of "comparative advantage" in the conditions of your agricultural production. And you have also understood the practical implications of comparative advantage: namely, the benefits of division of labor. And once again, these developments come about solely and directly from voluntary transactions between knowledgeable parties seeking to advance their own self-interest: neither altruism nor some plan implemented from above plays any part in these wealth-enhancing developments.

The core consideration of comparative advantage and the strategy of division of labor, of course, need not remain confined to the one-pair exchange between you and your neighbor. The growers of sweet potatoes and corn we mentioned above can adopt the same strategy. And as this pattern spreads, arranging the most advantageous exchanges becomes increasingly complicated and cumbersome. Everyone is faced with the daunting task of finding multiple exchange partners, each of whom has to have more than they need of some good we want and also less than they need of some good we have to sell. Moreover, every exchange requires the parties to arrive at a mutually acceptable swap ratio between their respective goods. How many sweet potatoes will neighbor A or neighbor B give me in return for a bushel of my beans? And can either of us find some alternative trading partner who will give us more or demand less in return? At this point, the sheer mechanics of exchange require an expenditure of lots of time and energy on the part of all concerned. Moreover, all parties to an exchange are left wondering whether they could have struck a better deal for themselves had they been able to search longer and more widely.

Clearly, the way to avoid these cumbersome complications would be the invention of some medium of exchange that could serve as a general and widely accepted measure of value. Such a medium would eliminate the awkward and complicated process required to effectuate a trade when the only way to do that was by quid pro quo swaps of particular goods. So once again, "naturally" and "spontaneously," such a medium of exchange comes into use by, as John Locke wrote, the "general consent of mankind." We call that medium of exchange "money."

With the introduction of money, the generalized value of a particular good can be established. I don't have to find out or say that a bushel of my beans is worth two bushels of corn, three bushels of sweet potatoes, a crate and a half of tomatoes, and on and on. Through the aggregation of the terms of all the exchanges made for beans in the whole marketplace, I and all my potential buyers or trade partners can know that a bushel of my beans is worth so many dollars, or pesos, or euros, or yen. And we all can also know the "market value" or price of all the other goods I may be interested in acquiring. Now exchanges no longer have to be quid pro quo swaps of particular goods. Any good can instead be priced by and acquired through the general medium of exchange, since the medium of exchange serves as a measure of the relative economic worth of any one good to all other goods available in the marketplace.

A final and important benefit of money is that it serves as a store of value. If all I have of value as a farmer are my crops, then all that I have is quite perishable. It is hard to be a saver in such circumstances. I cannot very well accumulate wealth in surplus crops to save for future needs. But by selling my produce on the market for money, I can convert my perishable wealth into a good that will not rot or decay. (Money can lose value through inflation or changes in exchange rates with other currencies, of course. But absent some calamity in the financial markets, this is only a partial erosion of value.)

The creation of a sizable market and the availability of money also allow prices to be established for all goods and allow these prices to change automatically in response to changing market conditions. These constant spontaneous adjustments thereby direct economic resources to where they will do the most good.[3] When people want more of a particular good than is available, the price will rise. In the short run, those who want the good the most will pay the higher price, while those who want it less will buy alternative goods. As the price rises, additional suppliers may enter the market, redirecting their productive efforts away from less desired goods. The result is a continual process of reconfiguring the supply and demand of all the goods in the marketplace toward a favorable equilibrium point—a point that maximizes consumer satisfaction and revenue within the constraints of current technologies.

These dynamics of the free marketplace, most importantly, create huge incentives for producers of goods to act in ways that benefit their customers, current and potential, and that thereby increase the economic well-being of the entire society. These incentives—the "profit motive"—represent a kind of "market discipline" that offers rewards for efficient producers and punishments for the less efficient. In the free market, all producers of any commodity are in competition with each other—and with other possible entrants into their line of work. Any business that can produce and sell a good of equal quality for a lower price than other producers (i.e., "the competition") or that can produce and sell a good of higher quality for the same price will attract more buyers and make more money. Producers who fail to "match the competition"—who cannot keep up in terms of their efficiency or quality—will suffer financially and possibly be forced to find another line of business.

The competitive pressures of the marketplace benefit the economy not only in the short run by rewarding the most efficient employment of the current means of production but also in the longer run by rewarding those who succeed in improving the techniques of production itself. If I am running a business, I can improve its efficiency in the short run in a number of ways. I can work myself or my employees harder. I can organize my workplace better, lessening the waste of time and effort by improved coordination. I can improve the skill level of my workers. All these improvements may make a difference, keeping my business competitive in the market and possibly raising my profit level. But I also may be able to make a quantum leap in my business success through technological innovation and invention. It's one thing to learn how to build a better horse carriage or to build one more economically. It's another thing altogether to figure out how to build a horseless carriage. It's a good thing to build a better radio, but much better to figure out how to transmit pictures and invent the television. Or to invent laptop computers, or iPhones, or Facebook. That's when you make big money—and by being motivated to do so, that's when you also really improve other people's lives and economic well-being.

So this in a nutshell is the logical case for free-market economics. Create a free market, establish and enforce protection of property rights, leave economic enterprises and transactions to the voluntary actions and agreements of private citizens, and good things will follow. The key to the superiority of free markets in maximizing economic productivity is their extraordinary ability (1) to transmit crucial economic information both rapidly and accurately and (2) to create incentives that draw upon the supremely powerful motivating force of personal self-interest to direct economic choices and efforts into activities beneficial to society as a whole. Markets let buyers and sellers, both current and potential, know what consumer preferences are. And they operate in a way that, as one famous phrase goes, turns "private vice into public good." (*Vice* here means "selfishness," which in the form of acquisitiveness and concupiscence—to cite language of disapproval from our moral vocabulary—is traditionally depicted as a moral failing. And public "virtue" here signifies the good of aggregate material well-being.) These beneficent results happen because of the unique capacity of markets to convey crucial information and draw upon the power of human self-interest to establish and continually adjust rational ("market-clearing") prices, to prompt productivity-enhancing cooperative endeavors through division of labor, and to enforce market discipline—that is, to reward those who are more productive and efficient while penalizing those less productive or efficient. And the supreme beauty of these benign causal mechanisms is that the system is self-regulating and requires no human superintendence. Hence no one exercises political control over other people when it comes to allocating economic resources and productive efforts. To the extent that anyone is "in charge," it is the entire body of consumers—"consumer sovereignty"—because it is the aggregate force of all the people's desires and choices that determines what will be produced, what will be sold, and at what price. Adam Smith's "invisible hand" does all the administrative work, it works for free, and it works for all of us. Such is the magic of free markets.

So these are the facts and the logic that lead to the mantra of those who champion maximizing the scope and sway of the marketplace: leave it alone! *It* refers here to the marketplace; and the admonition is directed to any person or institution with the power to interfere with it—that is, the government and, in a democracy, the sovereign public. Any interference with the dynamics and the allocations of the market lessens productivity, efficiency, and the overall wealth of the society. As Richard Armey, the Republican House majority leader from 1995 to 2003 and a libertarian-leaning former professor of economics, famously put it: when it comes to economic decisions, "Markets are wise, government is foolish."

That does not mean that laissez-faire advocates are anarchists. Except for the far-out radicals among them, they recognize that we need government institutions—and with them government power—to accomplish a few important things. But these legitimate purposes and functions are to their mind few and specific, centering on the need for security and the preservation of law and order. We need a military to defend ourselves against predators without, we need police to defend the law-abiding from thieves and thugs within, we need courts to adjudicate legal disputes and enforce contracts, and we need the institutional means to collect and disburse the funds needed to finance these limited government functions. The laissez-faire goal is minimal government—a government that essentially confines itself to the protection of life, liberty, and property. All other allocations of resources, all other economic transactions, should be left to voluntary agreements among individuals and private institutions.

This logical case for minimizing government and maximizing reliance upon free markets seems clear and, on its face, extremely compelling. But at this point the adherents of laissez-faire are faced with a conundrum that calls for some additional explanations. For the fact is that there is not now and never has been any real-world example of a political society that has organized its economy in the way that free-market fundamentalists recommend. All existing and past societies have in a number of significant respects "interfered" with the operation of economic transactions within their domains. So the questions that present themselves in the face of this apparent puzzle are: If the logic of laissez-faire is so compelling, why in the world would it be the universal practice of governments to fail to act upon it? Why, assuming that no society sets out deliberately to make itself worse off, would they all engage in some form of government control, regulation, and redistribution of market allocations? Are there no rational and legitimate grounds for these policies that seem to fly in the face of the logic and the counsel of free-market enthusiasts? The answer given by free-market theorists to these related questions is twofold. First, these deviations from what they see as good social and economic principles and policies are the product of several powerful causes that stem from human flaws and failures. Second, there are in fact a few legitimate exceptions to the rule of laissez-faire that arise from real-world circumstances inhibiting the benign consequences of free markets. But these exceptions are few and specific.

Let us look first at these exceptions that even the most ardent advocates of free markets are usually willing to recognize as legitimate. There are basically three of these. The first is what economists refer to as "externalities," or what Milton Friedman calls "neighborhood effects." The problem here is that some economic transactions create economic consequences for others who are not parties to the agreement. These consequences may be good or bad, benefits or costs. The critical thing is that the terms of the voluntary free-market agreement do not take these larger consequences into account: outsiders who suffer are not compensated under the agreement, and outsiders who benefit are not charged. If the externalities are beneficial to them, these third parties are obviously not going to protest. If the externalities are damaging, on the other hand, the parties who suffer have clearly been wronged and will both understandably and legitimately seek some form of recompense. In such cases, therefore, both economic efficiency and norms of equity and fairness can justify empowering a third-party agent such as the government to take action in order to allocate the costs and benefits appropriately where the market did not do so. An obvious and important example here is that of pollution. I contract with a company to buy paper, and the company's mill creates effluent that drains into a nearby river—thereby polluting the water supply of cities downstream. Neither the company nor I are paying these cities anything as part of our agreement. So here some agency of government is entitled to "interfere" in our private transaction that has imposed negative effects on others. Presumably, the agency in question will either issue a prohibition against the discharge of the manufacturing waste into the river or else require the polluters to provide compensation to the cities affected sufficient for them to purify their water. As a consequence of this government "interference," the cost of my paper will certainly go up. But this is a proper outcome in both economic and moral terms: the cost of the economic transaction between me and the paper company will have—by the government's "interference"—in effect become internalized, as the logic of the marketplace in fact requires. So this exception to the rule of laissez-faire does not represent an exception in the sense of a deviation from the underlying goals and standards of free-market economics. It is instead an exception to the standard means—namely laissez-faire—of attaining these goals.

A second legitimate exception to the "Butt out, government!" mandate may arise in the case of what are called "technical monopolies." A technical monopoly occurs when the conditions for the production and distribution of a particular good or service are such that it would be economically inefficient to have more than one provider. The standard significant example here is your local power company. Until the cell phone revolutionized the communications industry, your phone company was another relevant case. And before the existence of the automobile and the interstate highway system, railroads were another. The basic problem here is that if consumers have no choice among providers, there is no competition among them; and when that happens, the consumer is at the mercy of the single producer. That is why the 1892 platform of the Populist Party in this country called for the most extensive form of government "interference" with both the railroads and the phone companies: namely government ownership and provision. It said: "Transportation being a means of exchange and a public necessity, the government should own and operate the railroads in the interest of the people. The telegraph and telephone, like the post office system, being a necessity for the transmission of news, should be owned and operated by the government in the interest of the people."

There are only three ways to deal with problems created by a technical monopoly. The first is government takeover and provision such as the 1892 Populists called for. The second approach is simply to tolerate the monopoly and live with the problems created by the disproportionate power between buyers and the seller. The third is to leave the monopoly company in private hands but to subject it to some form of government supervision when it comes to pricing. In the paradigmatic instance of technical monopoly—electrical power companies—the standard practice in this country usually is the last of the three courses of action: utility commissions are created and staffed by state governments and given the authority to review and control the pricing policies of companies like Duke Power and Consolidated Edison. In a number of areas, mostly rural, electricity is provided by member cooperatives. And the Tennessee Valley Authority represents the major extant case (in the United States) in which a government corporation owns the means of production and serves as a nonprofit provider of electricity.[4] For their part, some laissez-faire advocates concede the need for government regulation in these circumstances, while others agree with Milton Friedman's conclusion that "if tolerable, private monopoly may be the least of evils."[5]

Last, free-market advocates generally recognize that children and those mentally or physically disabled cannot be left to cope with the demands and discipline of the marketplace. These, then, represent exceptions to the classical liberal opposition to government paternalism. Economic libertarians may disagree about the proper way to deal with the economic incompetency of the immature and disabled: some concede that government will have to play a major role here, while others argue that the combined efforts of nongovernment organizations such as churches and private philanthropies might be up to the job. But they all recognize that the market allocative process of "to each according to his/her marginal productivity" will not suffice in this area.

Government is needed to provide security for persons and property, then. And some government action may be justified to deal with the problems presented by market externalities, by technical monopolies, and by the dependency of children and the infirm. Beyond that, however, laissez-faire advocates insist that government involvement in the economy is damaging and in some respects morally improper. Since markets spontaneously direct economic resources to where they will produce the biggest bang for the buck—to where they will maximize the aggregate preference satisfaction of the society—collective interference with the workings of market mechanisms always will lead to the misallocation of resources. Efficiency, productivity, and the country's GDP will all be lower than they could have been and would have been had the free market simply been left alone to perform its magic.

Why then do societies and their governing authorities persist in going beyond the above three circumstantial situations in order to redistribute and redirect the allocation of resources through various forms of regulation, public enterprise, subsidies, and prohibition? On the face of things, such persistence in presumably making things worse off seems difficult to understand or justify. Such presumptively irrational intrusions can become understandable, free-market purists argue, only by taking into account what were alluded to above as "human flaws and failures," specifically the flaws and failures of ignorance, self-seeking, and moral arrogance. Consider each of these in turn, beginning with ignorance. Governments display their ignorance of economics when they think that they can make their countries wealthy by forcefully appropriating gold and precious jewels from weaker peoples instead of building their own productive capabilities. And they evince their economic ignorance, to their own detriment, when they think their economies will benefit by erecting permanent tariff walls to keep out foreign competition to their industries. In democratic societies, where the people ultimately rule, public ignorance and short-mindedness may lead them to imagine that there is such a thing as a "free lunch" or that "deficits don't matter." And when they choose decision makers who act upon these delusions of their constituents, the long-run economic consequences will not be all that pretty.

Second, there is the problem of partisan self-seeking. In principle, free-market champions are not at all averse to self-interested behavior. Markets actually run upon it. The profit motive is a good thing in their view; and they look down on those they see as misguided moralists who go around denouncing the "greed" of economic actors or institutions such as investors, banks, and corporations. So self-seeking per se is certainly not all bad in their view—and indeed can be socially beneficial when it is channeled within and constrained by the discipline of the marketplace. Self-seeking by organized subsets of the population in the political sphere, however, is another thing altogether. For by operating in this domain, what we often call "special interests" often work diligently and successfully to persuade—or bully—political authorities to carve out special benefits for them. Groups of various sorts thus are able to achieve outcomes and resources they could not earn in the marketplace—through legislative set-asides or "earmarks," government subsidies, exemptions from taxes, tariffs to exclude more efficient foreign competitors, and so on. In the lexicon of public choice theory, this is referred to as "rent-seeking," or what Friedman calls "special pleading." That's what the army of lobbyists clustered about K Street in Washington, D.C., are there for. And when the threats and blandishments of special pleaders are successful, free-market advocates argue, this not only represents a classic instance of what the civic republican tradition called "corruption" but also creates an economically disadvantageous allocation of resources for society as a whole, because of its evasion of the discipline of the marketplace.

The third principal malign source of collective interference in the marketplace that laissez-faire economists and social critics condemn is what they see as a form of moral arrogance that leads to paternalistic overriding of market allocations. The arrogance they denounce is the presumption that you know better than I do what's good for me. That inaccurate and improper belief, they claim, is the implicit assumption required to support intervening in the market to allocate resources to goods you think people should have wanted instead of what they actually want and would have purchased on their own. Examples here might include things like government authorities believing it would be better for you to read books than to play video games and therefore to impose taxes on these games to fund public libraries. Or believing you should not smoke and therefore placing a high tax on cigarettes and using those funds for purposes they favor. Or believing that classical music is more elevating than rock or rap and therefore using public funds to subsidize a symphony orchestra. Or believing that you should have access to what they think is a more objective account of current events and therefore subsidizing, however minimally, enterprises such as National Public Radio. The libertarian view is that the only legitimate meaning of the general welfare is the aggregate satisfaction of what individual people desire for themselves, not what some other people think would be good for them. It follows that the general welfare is best served by leaving it to all people to decide what is best for themselves and to be free to allocate their wealth and income as they choose. And that is what the free market accomplishes.

To summarize, then, the core claims of laissez-faire liberals (aka in current American terms "small-government conservatives") are these. First, we are all best served by economic arrangements that leave individuals as free as possible to pursue their interests as they see them through voluntary transactions. Second, legitimate exceptions to that fundamental precept do exist, but they are few—the need to deal with externalities, technical monopoly, and those unable to care for themselves—and these should be construed narrowly. Third, many significant governmental restrictions, regulations, and enterprises are driven by special pleading, rent-seeking, and paternalistic arrogance and do not qualify as legitimate exceptions to the central precept of laissez-faire. The public agenda that follows from these core beliefs may best be captured by a single-word imperative: privatize. Minimize government. Minimize the public sphere. Rigorously scrutinize claims made about externalities and technical monopoly. Fight strenuously against all attempts to commandeer economic resources by those groups engaged in special pleading, rent-seeking, and paternalistic do-gooding. Wherever possible, privatize, privatize, privatize. The market is wise, government foolish.

Free-market "conservatives" differ with each other at times when it comes to the specifics of public policy and what they might allow government to do. Milton Friedman, for example, believed that some collective action was justified to prevent outright destitution; and he therefore argued that, although what he saw as paternalistic poverty programs should be eliminated, these could be replaced by what he called a "negative income tax." This policy would in its effect constitute a minimal level of guaranteed annual income, a notion that is anathema to most economic libertarians. They are unanimous, however, in believing that many important government programs are inappropriate and should be rolled back wherever possible. And they usually are unanimous in their opposition to any new policies and programs that expand the welfare state and extend the reach of government.

A leading example of this opposition to new initiatives as I write is congressional Republicans' adamant obstruction of and continual attempts to repeal the Affordable Care Act (aka "Obamacare"). And the list of government programs that laissez-faire partisans would like to eliminate or cut back is a long one. A paradigmatic case here is the attempt to abolish the federal Old Age, Survivors, and Disability Insurance Program, better known as Social Security. When George W. Bush won his second term as president, one of his first major proposals, for example, was to dismantle Social Security over time and to leave people to rely for their retirement income upon the proceeds of private savings and investment funds. That proposal did not get very far, as it turns out that this is one "socialist" program that is popular and widely supported by the American public. Similarly, some congressional Republicans have endorsed legislative proposals to abolish the Medicare and Medicaid programs in their current form, providing in their stead block grants to the states to subsidize at their discretion private health insurance policies for their senior citizens. That government rollback reform also struggles for traction with a public that includes the somewhat confused fellow who strongly admonished his congressman to "tell the government to keep its hands off of my Medicare." Other examples include opposition to minimum-wage laws, opposition to regulation of the financial industry, opposition to governmental mortgage insurance programs, proposals to privatize public parks and other public land holdings, and proposals to replace funding of public schools with private education vouchers.

The Reform Liberal Critique of Laissez-Faire Economics: The Problems and Dangers of Free Markets

Advocates of laissez-faire economics and the minimal state often like to characterize and denounce New Deal liberals as "socialists." Right-wing bloggers, Tea Party Republicans, and others of like mind habitually say that Democrats in general are pushing "socialist" or even "Marxist" policies. During the 2008 election campaign, in fact, a television newswoman, interviewing the Democratic vice presidential candidate Joe Biden, asked him on the air, "Is Barack Obama a Marxist?" An incredulous Biden managed to blurt out, "Are you serious?" And when it became clear that his interviewer was not joking, he tried as politely as possible to assure her that the answer was definitely "No."

The socialist and communist parties or regimes that played a significant role in twentieth-century European politics advocated the replacement of capitalist free-market systems with collective ownership of the means of production and government operation of major economic enterprises. Support for such state-centered management of the economy, however, declined significantly after the implosion of the Soviet economy and regime in the 1980s. Moreover, socialist parties and programs have never garnered much support in the United States. The Populist Party did advocate government ownership and operation of banks and railroads in the 1880s and 1890s. The Socialist Party of America led by Eugene Debs managed to get 6 percent of the vote in the 1912 presidential election and also to elect two US representatives and a number of local officeholders. A handful of labor unions, such as the IWW, have championed the overthrow of capitalist institutions. Finally, the economic disaster of the Great Depression of the 1930s gave life to the Socialist Workers Party and provided some recruits for the Communist Party USA; but these never amounted to anything more than fringe parties.

So the characterization of Democrats as "socialist" or "Marxist" is simply inaccurate if the meaning of that term is the traditional one:

that is, state ownership of the means of production. On the other hand, some partisans of unfettered market economics may have in effect redefined "socialism" as meaning any government intervention in the economy whatsoever, including any form of regulation, subsidy, or redistributive social insurance such as Social Security and Medicare. And if that very broad and inclusive definition is intended, then reform liberals, New Deal liberals, and the Democratic Party do qualify as "socialist." Perhaps that is why senator and former presidential candidate Bernie Sanders has decided to call himself a "democratic socialist." Of course, it also follows from accepting that watered-down meaning of "socialism" that every organized society in history has been to some degree "socialistic." For there is not now and there never has been an organized society that left the production and distribution of every good and service entirely to private transactions. The pure ideal state of laissez-faire is then utopian in the literal sense of that word—which comes from the Greek words for "no" and "place." There is now no society that is purely laissez-faire, and there has never been one. As the political theorist Michael Walzer has written: "Every political community is in principle a welfare state" in the sense that "there has never been a political community that did not provide, or try to provide, or claim to provide, for the needs of its members as its members understood those needs."[6] To be clear, Walzer does not mean to say that all political communities provide for all the needs of their members or provide everything that some of its members may consider to be their needs. He simply means to say that all societies devote some collective efforts to providing their members with some of the specific goods or resources they need in order to function as members of the society.

It is neither the claim nor the intent of reform liberals, New Deal liberals, or "welfare state liberals" that our capitalist free-market economy should be done away with and be replaced by a system of government-run enterprises in the service of collectively determined resource allocations. I think it safe to say that virtually every significant political party or political leader in this country understands the social benefits of the free marketplace. What reform liberals do argue, however, is that—in the real world—entirely unregulated market economies are likely to encounter serious difficulties and to produce some problematic results. And they therefore insist that free-market institutions need to be complemented and in some respects constrained by government policies. They also believe that leaving the allocation of all goods and services in a society to the marketplace will lead to some distributive outcomes that are morally indefensible. Finally, they believe that a society governed by the market alone will not result in a society that conforms with important democratic ideals. In the rest of this chapter, we shall concentrate on the first of these three reform liberal arguments about the inadequacies of laissez-faire policies—those concerned with economic performance—leaving the latter two concerns about distributive justice and democratic goods to the chapters that follow.

The Blackboard Dream World

The economic criticisms that reform liberals levy against laissez-faire arguments can best be introduced by a joke that economists sometimes tell about themselves. It goes like this. Three academics find themselves stranded on a deserted island after a shipwreck. As they explore their surroundings, they are happy to find crates filled with cans of food that someone has abandoned there. Their discussion turns to the best way to open the cans. The first survivor, a chemist, proposes placing the cans under sea water and letting the salt corrode the metal. The second survivor, a physicist, retorts that this procedure would be too slow and that they should instead shinny up one of the palm trees and smash open the cans by throwing them onto the rocks below. The third survivor is an economist. "That's too dangerous," he says. "The last thing we need is to have one of us fall from the tree and injure himself." Then, like the other two, he draws upon his own academic discipline for inspiration and offers this strategy: "It's really simple," he says. "First, we assume that we have a can opener . . ."

Now, this seems like a kind of "stupid joke"—more weird than funny. But the point of the joke—and what makes it funny—is that it recognizes and exposes the fact that the standard economists' models of the functioning of the marketplace are based upon a number of assumptions that are in fact obviously not true. When your professor in

Econ 101 steps to the blackboard at the outset of the semester, he or she will usually begin by noting those assumptions: "Let us assume that . . ." followed by a number of propositions that are obviously counterfactual. And then the professor is off and running with his or her graphs of supply and demand curves.

Now, economists are intelligent people who are not clueless about the basic facts of life. The reason they proceed this way—the method behind their madness, as it were—is that it is impossible to construct any useful model of the core dynamics of free market exchanges without making some simplifying assumptions. For example, were we to begin our theoretical inquiry into market functioning by supposing that the choices and actions of participants in the market were driven by a complex host of motivations, some of them conflicting and some of them unknown, our attempts to deduce the operations and outcomes of market transactions could never get off the ground. It would be like trying to do geometry without having any axioms. So economists base their models on assumptions that they know represent simplifications of what happens in the real world but that they also believe are broadly accurate "for the most part" and "ceteris paribus" (i.e., all else being equal). They assume, for example, that people, all else being equal, will make economic decisions intended to maximize their financial well-being. Whenever we have options, we will sell dear and buy cheap. Now that is not always and invariably true: you might choose to "buy local" to support your neighbors, or you might sell your car to a member of your church for less than you could get from some stranger, for example. But for the most part, all other things being equal, we are going to make choices that make us better off than the available alternatives. And it makes sense, therefore, given the theoretical need to make axiomatic assumptions, for economists to suppose that this kind of "natural"—that is, self-maximizing—behavior may be taken for granted. Together with other similar assumptions, such simplifications of our economic circumstances and behavior add up to what we can think of as a model of a "perfect market."

The principal assumptions upon which the model of a "perfect market" depends, then, are these. First is the assumption we have just used as an example: economic actors behave "rationally"—in the sense that they act to maximize their economic self-interest. A second assumption is that the marketplace encompasses an infinite number of buyers and sellers. The point of this assumption is to suppose that no single producer or consumer has the power to interfere with the market's determination of the price or the amounts of goods and services that are exchanged. Third, it is assumed that all parties to the transactions are acting freely. Fourth, it is assumed that all parties in a particular market have all the information relevant to making a rational decision. Fifth, it is assumed that all factors of production are perfectly mobile. This does not mean that there are no costs of transportation but simply that no outside constraints prevent people, goods, or services from moving to where they are most productive. Sixth, it is assumed that all the costs and benefits of economic transactions are distributed among the contracting parties. Finally, it must be tacitly supposed that the initial distribution of economic holdings in the marketplace is not morally illegitimate. This does not mean that the pattern of initial holdings can be proven to be fair and just. It means only that the pattern of initial holdings is not produced by some form of theft, extortion, or rights violation.

Now the economics professors who use these assumptions as the basis for their theoretical models of market functioning would happily concede that none of these stipulated conditions of the ideal or "perfect" market are ever likely to be completely satisfied in the real world. They make their assumptions "for the sake of argument," as it were. For just as there can be no geometry without some axioms to serve as foundations, so also we cannot see the functional logic of an operating system or pattern of human behavior unless we make certain assumptions about the conditions or circumstances within which these systems and behaviors take place. So these unrealistic assumptions about perfect knowledge, an infinite number of buyers and sellers, and so on are used as "simplifying" assumptions we have to make in order to understand the way the market system works—at least in the abstract.

The economists who construct their models of the functioning of "ideal" or "perfect" markets know full well, then, that markets actually perform in the way presented in their models only to the extent that the assumptions upon which the models are based are in fact fully satisfied. And they are certainly aware that none of these necessary conditions of ideal markets are ever fully met in the real world. Those who champion laissez-faire policies, however, believe that the conditions necessary for unconstrained market forces to deliver optimal economic efficiencies and productivity are sufficiently approximated in the real world for markets to deliver as advertised. And this is in fact what they claim—or perhaps simply take for granted—although the more thoughtful among them are willing to concede that in a few cases the conditions are in fact not met and some form of government intervention may be justified. Even in these cases where they recognize the imperfection of market outcomes, however, partisans of laissez-faire often opt for simply living with these market imperfections in preference to government action to remedy them.

Reform liberals and other critics of laissez-faire, in contrast, believe that the gaps between the assumptions underlying the idealized model of free markets and the facts of the real world we live in are wide enough and deep enough to create significant derangements in the real-world results of unregulated markets. They believe, in other words, that the idealized depiction of the market system pushed by advocates of laissez-faire policies is a "blackboard dream" that works perfectly only in an imaginary world that does not exist and never can exist. They also insist that what laissez-faire economists concede to be difficulties that impede markets from functioning in the way they are supposed to are much more problematic than depicted. In the remainder of this chapter, then, we shall examine some of the most important problems and dangers that reform liberals see as the real-world consequences of unconstrained free markets. In most of these cases, it is useful to note, the source of the undesirable outcomes is the result of divergences between the enabling conditions of ideal markets and the actual conditions of the world we live in or a consequence of complications and complexities with the real-world institutionalization of markets—or some combination of both of these facts of life. In effect, the doubts and criticisms reform liberals raise about laissez-faire economics and policies are an instance of the oft-heard complaint: that's all very nice in theory, but it doesn't (and can't) work that way in practice.

In the rest of this section, then, we shall return to the core enabling conditions of the perfect marketplace identified a bit earlier in this chapter. We shall then look at what might be called the "nonexistent can opener" problems associated with each of them in the real world—as opposed to the "blackboard dream world" of abstract economic theory. And we shall observe how each of the gaps on display between the abstract ideal blackboard world and the real world create problems that, in the view of reform liberals, call for remediation by some form of governmental action. In addition, we shall note a few areas in which markets seem destined to perform inadequately or perversely because of other real-world complications.

The first enabling assumption of proper market functioning is that economic decision makers behave rationally. To make that assumption is not necessarily to suppose that people always make perfect choices in the service of their well-being in some objective sense of that term. We all make mistakes of judgment—some people more than others—about what our well-being truly consists in and about the intermediate steps most likely to help us reach our goals. All that the rationality condition requires is that people will make their economic choices on the basis of their best judgment about what will maximize their interests, or what economists sometimes refer to as their "preference satisfaction." And to be clear, this assumption need not imply that rational actors are entirely "selfish" people in the usual sense of that word: they may well see the interests they want to advance as including the welfare of their families or community and fidelity to their moral beliefs. The rational-actor assumption requires only that people are competent and will make choices designed to maximize their interests as they understand them.

Properly understood, the assumption of rational market participants is a condition that the real world embodies quite well. If someone offers us the same good or service at a lower price, we will buy from him or her rather than from the more expensive provider. If someone offers us a better-quality product at the same price as inferior ones, we will buy from that person. If multiple employers offer us similar jobs, we will accept the one carrying the highest salary. We will be averse to risk taking, but we will take some risk if the prospect of higher returns seems substantial. And the overwhelming majority of people do actually behave and choose rationally in this sense.

So far, so good on this enabling assumption. But even here, several real-world complications cause problems with the assumption that market actors will act rationally. The first of these problems is that most of us suffer from a form of myopia created by our natural passions and cognitive limitations. As a result, we often behave in a "short-sighted" manner that causes us big trouble down the road. Political theorist Thomas Hobbes placed a lot of emphasis on the dangers of this deficit of rationality, which he accounted for in a justly famous passage: "All men are by nature provided of notable multiplying glasses [magnification lenses], (that is their Passions and Self-love), through which, every little payment appeareth a great grievance; but are destitute of those prospective glasses [telescopic lenses], (namely Morall and Civill Science) to see a farre off the miseries that hang over them, and cannot without such payments be avoyded."[7]

Because of the natural inclination to choose immediate over deferred gratification and the speculative uncertainties attending our future, then, our "long-run rationality" is not all that good. The principal losers from this myopic failure to plan adequately for future contingencies are those who make this miscalculation. But when things go badly for them down the road, others may also wind up paying a price or carrying a heavy burden. Failures to save for retirement provide a good example here. I know people who tell me that they don't really need to plan for their postretirement years because none of their parents or grandparents had long lives. But what they are also saying by implication is that, if they surprise themselves with their longevity, then someone else—whether family or community services or philanthropic organizations—will have to provide for them. Whereas laissez-faire liberals tend to see compulsory participation in retirement programs like Social Security as morally unjustifiable, therefore, New Deal liberals see it as a reasonable and appropriate expedient needed to save the improvident from destitution and also to prevent them from becoming a burden to the rest of us.

A similar problematic shortcoming in the rationality of people in the real world is that they are often very poor assessors of risk. That is evident when we contemplate the large number of people who try to drive while inebriated—a bad decision we try to deter by criminal penalties. To cite another currently relevant example of bad risk assessment, consider also the many people who spurn health insurance because they think they are healthy and will not get sick. That calculation often fails, with sometimes disastrous financial consequences for them and with consequent burdens placed upon others. That reality might be more apparent if health insurance policies came with an identifiable entry on them, as car insurance policies do, that read, "Your contribution to health costs of the uninsured." A recent example of the generalized costs of people's poor judgment about their health risks came when a plaintiff in the first major legal attack upon the constitutionality of the Affordable Care Act was removed from the case because she suffered an unexpected major health problem that caused her to lose the business she owned and to undergo extensive treatment at public expense. Inadvertently, she became an exemplary case of why reform liberals tend to support the idea of some form of universal health care that includes some form of mandatory participation.

A final and quite important area of distortions of the rational calculations and risk assessments presupposed by the free-market model—one that has also been highly visible recently—is the product of the dynamics of corporate institutions. The classic market model conceives all buyers and sellers, producers and consumers, employers and employees as rational individuals. That includes institutional actors, including the large-scale corporate entities that play such a prominent role in modern economies. Mitt Romney famously admonished a questioner during his presidential campaign of 2012 that "corporations are people, too, my friend." And applying the market model to corporate actors proceeds upon that logic. This assumption, however, is not really true. Corporations are institutions populated and run by people, but the corporations themselves do not have the properties of the flesh-and-blood people who populate and run them—properties such as minds, emotions, self-established purposes, or moral beliefs. Equating corporate institutions with individual persons therefore represents a misleading "fallacy of the whole" that obscures potentially serious economic perils presented by the way corporate institutions actually function in the real world. The most important of these perils are captured by the phrases "limited liability," "I'll be gone by then," "too big to fail," and "heads I win, tails you lose."

Limited liability laws these days provide significant protection to the personal assets of corporate stakeholders against business debts, including those that may be the result of poor or risky decisions made by those in charge. Individuals in modern societies also are widely accorded a form of limited liability by bankruptcy laws. In both instances, the danger is that these protections against bearing full liability for the costs to others of economic decisions that turn out badly alters people's risk calculations. This change in decision makers' cost-benefits equations thereby creates a real-world divergence from the conditions and incentives of "rational behavior" built into the market model; and in doing so it compromises the logic that sustains the models' claim to optimality. Instead of incorporating the full potential risk of their actions into their decision-making, corporate managers and stakeholders can calculate their risk at a discount. This creates a form of "moral hazard," which is the rational temptation to take excessive risks because other parties will have to pay part of the price when things go wrong. (Once again, bankruptcy laws create similar temptations.)

The moral of this account is not that the practice of granting corporate managers, directors, and shareholders limited liability should be eliminated. Almost all knowledgeable observers believe that the social benefits of providing some limits to the liability of people who play roles in corporate institutions outweigh the costs of doing so.[8] Were no such limits on participants' liability for the costs of bad corporate decisions available, it would become impossible to induce people to engage with others in such large-scale business enterprises. Why, for example, would anyone agree to work for a large company like General Motors, say, if a consequence of employment would be that one could personally be held financially liable for the full cost of whatever the corporation as a whole did? Further, rendering corporate institutions nonviable in this way would deprive us of the great economic benefits of structured cooperative work by people with complementary special talents and would undermine the raising of capital needed to finance such valuable and important large-scale entrepreneurial endeavors. The moral of this story, then, is not that granting a degree of limited liability to the managers, directors, employees, and shareholders of corporations is bad policy. The moral of the story from the standpoint of reform liberals is instead that some forms of government regulation may very well be necessary and proper to prevent or to lessen the social damage caused by excessive risk taking that liability limits can encourage.

The dangers of such excessive risk taking on the part of individuals acting within the incentive structure presented to them by their role in corporate institutions were on full display during the financial crisis of 2009. The gap between the welfare of these individual actors and the welfare of the corporation as a whole—and the threat to the economy as a whole engendered by this gap—were captured by the mantra of "I'll be gone by then." The actual decisions on deals and trades by investment banks and other financial institutions are not made by some mythical macroperson (the corporate institution) but by individual traders. These traders are compensated to a considerable extent on the basis of the profits generated by their transactions. The incentive structure under which they work therefore makes it rational for them to take long-term risks that produce short-run gains. They are well rewarded for their gains in their annual bonuses, and if the risks prove costly down the road—well, they can be gone by then, leaving the losses to be borne by the institution and its shareholders. The problem here is the faulty supposition that, to recall Mitt Romney's words once again, "Corporations are people, too." Because they enjoy limited liability, corporate decision makers may very well act in a way that individuals who had to bear the full risk of their choices likely would not. To be specific, the important result of these legal and institutional arrangements is that corporations may fail to act with the rational care and circumspection that the logic of laissez-faire attributes to economic actors.

This gap between corporate behavior and the logic of free-market optimality can also be exacerbated in cases where the corporations in question are very large ones that play a critical role in the economy. In such circumstances, these corporations may be shielded from bearing the full cost of their bad decisions because they are deemed to be—to invoke another mantra from the 2009 financial crisis—"too big to fail." If the consequences for the national economy and the larger society of an implosion of the financial system or the failure of a huge and strategic company such as General Motors or Boeing seem sufficiently disastrous, the taxpaying public may be forced to bear the costs of "bailing them out." The failure—and attendant danger to the larger society—here is not an absence of rationality on the part of individual actors. The failure is a structural one. When institutional dynamics interfere with the discipline of the marketplace by allowing economic decision makers to off-load onto others the costs of risks they take that go bad, problems ensue. Games in which important players can operate on a logic of "heads I win, tails you lose" will often end badly for those who wind up shouldering the losses.

From the perspective of reform liberals, then, the central lesson of the examples canvassed here is that one important reason markets do not function in the real world as benignly as they do on the economists' blackboard is that in the real world both individuals and institutions may not act in the rational way the market model assumes. Individuals act imprudently because they are short-sighted and incapable of assessing risk properly. Institutions act imprudently because the risk schedule they face as economic "actors" may diverge from the personal risk schedules of the individuals within them who actually make the decisions for them. And in both instances, the damages that result from these failures of rationality and the breakdown of market discipline are imposed upon the larger community.

The policy implication of these market failures, according to reform liberals, is the need for some forms of government regulation to protect the larger community. To prevent imprudent individuals from shifting to others the cost of their medical treatments or the burdens of providing subsistence funds for their retirement years, it is both practically and morally appropriate to require individuals to make provision for these costs. And that is what Social Security and the Affordable Care Act do, the former by imposing a tax upon earned income to fund a modest retirement safety net for those who pay it, and the latter by requiring everyone to purchase some form of health care insurance while providing enough subsidy to lower-income individuals to make that possible. And while there are no sure cures for large corporate institutions imposing risks upon taxpayers, unwary customers, and shareholders, provisions in the Dodd-Frank Financial Reform Act were enacted to mitigate these costs and dangers. For example, one of its provisions seeks to lessen the dangers of "too big to fail" by raising reserve funds requirements upon banks; and another provision sets limits in place upon the ability of financial institutions to make risky investments with other people's money. Unsurprisingly, all of these programs and provisions continue to be controversial. Unsurprisingly, laissez-faire market enthusiasts decry these programs and policies as improper government regulation and interference with free markets. But reform liberals would insist, to the contrary, that some form of collective action through government legislation is necessary and proper to prevent the high costs and damages visited upon the public by failures of rationality and attendant breakdowns of market discipline in the real world of imperfect people and imperfect institutions.

Another important set of problems for unregulated free market economies also can arise from the development of large corporate institutions. These are the problems presented by the emergence of very large firms that are able to use their size and power to drive out or to bar the development of competitors and thereby to extract profits that exceed those that would have been produced by competitive markets of the sort depicted on the economists' blackboards. This is the phenomenon of high concentration in particular industries—or, in other words, the phenomenon of monopoly and/or oligopoly. The fundamental problem here is that the capacity of free markets to establish optimal pricing and thereby to maximize economic efficiency depends upon the pressure placed on firms and on individuals by those who are competing with them for customers or jobs.

Before the Industrial Revolution, monopolies were largely products of government action: they were grants of exclusivity to conduct business in particular industries or geographic areas given to particular firms by political authorities. Famous examples of such government-created monopolies were the British and Dutch East India companies, both of which were private companies given royal charters around 1600 that accorded them the exclusive right to conduct trade in lands east of the Cape of Good Hope. Some of the British colonies in America were also originally governed by companies that had been granted charters by the crown that accorded them exclusive rights to govern and develop specified parts of British-claimed land in North America. And, to note another example of government-granted monopoly rights, in late medieval times organized associations of craftsmen or traders known as guilds functioned in effect as professional cartels that often were afforded effective monopoly power within their areas of production or trade by "letters patent" bestowed upon them by a monarch or other ruling authority.

Part of the logic and intent of laissez-faire reformers in the eighteenth century was precisely to eliminate such grants of monopoly that functioned as restraints on free trade and the benefits that market competition could provide. Laissez-faire liberalism, then, in its inception was in part an antimonopoly movement; and the abolition of government restraints upon trade was a means to that end. It came as a disconcerting irony, then, when it turned out that these very free markets could themselves—under the new modes of production created by the Industrial Revolution—wind up producing their own new kind of economic monopolies by the very working of the "invisible hand" that was supposed to have done away with such concentrations of economic power.

In the United States, the full impact of the social and economic changes generated by the Industrial Revolution was delayed somewhat by a number of factors—including the gigantic disruption of the Civil War. At the end of that war, however, the transformation of this country into an industrialized nation occurred with surprising rapidity. The number of people in America who lived in cities increased 500 percent between 1860 and 1900. The number of manufacturing workers quadrupled over the same period. The number of factories in this country doubled in the twenty years between 1880 and 1900. In 1867, US steel companies produced two hundred thousand tons of steel, but by 1900 the country's steel production had grown to ten million tons annually. The transportation infrastructure of an industrial society developed rapidly over this period, with roads, canals, and railways being constructed at a fast pace. Partly as a result, new industrial towns such as Paterson, New Jersey, Scranton, Pennsylvania, and Youngstown and Akron, Ohio, appeared on the map.

The technological requirements for industrial manufacturing led to the creation of unprecedentedly large-scale corporations. And that led in turn to increasing concentration in many sectors of the economy. Small firms could not keep pace with these new economic leviathans such as US Steel, Standard Oil, American Tobacco, and the large railroad companies. The result was that at the onset of the twentieth century around three hundred midsize companies per year went out of business, and there were fifty industrial sectors in which a single firm accounted for more than 60 percent of production. The capital needs of a large-scale industrial economy also led to the creation of new large-scale financial institutions such as J. P. Morgan and Company.

American politics between 1880 and the onset of the First World War thus became dominated by battles about how to deal with the new phenomenon of monopoly capitalism. The basic problem here was that the working of free markets in the context of industrialization had undermined one of the fundamental conditions required for markets to function in the benign fashion depicted on economists' blackboards: namely, the presence of sufficient numbers of producers and consumers to prevent any one (or few) of them from exerting leverage over pricing and the allocation of economic resources. This was the impetus for the demands of the Midwest-based Populist Party that the government own and operate the railroads and also establish banks "for the safe deposit of the earnings of the people." It also set the stage for the passage of the Sherman and Clayton Anti-Trust Acts of 1890 and 1914 and for the "trust-busting" agenda of Theodore Roosevelt.

In cases where the conditions of production make having a single producer an unavoidable outcome, in policy terms there are basically three possible alternatives. The first is to live with the private monopoly and hope that it will not exploit its leverage over its customers to the maximum but will instead be satisfied with enjoying relatively modest monopoly profits. The second is for the government to take over the monopoly enterprise and run it as a public service. And the third is for the government to use its regulatory authority to impose service requirements and to exercise some control over prices. Even the most ardent champions of free markets recognize that keeping the government out of the market will not produce the optimal pricing and resource allocation promised by the ideal logic of the market. But they tend to believe that living with a private monopoly is, in Milton Friedman's words, "the least of the evils."

That judgment of Friedman represents in part his belief that, if and when conditions of production change in a way that no longer makes monopoly inevitable, unregulated private enterprises will adapt and adjust more quickly to eliminate the monopoly.[9] Reform liberals, in contrast, are less sanguine about both the moderation of private monopolies and the ease with which enterprises will relinquish their monopoly privileges when conditions make that technically possible. Accordingly, they generally insist upon the creation of state-level utilities commissions that have the authority to review and control the prices and practices of monopoly electricity and natural gas suppliers. Where it becomes an issue, reform liberals are also likely to support publicly owned and operated water and sewer systems over the alternative of leaving these to provision by private enterprise.[10]

Where monopoly or oligopoly escape from market discipline is not the result of purely technical causes but instead is produced by collusion or other anticompetitive practices, reform liberals endorse the use of government power to enforce the provisions of antitrust law to prevent this from happening. Laissez-faire liberals are conflicted about this, because they are forced to choose between allowing the undermining of the enabling conditions of proper market functions or allowing their bête noire of government intervention in the economy to constrain private enterprise. Some would follow Friedman, who seems to opt rather straightforwardly for "the effective enforcement of rules such as those embodied in our anti-trust laws."[11] But other free-market champions would rather tell the government to leave private business practices alone, even when these practices result in effective restraint of trade.

Another important assumption packed into the ideal-market model is that consumers have perfect information. Even if consumers are entirely rational (i.e., preference optimizing) when making their choices, these choices will not lead to efficient outcomes in the absence of necessary information. This necessity is most obvious in the case of price information: it does me no good as a consumer that an item I am purchasing can be had more cheaply elsewhere if I do not know that. Fortunately for us as consumers—and for market efficiency—it has become relatively easy these days to acquire this crucial information. Not all that long ago, the cost in time and effort to acquire relevant price information could be significant. Perhaps I had to drive my horse and buggy around to potential suppliers. Or I might be able to scour my local newspaper to see what prices were at establishments that advertised there. Or I might, after Alexander Graham Bell invented the telephone, call around to ask suppliers about their prices. Now we can find and compare prices on our computer screens quickly and easily by typing the item we want into a search engine or by deploying programs like Amazon, Priceline, or Trivago. The result has been a considerable improvement in the functioning of markets as price information actually approaches the perfection modeled on the economists' blackboard.

Other information important to consumers may be much less easily accessible. The marketplace in health care in this country is a good case in point. First, basic price information here can be hard or even impossible to get—as many of you no doubt know from firsthand experience. A member of my family, for example, was recently trying to decide among treatment options for a health condition. So she called both her insurer and her health care system to find the cost of the various options. Neither of them was willing or able to provide this information to her. The message was: here's the (quite wide) range of costs, and you'll only know when you get the bill after the fact. In other situations, price shopping is also impossible for practical reasons. People having heart attacks are not in a position to perform a price comparison among different hospitals, for example; nor would it be feasible for them to instruct the ambulance driver to take them to the place with the best price for their emergency treatment. It can also be extremely difficult to find out important information about the training, experience, and skill level of different surgeons or treatment specialists.

It is similarly difficult for consumers to know exactly what the content and background are of food they buy in grocery stores or restaurants. We also often have extremely imperfect information about the contents, functions, and side effects of medications and food supplements. A recent investigation by New York State officials, for example, found that many food supplement products actually contained very little of the herbs or biological agents they claimed to provide. How much do dieters know about the caloric content of restaurant items? How much information did smokers receive about the carcinogenic effects of cigarettes before their manufacturers were required to post warnings on their packages? And apart from government ratings, how much would consumers be able to know about the sanitation standards and practices of the restaurants they patronize?

Moving beyond the unknowns in consumables, how much information do passengers have about the pilot training and aircraft maintenance practices of the various airlines before they choose their flights? If an airline decided it needed to cut its costs to be competitive, and it did so by outsourcing its plane maintenance to foreign subcontractors with lower standards for technician training or by checking and servicing its planes less frequently, how would you know that? When you buy pajamas or nightgowns for your children, how do you know how flammable they are? When you have to sign loan or mortgage contracts that run to many pages of small print, how sure can you be that crucial information is not encrypted there in impenetrable legalese? For reform liberals, the answer to these questions is that the free-market admonition *Caveat emptor* ("Let the buyer beware") is in many important cases not adequate or appropriate. When buyers have no option but to base their purchase on inadequate or false information, they cannot be the rational consumers that markets require in order to be efficient and benign. Reform liberals therefore insist that free markets require some government regulation and safeguards in order to function in the way they are supposed to function. Specifically, in the context of the "perfect information" enabling condition of the ideal-market model, laws and agencies of government are necessary to provide or to require the provision of important product information. Or, in cases where accomplishing that transparency is important but very difficult, it may make sense for governing agencies to conduct fact-finding investigations and in some cases to set and enforce safety standards that rational consumers would insist upon if they were able to have the relevant information. So, say reform liberals, it is necessary for us to create government oversight agencies such as the Federal Aviation Administration, the Federal Trade Commission, the Food and Drug Administration, and the Consumer Financial Protection Bureau to make good this failure of private actors to provide consumers the information they need to protect themselves and make rational choices.

Another assumption of the ideal-market model is the perfect mobility of all productive resources. Such mobility allows economic resources to be moved to where they can be most productive. In the real world, of course, factors of production cannot move around as easily as they do on the economists' blackboard. That kind of "friction" or stickiness can cause problems in the functioning of real-world markets. Several examples illustrate the nature of these problems. Consider first the concrete realities of the agricultural marketplace. Most foodstuffs are products of nature: meat, milk, and eggs come from animals; and bread, pasta, rice, vegetables, fruit, nuts, cereal, potato chips, and many other foods encountered in the aisles of grocery stores come from plants. Plants and animals have biological life cycles and take time to cultivate. That's the lack-of-mobility factor. The result is that producers—the farmers, fishermen, cattlemen—cannot change what they choose to produce very quickly. Moreover, the vagaries of nature—especially weather—make it hard to predict what the level of supply of agricultural commodities will be in a given year. This means that—as economists would put it—both the supply and demand curves for agricultural goods are quite inelastic. That is, at least in the short run, producers cannot in a timely fashion supply more when prices turn out to be high, and consumers won't demand much more when prices are low: ranchers cannot quickly produce more cattle when beef prices go up, and food consumers (all of us) both have to eat and can only eat so much, so we can't stop eating when food prices go up and generally will not want to gorge ourselves just because food costs go down.

This combination of resource immobility and supply/demand inelasticity produces a lot of volatility in the market for agricultural goods, and this volatility can be quite destructive to producers in the short run and destructive in less direct ways to all of us as well. When prices plummet, farmers and growers may not make enough to cover their costs. When prices soar, those with limited resources will struggle to put food on the table. The consequences can include not only economic suffering but social and political conflicts and disruption as well. Think, for example, of farmers in the American Midwest in the 1870s and 1930s, the devastation to some developing countries when coffee prices plunge, and the sometimes violent political instability that soaring bread prices have caused. (This last example, one may recall, provided the background for Queen Marie Antoinette's famously callous remark about the French populace's protests that they could not afford to buy bread: "Let them eat cake!" Not long after, the French monarchy fell, and she—and many others—were hauled off to the guillotine.)

Another example of the economic distress and social dislocations that resource mobility issues can cause was what Ross Perot famously called the great "sucking sound" of American manufacturing jobs being lost as technological advances and the lowering of trade barriers (aka more international free trade) made it more profitable for companies to outsource their manufacturing operations to other countries. Labor is an activity of people. People have lives and are not inanimate things. Lives are rooted in places and relationships. So the newly jobless workers in cities like Flint and Youngstown—and hence cities like these as well—suffered great damage. On the economists' blackboard, they would have quickly moved to where jobs were more plentiful. But that instantaneous mobility is not easy or even possible for labor/people as it is for the other factors of production—namely capital and raw materials.

These very different levels of mobility among the different factors of production can create serious problems in the real-world marketplace. Economic production requires capital, labor, and materials. For all sorts of both practical and legal reasons, labor is relatively immobile, materials are—with modern transport technology—relatively mobile, and capital can move almost instantaneously from one end of the globe to the other. This disjunction among the relative mobility/ immobility of the three central components of the production of goods can cause financial instability, economic damage, and painful social dislocation—with emerging and distressed national economies especially vulnerable. When these countries hit a difficult patch economically, they can see their difficulties metastasize at warp speed through the phenomenon of "capital flight." In capital flight, financiers and investors around the world abruptly pull their capital out of the particular countries whose economies are seen as problematic.

When that happens, of course, these countries become immensely more troubled, a vicious cycle ensues, they suffer a financial meltdown, and their people's economic circumstances plummet. Moreover, the economic stress and damage can quickly become contagious, spilling across national borders and affecting other countries that have economic ties with their sinking neighbors. The "Asian Crisis" of 1997–98 represents a classic example of this disturbing and dangerous scenario. And more recently, the economic crisis in Greece and its contagion to that country's European neighbors exhibit some similar dynamics. It could also be said that the financial meltdown and Great Recession in the United States in 2008–9 exhibited in a scary way the derangements and resultant economic and social damage that unregulated capital markets can cause, even though the problem here was more of a capital freeze than a capital flight.

Now, reform liberals do not come armed with easy or even good answers to these kinds of problems caused by the immobility of some factors of production and the excessive mobility of capital. It is practically infeasible and would be morally problematic to fight labor immobility by forcibly shipping workers around the world, for example. And it would be economically destructive and a violation of people's rights to use their property as they see fit to prohibit or significantly impede the free deployment of capital. But reform liberals have two main contentions to make in this area. First, they would insist that the cases discussed here represent another important instance of the incapacity of unregulated markets in the real world to produce the efficient and benign outcomes promised by their performance on the economists' blackboard. And second, as a consequence of this divergence between the ideal results depicted in abstract theoretical markets and the actual economic derangements and attendant social damage caused by the inevitably nonideal markets found in the real world, laissez-faire is not always sound advice. Instead, it may at times be necessary, or at least better, to regulate or constrain the operations of the marketplace to lessen their volatility, to prevent dangerous financial instability, and to protect countries or economic sectors from suffering irreparable damage as a result of drastic short-term swings of the market.

This is the logic and animating purpose of a variety of government programs and policy proposals. In the United States, Congress established the Agricultural Stabilization and Conservation Service and authorized it to establish and administer programs designed to stabilize prices for agricultural commodities. These programs included the establishment of production quotas for some products, loan programs to allow farmers to sell their produce over a longer time frame instead of being forced to sell it all at harvest time when prices are lowest, and programs to purchase surplus products and distribute them to school lunch programs and foreign aid programs. Canada has a similar program, which began as the Canadian Agricultural Income Stabilization Program and which now is called AgriStability and AgriInvest. When it comes to geographic pockets of high unemployment caused by failing industries or the outsourcing of manufacturing operations, there are no easy answers. But one way to mitigate the damage caused by job loss resulting from the "creative destruction" of the marketplace is to offer job retraining programs to those who have been economically displaced. Some European countries, Germany in particular, have made such programs a staple of their labor policy. Attempts to lessen the damage of dramatic episodes of capital flight, on the other hand, would seem to require some form of international regulatory framework that does not currently exist. Some transnational organizations are, however, lobbying for the creation of such a framework; and new episodes resembling the Asian Crisis of 1997–98 would likely provide strong impetus to their proposals.[12]

Next, the problem of externalities. A crucial but often-violated assumption built into the ideal-market model is that all the costs and benefits of economic transactions go to the parties making the contract. Any and all deviations from this requirement render markets less than fully efficient and less than optimal in their utility. If non-participants in the contract receive benefits, they become free riders. And if costs are visited upon people not participating in the contract, they become in effect uncompensated contributors to the gains of others. Now, even the most ardent advocates of free markets and laissez-faire policies recognize that such third-party costs and benefits often happen in the real world; and they concede that these deviations from the necessary conditions of ideal market functioning can justify compensatory action by some governing authority. As we noted in the previous sections of this chapter, for example, laissez-faire economist Milton Friedman cited these economic externalities, or "neighborhood effects," as he called them, as one of the only two justifications for government intervention in the free-market system he considered legitimate, the other being technical monopolies. So, in principle, both laissez-faire liberals and reform liberals are in agreement here. From the perspective of reform liberals, however, the problem is that Friedman and those like him vastly understate the scope and magnitude of these externalities.

For good or for ill, reform liberals say, we live in an increasingly small world in which positive or negative events elsewhere have significant effects on us. Greece has debt problems or Thailand has credit issues, the economic contagion spreads, markets tremble around the world, and your IRA shrinks. And certainly, within countries the circumstances and conditions of one economic sector or population have consequences for all the rest of us. From the reform liberal perspective, then, government needs to take an active role in promoting positive externalities and prohibiting, discouraging, or compensating negative externalities. Consider here five important areas where reform liberals argue that government has legitimate work to do: protecting the environment, remedying market failures in human capital formation, building infrastructure, creating and protecting public spaces, and fighting threats to public health.

Take first our natural environment. We need clean air, clean water, good land, and other natural resources not only for a healthy economy but for life itself. But actions and transactions that make sense in the short-run calculus of the marketplace can inflict serious damage—in some cases irremediable damage—on these natural resources. Agricultural and manufacturing industries can foul our rivers and streams with hog waste or coal ash, utility companies and manufacturing plants can belch carbon wastes into the air that kill trees and sicken people, strip mines can lay waste to hills and valleys, and so on. These damages are the product of market incentives when the contracting parties are able to ignore the costs they are inflicting upon outside parties. Although suing for damages under tort law could conceivably mitigate some of these negative externalities, this process taken alone would be both cumbersome and inefficient. It also would come ex post facto, compensating for sicknesses and deaths rather than preventing them. So here, reform liberals insist, there is a clear need for government regulatory laws and enforcement efforts to protect the public against these environmental negative externalities.

There is also, moreover, an important intergenerational consideration at work here when it comes to environmental protection, for succeeding generations will pay a heavy price for any serious degradation of the natural world they will inherit from us and have to inhabit. But they don't get to be parties to any of the economic calculations and incentives of the present generation—calculations and incentives that simply exclude from consideration long-run consequences that none of the decision makers will have to deal with. Economically, it makes sense for us to fuel our automobiles and generate our electricity by burning fossil fuels and burning coal as long as doing that is less expensive than any available alternatives. But the costs to future generations could be enormous. So if we care about our progeny, at some point we may have to force ourselves to give up the cheaper but environmentally dangerous option and move to other more expensive but environmentally safe options for our energy needs. And that won't happen without taking some collective actions through regulations that override the short-run market incentives that would produce destructive consequences down the road.

Second, a number of real-world rigidities and complications create a market imperfection in the area of the development of human capital. This phenomenon is recognized even by some economists of a laissez-faire disposition. Thus Milton Friedman writes that "there is considerable empirical evidence that the rate of return on investment in training is very much higher than the rate of return on investment in physical capital. This difference suggests the existence of underinvestment in human capital. . . . Whatever the reason, an imperfection of the market has led to underinvestment in human capital."[13] As opposed as he is in general to government intervention in the marketplace, Friedman nevertheless goes on to concede that government intervention might here be justified to address this problem of underinvestment "on grounds both of technical monopoly, insofar as the obstacle to the development of such investment has been administrative costs, and of improving the operation of the market, insofar as it has been simply market frictions and rigidities."[14]

Friedman's focus here is upon intervening in order to enable individuals to make what would be more rational choices when it comes to investing in themselves. But the market imperfection that impedes optimal levels of investment in human capital through education and other training programs also has the broader consequence of producing negative externalities (or discouraging the creation of positive externalities) for society as a whole. Think of it this way: Would you rather be born into a country whose people have the health, education, and training to maximize their productivity or into a country where people's talents go underdeveloped? Obviously, your own welfare and economic prospects will be much better in the country where investment in human capital is optimized. Underinvestment in human capital, then, carries negative externalities for everyone. So, reform liberals argue, this is an important area in which government action is necessary to remedy a real-world market imperfection that negatively affects the country as a whole by lessening the economic productivity of its people.

Another area where it is not really feasible to depend upon the marketplace to produce optimal outcomes is infrastructure development and maintenance. This is also an externalities problem, since the incapacity of private exchanges stems from the great practical difficulties of allocating the costs and benefits at stake. Transportation infrastructure is the exemplary case here. For any national or regional economy to function at all well, it has to have a good transportation system available to enable the production and exchange of goods. That means an extensive network of good highways, rail systems, airports, ports, and possibly canals. Private enterprise can play a role in creating this kind of infrastructure, but there are structural problems that place some limits on what they can do. A private company could build a long-distance limited-access highway and recoup its investment and make a profit by imposing and collecting tolls. Even here, of course, it would almost certainly be necessary to have recourse to relevant governments for land acquisition. And collecting tolls on local road systems would be technologically very complicated and expensive at best. So infrastructure development is an area where laissez-faire often is not a good way to get a necessary job done. Despite the widespread invocation of laissez-faire mantras—such as "Markets are wise, governments are foolish" and "Government can redistribute but can't produce anything"—this is usually not a partisan issue. The huge public works project of building the Hoover Dam, for example, was undertaken by Republican administrations and bears the name of a Republican president. It was President Dwight Eisenhower who promoted and presided over the creation of our system of interstate highways. And, of course, private businesses are always happy to have governments finance the building of things they can use.

Finally, consider the area of public health. In the service of protecting and promoting public health, programs that provide universal—or nearly universal—access to health care are found in every advanced industrial country, in part because such programs represent investment in the countries' stock of human capital. A sickly workforce is a drain on economic productivity. In addition to health care provision, moreover, the protection of the public against communicable diseases exceeds the capacities of the marketplace: providing this kind of protection demands universality, coordination, and authority unavailable to private actors. The near eradication of the ravages of childhood diseases such as measles and polio is a result of universal vaccination programs possible only through government organization, authority, and subsidy. Minimizing the annual epidemic of influenza and the spread of diseases like hepatitis also requires levels of coordination and subsidy available only to public authorities. And during scares over the threat of devastating diseases like Ebola, people go running not to their doctor, whose powers to protect them are quite limited, but to various agencies of the government such as the Centers for Disease Control. (As this book was going to press, the emergence of a new coronavirus was in the process of inflicting very serious damage upon the health and the economy not only of this country but also the entire world. And, say many, we are now suffering the costs of having cut back the staff and resources of the CDC and also of other federal public health agencies whose mission is to protect us against the ravages of such diseases.)

To summarize, then, many of the situations where reform liberals see a need for government regulation or intervention into the economy arise from the ways in which actual conditions in the real world diverge from the enabling conditions of properly functioning markets. In the real world, some important goods or services are indivisible: we cannot each decide and purchase individually what kind of military programs we want to protect us from external threats to our security. In the real world, some markets are monopolistic or oligopolistic, undermining the competitive pressures that produce the economically optimal pricing depicted on the economists' blackboard. In the real world, buyers often lack access to the information they need to make rational decisions. In the real world, private transactions often impose uncompensated costs on third parties. In the real world, "friction" is ubiquitous, impeding the optimal allocation of resources and in some sectors creating destructive market volatility. So, reform liberals argue, in these areas collective action through government is not only justifiable but also at times truly necessary.

Unsurprisingly but revealingly, therefore, if you seek out the mission statements and program descriptions of the major departments and agencies of the federal government and of the independent regulatory commissions you will readily see that a significant portion of their activities is directed at remedying the kinds of market failures and imperfections canvassed above. Much of what the Department of Interior does and all of what the Environmental Protection Agency does serve to protect against negative externalities that damage the nation's air, water, and land. The Department of Labor and its Employment Training Administration provide job training programs. The Department of Education—which among other programs administers the federal Pell Grants that subsidize higher education for low-income students—is engaged in remedying what Friedman referred to as the imperfections in the market for human capital formation. The Food and Drug Administration and the Product Safety Commission test and regulate the content of products that could threaten the health of consumers for reasons they could not ascertain on their own—that is, these agencies work to remedy the unavailability in the real world of the information required by adequately functioning markets. The Department of Transportation seeks, among other things, to promote needed investment in the nation's transportation infrastructure—an essential component of a successful modern economy. The Centers for Disease Control and the Surgeon General's Office work to protect the public health. And so on. In all of these cases, reform liberals argue that what is going on is not some "socialist" desire to supplant private markets with government enterprises but instead a series of efforts to remedy market failures caused by the inability of the real world to provide the necessary enabling conditions for markets to function in practice the way they should in theory.

Costs of Government Intrusion into the Economy: A Laissez-Faire Riposte

Before turning to some macroeconomic issues that tend to divide laissez-faire advocates and New Deal liberals, we need to note here how free-market enthusiasts can and have critically responded to reform liberal arguments on behalf of government's role in the economy.

The first part of the laissez-faire critique of reform liberal policies is a pointed reminder of the prima facie legitimacy of freely-entered-into market transactions. The legitimacy is both practical and moral. The practical value of abiding by the resource allocations generated by free contractual agreements is their utility in maximizing economic efficiency. The moral legitimacy of such transactions is that they represent an economic version of the fundamental liberal principle of government by consent. So even through it is certainly true that the way markets function in the real world is not so perfect as the way they function in the idealized world of the economists' blackboard, arguments for overturning market outcomes should be treated with skepticism and suspicion. Given the twin practical and moral justifications for free-market outcomes, free-market enthusiasts insist that proposals to deviate from these outcomes require a high burden of proof. And in their view this high standard of proof is rarely met. Whenever in doubt, they argue, the benefit of the doubt should go to the marketplace. That is the proper default position.

The second part of the laissez-faire rebuttal of reform liberals' economic case is what philosophers would call a tu quoque response.

That is: your argument is subject to the very same kind of weakness you attribute to our argument. You say that our defense of free markets is flawed because our depiction of them is an idealized model not found in the real world. But you reform liberals do the same thing in your idealized assumptions about democratic decision-making and the content of government policies. You seem to assume that government policies of economic allocation and regulation embody rational judgments directed to the public interest. But this is a misleadingly idealized and sanitized version of what actually happens in the real world of democratic legislative and bureaucratic politics. For one thing, we free-market advocates don't believe that there is any such animal as "the public interest" that is anything more than or different from the aggregation of individual preference satisfaction. But even if there were such a thing as a public interest, it seems pretty clear that democratic legislatures are not driven by it and should not be seen as achieving it. Look at any democratic legislature in the real world and you will see that its decisions are driven by the promotion of quite particular ("special") interests. And the beneficiaries of the tax and spending laws that are passed are usually the most favored constituents of the most powerful legislators. When these laws are interpreted and implemented by administrative agencies, moreover, a similar bias prevails: these implementary policies and standards—of the sort found in this country in the Federal Register—are in practice hammered out in negotiations among the bureaucratic agency, the dominant and established relevant interest groups, and their congressional advocates who inhabit the relevant congressional committees. These are the constituent groups of what political scientists have called the "cozy triangles" that dominate public policy making.[15] The fundamental point here was well stated a century ago by one of the leading economists of that era, A. C. Pigou, who wrote: "It is not sufficient to contrast the imperfect adjustments of unfettered private enterprise with the best adjustment that [we] can imagine. For we cannot expect that any public authority will attain, or will even whole-heartedly seek, that ideal. Such authorities are liable alike to ignorance, to sectional pressure and to personal corruption by private interest.

A loud-voiced part of their constituents, if organized for votes, may easily outweigh the whole."[16]

A similar dynamic, according to scholars who have studied the matter, often afflicts the way that the independent regulatory agencies work in practice. In theory, these agencies and commissions protect and promote the interests of the public as a whole by regulations that govern the functions of firms and markets in particular sectors of the economy such as transportation, telecommunications, advertising, financial services, and so on. In practice what often happens over the years is what has been called "regulatory capture." That is, the agencies charged with constraining the firms in a particular sector on behalf of the interests of the broader public come to see the public interest as equivalent to the "good functioning" of that sector and to see "good functioning" as largely constituted by the health of the firms they are regulating. The result is that the agencies function in effect as the protectors of a kind of economic cartel. And part of what these firms are protected from are the competitive challenges that they would confront in a less regulated marketplace and that would benefit the consumer public.[17]

Drawing upon these pointed observations about the ways that government interventions and regulation actually work in the real world, laissez-faire critics of reform liberal programs that supplant or constrain the economic marketplace say in effect: you are no doubt correct to say that real-world markets are imperfect approximations of the "perfect markets" depicted in economic theoretical models. But the government policies and programs you promote to "remedy" these market imperfections are themselves very imperfect. They in practice do not perform as advertised in theory. They thwart the beneficial dynamics of market competition while producing in their stead not some putative "public interest" but instead a politically brokered self-serving bargain among rent-seeking special interests. And given the choice between imperfect approximations of market efficiency on the one hand and imperfect attempts to achieve better results by government contrivances on the other, we will choose imperfect real-world markets almost every time.

Two Macroeconomic Disagreements

We do not have here either the space or the need for an extended treatment of macroeconomic theory. There are, however, two issues under the heading of "How does a free market system perform over time, and what policies will optimize its performance?" that require mention—both because they are practically important and because laissez-faire and reform liberals argue about them. One of these questions is "How should we understand the dynamics of business cycles, and what, if anything, should be done to manage them?" The other question is "What kind of fiscal policies work best on behalf of economic growth?"

First, consider three divergent accounts of the causes of business cycles and their long-run implications for the stability and productivity of a capitalist free-market economy. The protagonists in this three-sided debate are (1) classical liberal laissez-faire economists such as Milton Friedman, Friedrich von Hayek, and Ludwig von Mises; (2) Marxist and socialist theorists such as Marx himself and his various followers; and (3) New Deal reform economists such as John Maynard Keynes and contemporary American economists such as Paul Krugman and Joseph Stiglitz.

Unsurprisingly, the most optimistic interpretation of the recurrent business cycle pattern—in which a period of heightened economic activity with full employment and rising prices is followed by a recessionary contraction with declining production, lower prices, and rising unemployment—is provided by the laissez-faire economists. On their account, business cycles are a natural, normal, and basically benign part of the dynamics of a market economy. The downturns may be painful at times, but they are an unavoidable part of the "creative destruction" of economic progress. Moreover, and most important, they argue that the ups and downs of the business cycle are self-correcting. A market economy, on their account, is a self-equilibrating system in which the equilibrium point toward which the internal forces of the system gravitate is one of full employment and efficient prices. Given this belief that the free-market economy is drawn by its own dynamics toward a benign equilibrium point, the implication for government policy is, unsurprisingly, that we should pretty much leave this self-optimizing system alone: laissez-faire. The role of government should basically be limited to providing a legal structure that protects private property rights and enforces contracts. The only other task for government authorities should be to enact and abide by rules that make the money supply stable and predictable.[18]

The opposite extreme account of the dynamics and long-run implications of business cycles in a free-market economy, again unsurprisingly, is Marx's. The costs and consequences of business cycles were an important part of Marx's account of what he called the "contradictions" (i.e., the alleged internal structural tensions) of capitalism that would ultimately lead to its destruction. So whereas laissez-faire economists see business cycles in a capitalist economy as minor perturbations that constantly correct themselves to a happy (full-employment) equilibrium, Marx and his collaborator Friedrich Engels saw these business cycles as producing increasingly destructive downturns that were fated to become increasingly intolerable both economically and politically.

Engels provided a succinct statement of this view of the depth and destructiveness of the up-and-down swings of a capitalist economy in his essay "Socialism: Utopian and Scientific" in 1877. In the previous fifty years, he noted, the British economy had experienced deep and costly economic downturns five times, or about once every ten years. In these downturns, he wrote:

> Commerce is at a standstill, the markets are glutted, products accumulate. . . . Hard cash disappears, credit vanishes, factories are closed, the mass of workers are in want of the means of subsistence. . . . Bankruptcy follows upon bankruptcy. . . . The stagnation lasts for years, productive forces are wasted and destroyed wholesale, until the accumulated mass of commodities finally filters off, more or less depreciated in value, until production and exchange gradually begin to move again. Little by little the pace quickens . . . into the headlong gallop of a perfect steeplechase

of industry, commercial credit, and speculation, which finally . . . ends where it began—in the ditch of a crisis. And so over and over again.[19]

Given this ongoing experience with the ups and downs of capitalism over Engels's entire life (he was born in 1820), it is not hard to understand his and Marx's very critical view of that system and their expectation that its future was limited.[20] And it was the experience of the Great Depression in the 1930s, in which unemployment rates reached 25 percent and which went on for a decade or more, that led some in the twentieth century to conclude that the Marxist account of capitalism's failure was convincing. As Arthur Koestler wrote of himself in *The God That Failed*, it was when "sane executives were ordering pigs to be drowned under the eyes of starving men" that he "in December, 1931 . . . joined the Communist Party of Germany."[21]

With the benefit of another 150 years' experience with modern capitalism, reform liberal economists would agree with their laissez-faire-oriented colleagues that the propensity of a free-market economy to generate recurrent painful recessions will not necessarily lead to its demise. But they also believe that the destructive consequences of these recurrent downturns can and should be greatly lessened—and that disastrous events like the Great Depression can largely be prevented by appropriate government management. Reform liberal economists would argue that Franklin Delano Roosevelt, reviled by many of the wealthy businessmen of his time as a "traitor to his class," was instead quite justified in calling himself "the greatest friend the profit system ever had."[22] That claim was justified, reform liberal economists would say, because his somewhat hit-or-miss interventions to get the stalled US economy moving upward included the kind of stimulative government measures that are necessary to keep recessionary downturns from turning into death spirals.

Governments' crucial role in dealing with the potentially destructive swings of free-market economies consists, in the view of reform liberal economists, of several forms of "countercyclical" policy—both monetary and fiscal. Monetary policy—governed in this country mostly by the Federal Reserve Board—can help keep expansionary parts of the business cycle from turning into dangerous "bubbles" by raising interest rates and tightening credit requirements. Conversely, when recessionary downturns occur, credit access can be made easier to encourage entrepreneurial activity and investment. Countercyclical fiscal policy consists in taxation policies that produce a balanced budget or a surplus when the economy is at full employment levels and allow for government investment in infrastructure and other programs that help support purchasing power—what economists call "effective aggregate demand"—when recessions come and unemployment rates rise. Equally important in this context are the built-in countercyclical effects of programs such as Social Security and unemployment insurance. Because many of the worst episodes in the history of capitalism have involved financial crises and panics, moreover, government banking insurance and regulation can play an important role in preventing or at least mitigating these destructive events. Important in this context is the role in this county of the FDIC (Federal Deposit Insurance Commission), which, by insuring funds deposited in banks, prevents so-called "runs" on banks where people rush en masse to withdraw their money and thereby create breakdowns in the credit system. Government can also set rules for cash reserves that financial institutions must keep and rules to prevent their taking of excessive risks with other people's money.

The reform liberal insistence upon the necessary and important role of government in countering the swings of the business cycle and preventing deep recessions is often associated with the economic theories of the eminent British economist John Maynard Keynes. That is because Keynes argued that free-market economies can settle at an equilibrium point below a full-employment level; and he provided an explanation of how that can happen.[23] His account, which appeared as the Great Depression ground on and on, seemed to many economists to be a plausible explanation of what was happening. And aspects of that explanation, such as his depiction of the consequences of "liquidity preference" (choosing to hold cash rather than spending or investing it) and time lags between planned savings and planned investment, have become incorporated into mainstream economics. His basic claim regarding the possibility of less-than-full-employment equilibria in a market economy remains contested, however. Neo-classical economists of a laissez-faire disposition have continued to maintain that, although the full-employment homeostatic forces they attribute to a market system may work slowly, these forces will in fact bring a market economy back to full employment in the long run. The retort of reform liberals to this claim, in turn, is that this is not sufficient grounds for telling governments to back off and leave the markets to do their alleged magic. For as Keynes himself pointedly observed in this context: 'In the long run, we're all dead.' So if governments have the tools at their disposal to bring their economies back from painful recessionary downturns more quickly, they should go ahead and use them.

The second issue that elicits competing responses from laissez-faire and reform liberal economists concerns the kind of fiscal policy—or taxation and government spending policies—most likely to boost economic growth. The answer of laissez-faire partisans is to call for cuts both in rates of taxation and in government spending. And the cuts in taxes should go principally to those in the upper income brackets. The rationale for this program of "cutting government spending and taxes on the wealthy" runs like this. The engine of wealth creation and economic growth is found in the private sector—that is, it comes from private business activity and not from government disbursements. Therefore, what is needed is policy to spur entrepreneurial activity in the private sector. To make that happen, you need to boost the amount of capital available for investment and also boost the incentives for those who have this capital to risk it by investing it in profit-making ventures instead of putting it under their mattress or bidding up the price of scarce beachfront property. Both of these things, they argue, will happen when taxes on the top income brackets and taxes on capital gains are lowered. So the tax proposals of Republican candidates for office these days usually embody this logic: we will cut taxes, including and especially on the "job creators," aka the wealthier members of society; they will then invest the additional funds they have because of these tax cuts into new productive enterprise; these enterprises, their employees, and their investors will make money; and the tax cuts will not increase the federal deficit because tax revenues from this new wealth (these candidates provide quite optimistic projections of the resulting rise in GDP) will make up for the losses in government revenue occasioned by the tax cuts.

This rosy scenario for boosting economic productivity and GDP is sometimes referred to as "supply-side economics." All economic transactions require both sellers and buyers, both those who have a supply of something for sale and those who have a desire for the goods in question and the means to purchase them; and this strategy focuses upon increasing supply. What, though, one might ask, about the other side of the equation? Will there be buyers willing and able to purchase the newly supplied goods? Perhaps relying upon a maxim attributed to the French economist Jean-Baptiste Say that "supply creates its demand," this line of argument seems to assume the answer is "yes." In effect, the supply-side argument affirms the famous mantra from the movie *Field of Dreams*: "If you build it, they will come." And it assumes in addition that those who come will have the wherewithal to buy what you built.

Reform liberals are skeptical of this supply-side scenario and, with particular reference to its proponents' extravagant promises of the productivity gains their strategy will achieve, dismiss it as "voodoo" economics, a derisive term they actually appropriated from President G. H. W. Bush, who had on the counsel of his advisers implemented such a strategy and was unhappy when the results were disappointing. When a market economy is not producing all that it could, reform liberals look mostly to the demand side of the equation. The root cause of lagging economic growth, they argue, usually is not some imagined lack of available capital. And if capital is not being invested in new enterprises and production of goods and services, the reason is not that the profits those enterprises would return to investors are taxed at 30 percent rather than 20 percent. (As the sage of Omaha, Warren Buffett, once said, he had never seen someone turn down the opportunity to make a profitable investment because he or she could pocket only 70 percent of the proceeds.) Instead, reform liberals contend that investment and productivity languish because potential investors and entrepreneurs have good reason to doubt that there are enough potential customers out there who are willing and able to buy their products. The core problem, in other words, is one of insufficient "effective aggregate demand": that is, consumers do not have enough purchasing power at their disposal for potential investors to think that people will buy enough of what they could produce to make it profitable to do so. So in place of the sunny optimism of the *Field of Dreams* mantra that they will come if you build it, reform liberals would offer a more cautionary mantra to explain laggard economic growth: "They won't build it unless they are confident that consumers will come with money in hand."

The policy implications of this demand-side explanation of the causes of an underperforming economy, in turn, logically run in a different direction from those promoted by supply-siders. Rather than change current fiscal policies in a way that will put more money in the hands of those well heeled enough to be investors, demand-side analysis leads to the practical conclusion that policy changes should emphasize getting more money into the hands of the consumer. More specifically, these policies should enhance the economic situation of consumers who will spend their additional resources and in so doing pump up the level of economic productivity. And because people toward the middle and lower income levels have a higher "propensity to consume," that means adopting policies that boost the income of these strata of the population. (A higher "propensity to consume" means simply a higher likelihood of spending additional resources rather than saving them. And because people in lower income echelons have more unmet needs than do the well off, they are likely to spend more of an economic windfall than are upper-class recipients.) For reform liberals, then, the pertinent lesson is that the best way to boost economic growth in most circumstances is to adopt policies that will improve the economic welfare of workers and consumers more generally, rather than looking to put more wealth into the hands of potential investors at the upper end of the spectrum.

One other government action to stimulate a recessionary economy is sometimes referred to as "priming the pump." The government can soften an economic downturn by putting people to work on infrastructure projects or other productive enterprises of some sort. Doing that cuts unemployment and puts purchasing power into the workers' hands, while also creating something of value. During the Great Depression in the 1930s, for example, the Roosevelt administration created the Works Progress Administration and the Civilian Conservation Corps. Critics complained that those hired under these programs were engaged in "make-work" activities of little value. But at least some of the work of these agencies created things of lasting value. Both the WPA and the CCC played a significant role, for example, in building the Blue Ridge Parkway—a national treasure that has been the most visited place in the national park system almost every year since World War II.

WE HAVE CERTAINLY not covered here every controversial issue regarding the economic performance of a capitalist market system, but we have canvassed the core logic behind the claim that a free-market system is superior to all others; we have looked at the reasons critics of the market system offer for why they believe that its real-world functioning does not and cannot produce the results it promises; we have looked at the reform liberal case for how and why collective action through government is necessary to constrain and supplement the economic marketplace; we have noted why advocates of laissez-faire policies see government interference with the market to be problematic; and we have examined two of the most important and policy-relevant macroeconomic disagreements between the defenders and critics of the market system.

All of these arguments take place within the logical domain of political economy. That is, they are all theoretically based accounts of the empirical consequences of market systems with reference to the criterion or goal of maximizing the aggregate production of wealth. Quite obviously, this criterion is a preeminent one in any assessment of economic systems, since the production of material goods—wealth and income—is what they are principally about. It is also true, however, that any economic system has very significant functions and consequences above and beyond its axial purpose of wealth production. From the standpoint of political philosophy, ideology, and public policy, two kinds of these additional functions and consequences are most important. First, economic systems not only produce wealth: they also distribute it. Second, if we can assume—and I think we should—that the purposes and goals of a political society are not exclusively economic but instead include other components of good and fulfilling human lives, then we must consider the ways that economic systems contribute to and/or impede achieving these larger human purposes when we evaluate them.

In the next two chapters, then, we shall turn our attention to assessing the capitalist market system in terms of these additional moral criteria. Setting aside for the moment the question of whether an unfettered market offers the best pathway to economic success, we shall look in the next chapter at competing arguments about whether the market's allocations of distributive shares can be seen as morally justifiable. And in the following chapter, we shall look at competing views about whether the functioning and results of capitalist market institutions contribute to—or possibly even define—the achievement of the constitutive purposes and ideals of a good democratic society, or whether, on the contrary, the functions and results of a market system are inadequate to—or possibly impede—the achievement of a good democratic society and therefore need to be politically constrained and supplemented in various ways.

CHAPTER TWO

The Moral Philosophy Debate

Are Market Outcomes Morally Acceptable?

The central question in the previous chapter was: Is a capitalist free-market system the most effective way to create wealth? Does its way of organizing and incentivizing the production of goods and services maximize the absolute amount of value/wealth possible for a society? Although any answer to this question is to some extent speculative, because it involves prediction of future consequences and conjectural comparisons with other hypothetically possible systems, it is fundamentally an empirical question within the domain of political economy. It is a question about the facts, about what alternatives might be possible within the real limits of the human condition, and about the relevant cause-and-effect relationships the real world presents to us. There is, of course, one implicit value assumption that makes these questions practically relevant: namely, that enhancing wealth production is a good thing to seek. But in a world of scarcity and great need, few would challenge that assumption.

All systems of political economy do more than produce wealth, however. They also establish and enforce rules for the distribution of the wealth they create. They determine not only what gets produced, how it gets produced, and how much gets produced but also who gets what share of the wealth produced. That in turn means that assessing the relative merits of an economic system, whether capitalist, communist, or whatever, cannot be accomplished entirely by invoking evidence and empirical theories from political economy. For judging the merits of schemes and standards for distributing things of value among contending parties depends upon our moral judgments. It requires answering questions such as: Who deserves what? To what are different people entitled? What rules for allocating scarce goods are fair? And why? In short, because they determine the rules for distributing wealth and not merely the arrangements for creating wealth, economic systems have to be judged not only within the court of political economy but also within the court of moral philosophy. Or, in the context of democratic societies where the people rule, the citizens have to make moral judgments about distributive justice when they are deciding what rules of the game they want to establish for their economic activities.

The distributive standard of an economic system is the answer given by its institutions to the question: To each according to what? The standard of the capitalist marketplace is: to each according to the market value of what they produce. Or, as some have added, according to the market value of what they and the instruments of production they own produce. It also should be noted that the "value" of the good or service you produce is here determined "subjectively" rather than "objectively." That is, the value of goods and services is determined by the needs, tastes, and desires of consumers and employers: there is no God's-eye standard of worth involved. And the market value of your production is relative rather than absolute: it is the *added* value of your specific contribution within the conditions of supply and demand for the goods or services in question. For example, the value of some special teacher, coach, or other mentor to your life might be extraordinarily great. But the price (salary) of that mentor will be far less than what LeBron James commands in the market, because there are many more people willing and able to provide comparable mentoring services than there are people who can do what LeBron does on the basketball court.

The central question in this chapter thus becomes: Does the market's distributive criterion of "to each according to the marginal subjective value of what they—and the productive instruments they own —produce" constitute an acceptable standard of distributive justice? Or, if this free-market allocative criterion cannot be persuasively defended as a standard of distributive justice, is there some other moral standard it does satisfy that can be said to override considerations of justice? In sum, the question is: Are the distributive standards and outcomes of market distributions morally appropriate?

Justice-Based Arguments for Market Allocations

Aristotle observed over two millennia ago that there are two basic types of conceptions of justice: egalitarian and proportional. Moreover, he believed that the battle between these contending conceptions played a central causal role in the political battles, including revolutions, that he had seen in the various city-states around him. The elites in these societies, the wealthy and powerful, adhered to the idea that it was morally appropriate for a society to allocate the good things in life at its disposal to people in proportion to their contributions to that society. Those who did more, those who were more valuable to the welfare of the society, should—as a matter of justice— receive more than those who contributed less. The common folk, on the other hand, inclined to a more egalitarian set of moral intuitions. All people have moral worth, all lives matter, they might have said. We are all Athenians or Spartans or Corinthians. So justice requires that we all share the goods we produce relatively equally, except and unless there are morally relevant overriding considerations on behalf of someone getting more.

Market justice, then, is a species of proportional justice. Markets allocate wealth, income, and the control of material goods unequally to members of a society—in proportion to the (marginal) value of what they produce. Those laissez-faire advocates who want to depict the way free markets allocate goods as in conformity with the de- mands of justice, therefore, have to provide reasons for us to accept the (unequal) proportional allocations produced by markets as fair and proper. These, then, are desert-based arguments—explanations of why people deserve what markets give them.

There are at least three grounds for the claim that people deserve the rewards—or deprivations—that market institutions give to them. These three bases for alleging that the wealth distributions of the market are deserved and therefore morally appropriate, moreover, are not inconsistent with each other. They can be compatible, even though they are not identical, and can be seen as mutually reinforcing. The first basis for asserting the moral propriety of the market's unequal distributions is the straightforward equation of worth and desert. To get what we are worth *is* to get what we deserve. And the market is the proper adjudicator of what we are worth—materially and economically speaking—because it represents the judgment of our peers, who express their appraisal of our worth in the most tangible way possible: by putting their money where their mouth is.

The second basis for asserting that we deserve what the market gives us is that the market rewards us for our effort—for the blood, sweat, and tears that we put into our creation of valuable goods and into our performance of valuable services. The classic locus of this argument in political theory is found in John Locke's famous justification of private property. God gives the earth to men in common, he tells us. So what can provide legitimacy to unequal holdings of property? The answer is that although we human beings have no grounds for claiming ownership of the natural resources that come from the hand of God, we each have a distinctive and legitimate personal possession in our individual bodies. My body is indeed and by right *my* body and not yours or anyone else's. So when I work to produce something of value, I accomplish that feat by "mixing my labor" with some of the heretofore economically dormant raw materials of the earth. The goods and the value so produced, then, are properly my own— separated from the original commons—because they represent my embodied labor. So once I plant corn in an unimproved plot of land, till it, weed it, and harvest it, that corn properly and legitimately belongs to me—and not to you, who contributed no toil to the process of wealth creation. And to the extent that I work longer and harder than you do, it is not an offense to justice; instead it is entirely fair and proper for me to prosper more than you do. We have both received our just deserts—proportioned in accord with our different levels of effort.

The third line of argument for defending the unequal distributions generated by the marketplace as a form of giving people their just deserts is the claim that people are being rewarded in some proportion to their moral character. People who come out ahead in the disparate allocations of the market do so because of their virtues. And virtue should be rewarded. Those who do not do so well in the marketplace, on the other hand, owe their lack of rewards principally to their own vices or poor behavior. Hence, the judgments of the market—like the judgments of God—are "meet and right." Locke himself gave some credence to this line of argument in the context of his justification of property rights. Though God "gave the world to man in common," he wrote, "it cannot be supposed He meant it should always remain common and uncultivated. He gave it to the use of the industrious and the rational . . . not to the fancy or covetousness of the quarrelsome and contentious."[1]

This argument was given voice in this country in the decades between 1880 and 1920 as the Industrial Revolution and the rise of large corporations brought about the Gilded Age, along with its magnification of disparities in wealth. Two exemplary exponents of this "wealth as a product of virtue" theme were William Graham Sumner, a prominent sociologist and Yale professor, and Russell Conwell, a lawyer, journalist, and entrepreneur who founded Temple University. Both of them also served as church ministers at some point in their careers, Sumner for an Episcopal church in New Jersey and Conwell for a Baptist church in Philadelphia. Sumner's vindication of the inequalities of a capitalist economy was a somewhat dour expression of the Protestant ethic. "God and Nature," he wrote, "have ordained the chances and conditions of life on earth once for all." We can deduce from these conditions "the rules of right living," which we must adhere to for success in "the struggle with Nature for existence." These rules require of us "very wearisome and commonplace tasks [that] consist in labor and self-denial repeated over and over again." Those who do well in the competitive marketplace are those who adhere to these rules and make the requisite sacrifices. They deserve their success. On the other hand, "The negligent, shiftless, inefficient, silly, and imprudent are fastened upon the industrious and prudent as a responsibility and a duty." These "are the ones through whom the productive and conservative forces of society are wasted. They constantly neutralize and destroy the finest efforts of the wise and industrious, and are a dead weight on the society." All "ought to have equal chances," but "the greater the chances the more unequal will be the fortune of these two sets of men. So it ought to be, in all justice and right reason [because] these results are proportioned to the merits of individuals."[2]

Some thirty years later, Conwell delivered a speech over six thousand times (earning in the process over $8 million) that he titled "Acres of Diamonds." In it, he urged his listeners, "You ought to get rich, and it is your duty to get rich . . . because to make money honestly is to preach the gospel." The wealthy deserve their riches because of their virtues, and the poor deserve their plight because it stems from their vices. Of the wealthy, he writes, "Let me say here clearly, . . . ninety eight out of one hundred of the rich men of America are honest. That is why they are rich. . . . Take me out into the suburbs of Philadelphia and introduce me to the people who own . . . those magnificent homes so lovely in their art, and I will introduce you to the very best people in character as well as in enterprise in our city." On the other hand, "The number of poor who are to be sympathized with is very small. To sympathize with a man whom God has punished for his sins, thus to help him when God would still continue a just punishment, is to do wrong."[3]

So if justice involves receiving what you deserve, as in receiving your "just deserts" or in rewarding people on the basis of "merit," then those who seek to defend the economic outcomes of the marketplace as morally proper have several justice-based arguments they can make—and have made. In the area of retributive justice—that is, accounts of just punishment for moral infractions—the common expression is "Let the punishment fit the crime." Just punishment should be proportionate to the amount of damage and the degree of malice of the criminal act. When it comes to distributive justice, say defenders of market distributions, it follows that what people receive as rewards or allocations should "fit" in the same way—that is, their share of wealth should bear direct proportion to the value or merit of their contributions. And the distributive outcomes of the capitalist market-place are entitled to be seen as conforming to the demands of justice because they do precisely that. In the marketplace, people get what they and their labor are worth; they receive in proportion to the effort they make or the hard work they do; and they are arguably also being rewarded for the virtues of honesty, self-control, thrift, reliability, and diligence that they exhibit.

Justice-Based Arguments for "Welfare State" Distributions

Reform liberals find the claim that the free marketplace produces a fair and morally unproblematic distribution of wealth and income unpersuasive. And some of them would insist that compelling standards of social justice obligate us to adjust the marketplace's distribution of wealth in ways that mitigate the unfairness and excessive inequalities of life. We begin here by looking at the reform liberal critique of the case for "market justice."

The first basis offered by laissez-faire enthusiasts for the justice of markets, as we noted in the previous section of this chapter, was that market price reflects the "worth" of goods and services. But this claim, its critics say, is problematic in important ways. When we think of "worth," we are presumably thinking about a kind of "value" that is in some sense real and objective, that is absolute rather than relative, and that serves the general interest rather than serving to benefit some at the expense of others. But the judgments and circumstances that determine the market "value" or price of a good or service are "marginal" and relative rather than absolute; and they often serve particular interests rather than—or even at the expense of—the interests of others or of society as a whole.

These abstractly stated distinctions and their bearing upon doubts about market price as reflecting the value or worth of something can be clarified by more concrete examples. The market prices—that is, the going salaries—of soldiers, firefighters, police officers, and elementary school teachers are relatively modest, whereas the salaries of movie and television stars and professional athletes run into tens of millions. Which of these are more essential to the safety and success of a society? Advertising executives who contrive advertising campaigns that seek to persuade teenagers that they will be seen as cool or macho or glamorous if they light up a particular brand of cigarette may be very highly compensated. But their value to the bottom line of the particular tobacco company whose products they promote surely does not represent a positive contribution to society as a whole. In fact, considering the devastating health consequences that a smoking habit has visited upon large numbers of people, the very work that commands a high price from their clients may have a significantly negative net worth for the society. Finally, the highest-paid public employees in most states in the US are college football or basketball coaches. This elevated status reflects the high marginal value they are deemed to have by the universities who employ them. Because they engage in zero-sum competition, being marginally better than others can make all the difference in the world in terms of bringing victories, hence honor and revenue, to their universities or professional franchises. But for the same reason—namely the zero-sum competitive nature of their industry—there arguably is little or no net worth to society of their collective labors. Or to take another example of the difference between the market reward for one's work and its actual worth, consider the virtually infinite worth of developing a polio vaccine and the relatively modest financial reward Jonas Salk received for doing that. You can surely come up with your own examples to make the point. Although market value may indicate the marginal worth of a good or service to particular purchasers, say reform liberals, that is not necessarily the same thing as the absolute real worth of that good or service to society as a whole.

Nor does market price accurately compensate proportionally to the effort in making a good or performing a service. It is surely true that all productive work requires the expenditure of some effort, which it is reasonable to say is rewarded by the marketplace. But there is not in the real world the correlation between levels of effort and reward in market outcomes that would justify any claim that these outcomes meet the criteria of proportional justice. Hard labor often produces meager returns. As Tennessee Ernie Ford famously sang about the plight of coal miners: "Sixteen tons and what do I get? Another day older and deeper in debt." And very handsome returns can result from work that is engaging and not particularly arduous.

Finally, the last of the three alleged bases for the proportional justice deservingness of the rewards people receive in the capitalist marketplace, reform liberal critics argue, is also not borne out upon reflection and observation. It may be true that some features of good moral character play an important role in achieving financial success. Honesty, diligence, and some degree of self-denial, as William Sumner insisted, are almost essential to succeeding in the marketplace. But the claim that fiscal success comes in some close proportion to the quality of one's overall moral character is very hard to sustain. Contrary to Russell Conwell's biased class stereotypes in his "Acres of Diamonds" speech, many of those toward the bottom of the income scale in today's society are hardworking, honest, responsible, and generous people. And some at the top are not paragons of human virtue. Gordon Gekko and Ebenezer Scrooge may be fictional characters; but it is not fiction to say that sins and character flaws such as covetousness, pride, pleonexia (an insistence upon taking more than one's proper share), and a willingness to exploit the vulnerable for one's own benefit can often be found among those living in urban penthouses or in the suburban mansions that Russell Conwell depicted as abodes of the morally best.

The hard truth is, say those who embrace more egalitarian conceptions of distributive justice, an enormous amount of sheer luck factors into determining where someone winds up in the economic pecking order of a capitalist system. Those who do well and brag about being "self-made" men or women are not only boastful but also somewhat delusional. As the sardonic gibe goes, they started on third base and thought they had hit a triple. Anyone who succeeds in life—and in the economic marketplace—undeniably had to work to get there. But they also had to have been the fortunate recipients of any number of important gifts they did nothing to deserve.

First, any one of us who becomes a success in life or in the marketplace has to have been endowed with certain natural talents, abilities, capacities. And, as the word *endowed* denotes, these abilities were gifts we lucked into rather than anything we either created or earned.

Intelligence, good health, a comely appearance, natural charm, marketable traits such as a fine voice or exceptional athleticism—these are theologically speaking "God-given" assets, or to the more naturalistically inclined the result of random outcomes in a genetic lottery. So no individuals can credibly claim to have done anything to deserve their particular complement of the "natural assets" that go a long way to determining how well they wind up faring in a competitive marketplace.

Second, all of us arrive helpless into this world. Without immediate and assiduous succor, care, attention, and support, we would quickly perish. Moreover, this condition of profound dependency extends for years on end—a fact of life quite perilous to children and quite burdensome to the adults charged with their care. (In his stage play *Seascape*, Edward Albee constructs a fanciful conversation between a human couple and a sea lizard couple, who compare their different lifestyles. When the human couple explain that humans have to care for their children for around eighteen years, the lizards respond with horrified disbelief.) The consequence of this fact of the human condition is that our chances of success in life are enormously dependent upon the quality of care and nurturance we receive from our parents—or their surrogates. And the quality of this nurturance varies dramatically. Some of us have highly competent and deeply devoted parents who provide unconditional love, material resources, and intellectual stimulation to pave our way to capable adulthood. Others suffer at the hands of abusive, incompetent, impoverished, or negligent parents who send their children into the world unhealthy, mentally unprepared, and emotionally scarred. The result is that nothing—perhaps not even the scope of our natural abilities—determines our chances in life more than the quality of our parenting. And since no one has any say over who their parents are, this crucial determinant of our life chances is a case of pure random luck—good or bad. That being the case, from the standpoint of justice—which demands that people get what they deserve—nothing could be more unfair and inequitable than the vast and totally undeserved disparities in the quality of the parents to whom people are born and bound.

Third, the larger circumstances of our birth and social support also go a very long way to determining how well we are able to do in life, economically and otherwise. We are born not only into different nuclear families but also into different countries that have different levels of material resources and different levels of institutional protection and support. Had he been born in Syria or the Sudan, for example, it is highly unlikely that Donald Trump would today be in a position that would allow him to disparage other people as "losers." He would himself have been a loser, for reasons beyond his control. These differing national circumstances have less significant bearing upon distributive questions among the citizens of the same country, since (setting aside the impact of discriminatory practices toward subgroups—an important but different consideration) all of us benefit, or suffer, from the favorable or unfavorable material, social, and institutional legacy we receive from our fellow citizens and forebears. Those who recognize the importance of such an institutional legacy, however, understand what President Obama meant by a comment to the effect that successful people "didn't create that on their own." And by so recognizing their indebtedness to many others, they are inspired to want to "give back" to a society that did well by them.

Finally, of course, there are all those out-of-the-blue serendipitous events that change the course of people's lives and careers. On the bad side are the disabling accidents or illnesses that damage or end the careers of those who suffer them. And on the positive side are those strokes of good fortune that dramatically advance someone's career path or present them with a financial windfall. A couple of examples can make the point. First, the career of my own father, who became a college president at the relatively tender age of thirty-five: How did he get on the path that took him there? He was a twenty-something employee in the Federal Budget Bureau (now OMB) in Washington shortly after World War II. A top university decided they needed an administrator with experience in government, because they realized that their interface with government agencies and programs was becoming increasingly important. They had settled upon my father's boss as their choice when he at the last moment suffered a significant health setback that forced him to decline. Out of some combination of desperation, convenience, and some appreciation of my father's abilities, they turned to him and said, "How about you?" So my family packed up and crossed the country for him to become "assistant to the president" at a top university. Seven years later, he became a college president—a position he held at one institution or another until his retirement. Or consider the case of my own university's number one sports fan. Not long after graduating from my university, he took a job with a startup grocery store chain that was controlling its cash flow in part by compensating its employees with stock shares or options in lieu of good salaries. The company took off, and its stock grew exponentially. After a while, he realized that his stock holdings could allow him to retire quite early. So he decided to do that and devote his expansive leisure time to assiduously pursue his fandom of as many of his alma mater's teams as time would allow. So for him as for my father, a stroke of good fortune brought him a life he could not have reasonably imagined. Had he gone to work for a different chain of grocery stores and had my father's boss not taken sick, their lives would have been different and most likely not as remunerative. Good luck, indeed!

The lesson of the previous paragraphs, then, is that strokes of luck—good or bad—play a huge role in determining our level of success in the economic marketplace. Once you factor in our natural talents, which we did nothing to deserve, the quality of our parenting, which we did nothing to determine, the country of our birth, which we neither chose nor deserved, and random strokes of good or bad accidents in our lives, a lot of our place in life—including our income level—has already been settled. And from the standpoint of justice, those truths present a problem. As the distinguished legal philosopher Edmond Cahn has argued, our ethical sensibilities as human beings have endowed us with a "sense of injustice." This sense of injustice prompts us to feelings of moral indignation when we encounter instances of manifest unfairness. There are, he continues, several kinds of actions or events that trigger this indignant reaction. One is a perception that someone has been punished—or rewarded—for something that person did not do or in a way all out of proportion to his or her actions. That leads to the demand in law that, as the saying goes, punishments must "fit the crime." Another standard for morally acceptable law is "that the inequalities resulting from law must make sense." And that derives from the fact that "the sense of injustice revolts against whatever is unequal by caprice."[4]

So consider now, say most reform liberals, the implications of the preceding paragraphs. If we accept Cahn's point that our sense of injustice comes alive when we are confronted with (1) capricious inequalities, and (2) disparate outcomes that cannot credibly be presented as proportional to people's deservingness, and if we also recognize that an enormous amount of sheer luck, good and bad, plays a huge role in determining where people wind up in the highly unequal distributions of wealth and income the market system creates, it then follows that the claims of people such as Sumner, Conwell, and their contemporary intellectual heirs that market distributions are just and fair lose their persuasiveness. Whatever else one might say in favor of "letting the market decide," when it comes to the distribution of wealth and income it cannot credibly be claimed that the resulting allocations will be truly and entirely deserved, or fair, or just.

One part of the case for reform liberals' goals and policies, then, is the insistence that if a democratic society is to be a just society it cannot be content to let the free market provide the final word when it comes to the distribution of wealth and income. Instead, they contend, some redistribution is morally appropriate, perhaps even morally obligatory, in order to redress the significant role of what Cahn called "morally capricious inequalities" in creating the disparities of wealth and income generated by the dynamics of the marketplace.

How then should a society motivated by a sense of (in)justice go about dealing with the moral and practical challenges presented by the arbitrary inequalities and the nonproportionate relationship between merit and reward within them? What is the appropriate standard of redress? And how might it be institutionalized?

The standard perhaps offered most often is to provide "equal opportunity" to all members of the society. In fact, that standard is endorsed to some extent by laissez-faire and reform liberals alike. But important ambiguities attend the notion of equal opportunity, and the two camps tend to understand its meaning in importantly different ways. Market-oriented liberals largely identify equal opportunity with institutional nondiscrimination. And that principle, they believe, is embodied in three ways—all of which are found in free-market democracies. First, there is the legal nondiscrimination embodied in the precepts of "rule of law," especially in the requirements of "equal protection" that were crucial to classic accounts of liberal legitimacy and that are in this country enshrined in our constitution. Second is the political nondiscrimination institutionalized in universal suffrage and the equal weight accorded to every vote. Third is the nondiscriminatory force of the free market, which renders its judgments and offers its rewards on the basis of individuals' economic worth or merits, without regard to any ascriptive social status (such as feudal ranks and privileges) or regard to anyone's race, color, gender, or creed.[5] So, say free-market liberals, the kind of society that we champion—a combination of popular sovereignty, equality before the law, and a free-market economy—represents and embodies the proper understanding of what "equal opportunity" is all about.

Reform liberals certainly agree that one-person/one-vote democracy and equal protection of the law are crucial to affording all citizens the opportunity to succeed. And they also recognize and value the ways that free markets may penalize discriminatory practices: as the saying goes, "The only color that matters in the marketplace is green." But they find quite unconvincing the claim that nondiscrimination alone can either count as or be capable of producing genuinely equal opportunity. For even with all these important and admirable constraints on discrimination in place, it could still be the case that vast numbers of young people would arrive at their point of entry into the competitive marketplace quite unprepared. With a childhood of dependency upon impoverished adults, and absent some communal resources to draw upon, they might well enter into adulthood poorly educated, undersocialized, and even physically and mentally stunted from malnourishment. In that event, it would be a mockery for a society to congratulate itself for providing equal opportunity.

So to provide some redress for arbitrary inequalities, which are as Cahn observed presumptively unjust, any society that aspires to be fair and just, reform liberals argue, must take some affirmative steps toward achieving greater equality of real opportunity. And these steps logically would include providing all our children with access to a good education (something that my state of North Carolina has in fact enshrined in its constitution, where the relevant provision reads: "The General Assembly shall provide by taxation and otherwise for a general and uniform system of free public schools . . . wherein equal opportunities shall be provided for all students"), protection against malnutrition, and access to health care.[6]

Providing people with genuine opportunity also may go beyond ensuring that all children receive the education and health care needed to have a chance to succeed in life. In a racially, ethnically, and religiously pluralistic society, equal opportunity may require placing some constraints on marketplace behaviors in the form of antidiscrimination laws. No one, of course, can be prevented—for both practical and moral reasons—from patronizing establishments of their own choosing. So if I want, for reasons of personal comfort or prejudice, to buy from people who look and act and believe like me, I should be allowed to do that. But if a company operates a business open to the public, or is a large-scale employer, or is a provider of large-scale rental housing, a society dedicated to basic principles of justice and to equal protection of the law can require of it some showing that it is not engaged in systematic discrimination against certain groups within society. Although reform liberals are not the only ones who have supported the concrete embodiment of this logic in the enactment of equal-opportunity legislation in public accommodations, employment, and housing, they have been the principal proponents of these laws. And many laissez-faire liberals have opposed these government regulations on the grounds that even large corporate businesses are private actors whose property rights entitle them to discriminate if they want to.[7]

Some reform liberals also argue that even robust equal-opportunity policies alone are insufficient to achieve social justice and need to be supplemented by policies that would redress other sources of unjustified inequality of wealth and income. Equal-opportunity policies seek to diminish the impact of discrimination against minorities and to lessen the gap between the life chances of children that stems from their disparate locations in the socioeconomic hierarchy. So far, so good. But, as these reform liberals point out, that leaves quite untouched the other major source of capriciously unequal economic outcomes—namely, the huge disparity among people's natural talents. As the influential moral philosopher John Rawls writes: "It seems to be one of the fixed points of our considered judgments, that no one deserves his place in the distribution of natural endowments, any more than one deserves one's initial starting place in society." Therefore, he argues, "There is no more reason to permit the distribution of income and wealth to be settled by the distribution of natural assets than by historical and social fortune."[8]

Rawls argues that the most logical way to determine the principles of justice—that is, the rules that should be used to produce a fair distribution of wealth and income in a society—would be to ask: What rules would people agree to live by if they knew nothing at all about either the natural talents they had been given or the family and social circumstances they had been born to? Screening their knowledge of these morally arbitrary (because capriciously unequal) facts about themselves would function like the blindfold worn by our depiction of Lady Justice as she holds the scales of justice. In both cases, those charged with determining a fair and just outcome would be kept from having their decision contaminated by considerations irrelevant to justice.

Rawls's own answer to this hypothetical rational choice thought experiment goes like this: First, he argues that people faced with momentously consequential decisions under conditions of great uncertainty—certainly the case here—will quite rationally be highly risk averse. They will want above all to protect themselves against a disastrous fate. They will therefore adopt a decision strategy of maximizing the worst possible outcome to which the rules they chose would make them vulnerable.

That logic might seem to lead to choosing an absolutely equal distributive rule. But Rawls allows his hypothetical decision makers to understand the basic facts of the human condition, and so they would understand an important practical danger of mandating total equality: namely, that if everyone is going to wind up equal, no one has any incentive of self-interest to work any more than he or she wants to or to perform any unpleasant tasks. The result would be that every member of the society could wind up being worse off than if some economic incentives—and therefore some inequalities—were permitted.

The rational principle of distribution to choose in the absence of morally arbitrary considerations—and therefore Rawls's core principle of social justice—thus becomes: inequalities of wealth and income, liberties, and opportunities are permissible, but only to the extent that they function to produce the best possible outcome for the least advantaged members of the society.[9] Rawls calls this the "difference principle."

Rawls's egalitarian standard for social justice remains controversial, even among reform liberals. Some reform liberals find the logic and moral intuitions that lead to the difference principle convincing and would judge our social policies accordingly, but other reform liberals are not so persuaded. Even within Rawls's thought experiment, for example, some argue that it could be just as rational to choose distributive arrangements that guarantee everyone enough wealth and income to live and to perform his or her responsibilities as a democratic citizen but that otherwise permit the social and economic inequalities that result not only from people's talent levels but also from their different values, inclinations, and willingness to work. Many reform liberals, moreover, would agree with the libertarian philosopher Robert Nozick that it is problematic to derive persuasive principles of distributive justice from assumptions that take no account whatsoever of people's variable levels of time and effort—as Rawls seems to do. In his original justification for giving people no claim of moral desert for working more or working harder, for example, Rawls wrote that one's work ethic was as morally irrelevant as one's social standing at birth or one's endowment of natural talents because it, too, was a function of moral luck: "The assertion that a man deserves the superior character that enables him to make the effort to cultivate his abilities is equally problematic; for his character depends in large part upon fortunate family and social circumstances for which he can claim no credit. The notion of desert seems not to apply to these cases."[10]

As Nozick and others have pointed out, this argument "attributes *everything* noteworthy about the person completely to certain sorts of 'external' factors. So denigrating a person's autonomy and prime responsibility for his actions is a risky line to take for a theory that otherwise wishes to buttress the dignity and self-respect of autonomous beings."[11] It also seems difficult to reconcile Rawls's dismissal of moral desert in deciding just shares with his assertion that "a propensity to commit [criminal acts] is a mark of bad character, and in a just society legal punishments will only fall on those who display those faults."[12]

In later writing, Rawls put forward a somewhat different rationale for giving no consideration to moral desert in arriving at principles of social justice, saying that claims of moral desert are dependent upon "comprehensive moral and religious viewpoints that are not appropriate to invoke in a morally and religiously pluralistic society." But this alterative justification has its own problems, and it does not resolve the inconsistency between his accounts of distributive and criminal justice.[13] In any event, his dismissal of any consideration of moral desert in determining what constitutes economic fairness, his rejection of the idea that people who work longer and harder actually deserve a larger share of resources than those who work less, remains the same. (He would allow giving the more productive workers a somewhat larger share, but only to the degree necessary to maximize the absolute welfare of the least well off. Any inequality in distributive shares, that is, would represent a practical concession to necessity— not a morally deserved reward for superior effort.) And that seems as problematic to many reform liberals as to libertarians like Nozick. William Galston, for example, who served as a domestic policy adviser to President Clinton, criticizes Rawls for "severing the link between what we do and what we deserve." In so doing, his "ruling out individual desert as a core element of America's collective self-understanding that should shape the principles of justice we adopt does violence not only to a reasonable account of 'the moral point of view' but even to the most plausible description of the shared understanding of America's public culture."[14]

Despite his sharp criticism of Rawls's claim that social justice should pay no heed to moral desert, what Galston presents as "a contemporary American consensus (at least in broad outline) concerning just principles and institutions" incorporates not only equal opportunity but also elements of redistribution to compensate those endowed with fewer marketable assets. Market inequalities, he writes, are acceptable to justice ("Individuals are permitted to achieve unequal rewards by developing their natural talents") but only after all attain a "level of minimal decency defined by the minimum wage, [earned income] tax credits, the welfare system, unemployment insurance, social security," and disability payments. This depiction does in fact well describe the current American mix of market allocations tempered by a significant admixture of welfare state arrangements. But if that represents a rough consensus, it represents at least as much a compromise between political forces and moral persuasions pulling hard upon it in opposite directions. For many reform liberals would add to Galston's list of communal provision some form of universal access to health care and higher education, financed by a tax system somewhat more progressive than the current one. And from the other side, some laissez-faire small government forces would cut back or eliminate altogether the minimum-wage requirement, earned income tax credits, the Aid for Families with Dependent Children program, unemployment insurance, and social security programs that Galston includes as part of his alleged consensus.

The gap between the views about distributive justice and fairness found within the laissez-faire and reform liberal camps is also on display in their differences on tax policy. Some of the disagreements about tax policy stem from the differences between supply-side and demand-side economics discussed in the previous chapter. But divergent beliefs about justice are also very important in shaping competing versions of appropriate income tax and inheritance tax policies offered by the two camps. When it comes to setting income tax rates, laissez-faire partisans lean toward having a single "flat tax" rate on all income above a subsistence-level income that would be tax exempt. In debates among candidates for the 2016 Republican nomination for president, for example, Ben Carson cited the practice of "tithing" in his church—in which all church members are asked to contribute 10 percent of their income—as a good model for federal income taxes. And the economist Milton Friedman has proposed moving to a more realistically calculated flat tax of around 23 percent.[15] Reform liberals, on the other hand, generally argue that considerations of fairness dictate having a "progressive" tax schedule in which higher levels of income are taxed at a higher rate. The legendary billionaire investment mogul Warren Buffett, for example, once calculated that because of tax-favored capital gains his overall income tax rate was lower than his secretary's—and that this seemed unfair and inappropriate to him. Similarly, former president Bill Clinton, now faring extremely well financially since escaping the Oval Office, has regularly argued that the tax rate on high incomes like his own should in fairness be higher than it is.

There is a similar divide when it comes to inheritance taxes. Those toward the right on the ideological spectrum view the question of fairness in this area from the perspective of the donor—the person leaving the inheritance. (That's why they like to call it a "death tax.") They point out that the donor paid income taxes on the funds he or she is passing on and contend that these funds should not be subject to an additional tax simply because the person who earned them wanted to gift them to others rather than to spend them upon himself or herself.[16] Reform liberals, in contrast, argue that tax fairness should be looked at from the standpoint of the recipients. The rhetorically clever term *death tax* is a deliberate misnomer, they say, because no one is taxing the deceased—who for obvious reasons are permanently tax exempt. Instead, an inheritance tax is levied upon those who have been fortunate enough to have been given these funds. How then, they ask, can it possibly be seen as fair and proper to exempt these fortunate recipients from paying any tax on income they did nothing to earn while taxing all income that people actually worked for? From the standpoint of justice, doesn't this get it backwards? As current policy stands in this country, only about 0.2 percent of estates are subject to tax. Estates of up to $5 million per person or $10 million per married couple may be passed on without tax. Proposals for revision of the current law are consistent with the contrasting claims about fairness cited above: some Republican candidates favor eliminating federal inheritance taxes altogether, while some Democratic candidates would like to close the capital gains tax loophole by imposing the existing capital gains tax upon all unrealized capital gains in an estate and by taxing inherited windfalls (perhaps above the first million or two) at the same rate as earned income.

Non-Justice-Based Moral Arguments

In the preceding two sections of this chapter we have looked at some of the justice-based arguments for and against letting a society's income distribution be determined almost entirely by the free market. These competing arguments represent an important part of the debate between free-market liberals and reform liberals. But not all claims about what constitutes morally proper resource allocations in a society are based upon claims about justice. In this section we shall look at some of the most important arguments on both sides that are based upon other moral standards than those of justice and fairness. The three most important of these "other moral standards"—and therefore the ones we will discuss in the remainder of this chapter—are the utilitarian standard of "the greatest good for the greatest number," individual rights and entitlements, and obligations of charity or beneficence.

First let us consider arguments on behalf of using the utilitarian maxim as the ultimate standard for a morally justified allocation of resources. One widespread view among both moral philosophers and the general public in moral intuitions is that justice trumps utility. John Rawls gives voice to this core moral belief in what he calls "the primacy of justice" at the outset of his magnum opus *A Theory of Justice.* "Justice," he writes, "is the first virtue of social institutions. . . . Each person possesses an inviolability founded on justice that even the welfare of society as a whole cannot override. For this reason justice . . . does not allow that [unjust] sacrifices imposed on a few are outweighed by the larger sum of advantages enjoyed by many. . . . An injustice is tolerable only when it is necessary to avoid an even greater injustice."[17]

A couple of examples here can serve to illustrate Rawls's point. Suppose that authorities knew that someone had planted a bomb at an unknown location in New York City and that these authorities had the bomber's children in custody. It would be tempting to carry out a threat to torture the children in a way visible to the bomber in order to force him to reveal where the bomb was planted. Doing that could conceivably save lives. But doing that would be a moral atrocity. Similarly, we would surely and properly not be impressed by arguments claiming that the institution of slavery in America was justified because the cotton industry helped provide the financial wherewithal needed to fund the industrial development of our country. To quote

Professor Rawls one more time: "Justice denies that the loss of freedom for some is made right by a greater good shared by others."[18]

Other moral philosophers insist, however, that the utilitarian norm of "the greatest good for the greatest number" should be the primary concern in judging social institutions. The greater good does not necessarily have to take a back seat to considerations of justice. In fact, these philosophers argue, rules of justice are important precisely because they have their origins in utility. We create and enforce rules of justice and try to conform them to what the members of society think is right and fair in order to make that society stable, harmonious, happy, and successful. As the utilitarian philosopher David Hume wrote in his *Enquiry Concerning the Principles of Morals*, "Public utility is the *sole* origin of justice, and reflections on the beneficial consequences of this virtue are the *sole* foundation of its merit. . . . This virtue deserves its existence entirely from its necessary use to the intercourse and social state of mankind." And, he continues, when we seek to determine what the content of rules of justice should be—what should determine the content of property rights, for example—once again "the ultimate point . . . is the interest and happiness of human society."[19]

Both free-market defenders on one side and advocates for the welfare state on the other have arguments directed to people who, like Hume, believe that "the greatest good for the greatest number" is the ultimate standard in social policy. The utilitarian case for free-market capitalism parallels the prudential argument in the previous chapter that free-market allocations will maximize a society's wealth. Allowing a society's economic resources to be allocated by the marketplace places them where they are most efficient and productive. Doing so also stimulates economic innovation and improvement by the virtue of incentives that the market offers to entrepreneurs and inventors. So if the goal is to maximize utility in the long run, then free-market policies and distributions are the best way to achieve that goal. Moreover, continue free-market utilitarians, maximum productivity will in fact equate with "the greatest good for the greatest number" because the fruits of this productivity will filter down to even the lower-income members of society. Of course, they concede, as it says in the Bible: "The poor you will always have with you." But in today's advanced industrial societies, whatever their inequalities, even those toward the lower end of the income spectrum can dress well in clothes from Old Navy or T.J. Maxx, walk around with cell phones, be entertained by color television, and own an automobile—thanks to the results of free markets.

Two of the most prominent advocates of free markets who offer this utility-based moral justification for their views are the Austrian economist Ludwig von Mises and Milton Friedman, whom we have cited before. As von Mises, who likes to refer to himself as a "classical liberal," writes: "Liberalism [in the classical tradition] has always had in view the good of the whole, not that of any special group. It was this that the English utilitarians meant to express . . . in their famous formula, 'the greatest happiness for the greatest number.'"[20] Like John Stuart Mill in *On Liberty,* von Mises opts not to invoke claims about individual rights but instead to rest his case for free-market policies on the utilitarian maxim. And he adds that "the poor man" is included among those who enjoy the benefits of capitalism:

> It is not on behalf of property owners that [classical] liberals favor the preservation of the institution of private property. It is not because the abolition of that institution would violate property rights. . . . If they considered the abolition of the institution of private property to be in the general interest, they would advocate that it be abolished, no matter how prejudicial such a policy might be to property owners. However, the preservation of that institution is in the interest of all strata of society. Even the poor man who can call nothing his own lives incomparably better in our society than he would in one that would prove incapable of producing even a fraction of what is produced in our own.[21]

Milton Friedman writes in a similar vein, also concluding that the free-market distribution of wealth ultimately is best justified morally not by one or another conception of justice or fairness or deservingness but by its superior utility. He also, like von Mises and others, argues that the productivity benefits driven by letting market forces determine economic allocations work to the advantage of people on the low end of the economic scale, at least in the long run. In a chapter titled "The Distribution of Income," Friedman considers justice-based arguments that defend or condemn market allocations and concludes that none of them are fully convincing. So he repairs to a version of utility as the best alternative for deciding the matter; and by that standard, he concludes, "The ethical principle that would directly justify the distribution of income in a free market society: to each according to what he and the instruments he owns produces" stands vindicated. "I am led," he writes, "to the view that [the capitalist distributive principle] cannot in and of itself be regarded as an ethical principle" but that "it must be regarded as instrumental or a corollary of some other principle such as freedom." And this instrumental justification, one that includes the pleasures of freedom, satisfies the goal of "the greatest good for the greatest number" because the interests of "the masses" are thereby served. "The chief characteristic of progress and development over the past century is that it has freed the masses from back-breaking toil and has made available to them products and services that were formerly the monopoly of the upper classes."[22]

On the other side, reform liberals and defenders of welfare state redistributive programs can and have also drawn upon the utilitarian standard of the greatest good for the greatest number to justify their policies and proposals. In fact, some of the seminal figures who originated the school of "welfare economics" in the nineteenth century saw their principles of political economy as a subset of utilitarian moral philosophy. To put it into its simplest form, the utilitarian case for welfare state programs that provide income support for the economically worse off and seek to lessen economic inequality in general take their leave from the simple commonsense proposition that the marginal utility of an additional dollar is greater for a pauper than for a millionaire. Think of it this way: Who would derive greater benefit and pleasure from an extra $10,000 in their bank account: you or Bill Gates? Seems pretty clear that it would be you. We've all seen audiences at the show The Price Is Right whipped into a veritable frenzy by the prospect of winning a twenty-thousand-dollar Chevrolet, while Donald Trump, who never ceases reminding us he is "really rich," could hardly care less if someone gave him that same car. Studies have also found that people tend to become steadily happier as their income rises to around $70,000 annually, while increases in income above that point have less effect upon how happy people are. So if you put these observations together with the practical utilitarian imperative to seek "the greatest good for the greatest number," the logical conclusion would point toward robust programs of income support for people's basic needs and for crucial goods such as education and health care, financed by a progressive tax system.

Those seeking support for the empirical proposition that welfare states perform better in terms of meeting the utilitarian goal of "the greatest happiness," moreover, point to the results of studies that seek to determine the happiness level of people in different countries around the world. An international team of economists, neuroscientists, and statisticians sponsored by the United Nations, for example, published their third World Happiness Report in 2015. In the Ranking of Happiness based upon their findings, the top ten countries were Switzerland, Iceland, Denmark, Norway, Canada, Finland, Netherlands, Sweden, New Zealand, and Australia. (The United States was fifteenth.)[23] As commenters on the *Huffington Post* story about this report were quick to notice, the highest-ranked countries were almost uniformly places with robust welfare state programs. (One wrote: "Them bloody socialists. LOL." Another wrote: "They all have universal health care, some have free college educations, some have paid maternity and paternity leave. What's not to be happy about?")[24]

Individual Rights Arguments

For those who defend the allocations of the marketplace as morally justified, the ultimate and most important moral consideration is neither justice nor the utilitarian standard of the greatest good for the greatest number but instead what they contend are certain fundamental and unabridgeable individual rights. It may, they argue, be well and good for laissez-faire advocates to point out how and why people should be seen to deserve the resources they receive from market transactions. And it is also relevant for market libertarians such as Friedman and von Mises to point to the way that reliance upon market institutions to distribute economic resources improves the long-run economic welfare of society as a whole. But the arguments from desert are not entirely conclusive, and all utilitarian arguments are valid only as far as the causal claims they are based upon are accurate. The true and more fundamental basis for seeing the allocations of free-market transactions as not only morally acceptable but morally sacrosanct, according to these theorists, is the morally unabridgeable rights of individual human persons.

The libertarian social theorist Murray Rothbard, for example, argues that the nineteenth-century English laissez-faire liberals who "substituted a supposedly scientific utilitarianism for a supposedly mystical concept of natural rights as the groundwork of that philosophy"—along with their twentieth-century progeny such as Friedman and von Mises—made a serious error: "They came to use laissez-faire as a vague tendency rather than as an unblemished yardstick, and therefore increasingly and fatally compromised the libertarian creed. To say that a utilitarian cannot be trusted to maintain libertarian principle in every specific application may sound harsh, but it puts the case fairly. A notable contemporary example," he continues, "is the free-market economist Professor Milton Friedman who, like his classical economist forebears, holds to freedom as against State intervention as a general tendency, but in practice allows a myriad of damaging exceptions."[25]

So rather than relying upon the untrustworthy utilitarian arguments for a free-market libertarian society, Rothbard concludes, "Let us turn then to the natural rights basis for the libertarian creed, a basis which, in one form or another has been adopted by most of the libertarians, past and present."[26] Rothbard is joined in that claim by the prominent moral philosopher and critic of Rawlsian social justice theory Robert Nozick, who begins his magnum opus with a pronouncement of this moral axiom: "Individuals have rights, and there are things no person or groups may do to them (without violating their rights). So strong and far reaching are these rights that they raise the question of what, if anything, the state and its officials may do."[27]

Drawing upon John Locke's famous chapter on property in his *Second Treatise of Civil Government*, where he wrote that "every man has a property in his own person" (though ignoring Locke's important codicil that we are all God's property), Rothbard explicitly and Nozick implicitly both arrive at what Rothbard calls the proper "primary axiom" of market libertarianism: "the universal right of self-ownership."[28] And, again following Locke, they argue that we as self-owning individuals acquire an ownership right to goods we produce by "mixing our labor" with some part of the natural world that God gave to us in common. For, as Locke argued, in mixing our labor with the raw materials of the earth we greatly add to their value and therefore are morally entitled to remove these goods from the commons and make them our "private right." Rothbard concludes, then, that "the central core of the libertarian creed" is derived neither from abstract propositions about fair distributions nor from calculations about aggregate utility: instead it is "to establish the absolute right to private property of every man: first, in his own body, and second, in the previously unused natural resources which he first transforms by his labor. These two axioms, the right of self-ownership and the right to 'homestead,' establish the complete set of principles of the libertarian system."[29]

From whence comes this absolute and axiomatic right of self-ownership? you might ask. Neither Rothbard nor Nozick offers what presumably would have been Locke's answer: from God. Perhaps their reluctance to give that answer stems from a reluctance to hinge their principles upon theological beliefs that not all their audience might share. Perhaps they are reluctant partly because they then would have to grant that our right of self-ownership is not in fact absolute—since God retains, as it were, a lien upon us, who are ultimately *his* property.[30] Rothbard answers the question this way: the basis of natural rights is grounded in the necessities of our human nature. "The nature of man," he writes, "is such that each individual person must, in order to act, choose his own ends and employ his own means in order to attain them. . . . [It is] vitally necessary for each man's survival and property that he be free to learn, choose, develop his faculties, and act upon his knowledge and values. This is the necessary path of human nature. Violent interference with a man's learning and choices is therefore profoundly antihuman: it violates the natural law of man's needs."[31]

Nozick more or less ducks the question about the moral basis or justification for his bold opening insistence that "individuals have rights" that are "strong and far reaching." "The precise statement of the moral theory and its underlying basis," he writes, "would require a full-scale presentation and is a task for another time." At crucial points in his argument, however, he invokes Kant's categorical imperative. His central concern to avoid rights violations, he says, "reflects the underlying Kantian principle that individuals are ends and not means; they may not be sacrificed or used for the achieving of other ends without their consent. Individuals are inviolable."[32]

This line of justification, we can say, is quite compatible and coherent with Rothbard's reasoning. Together they say: Human persons are "rational and spiritual beings" in that they possess free will and know the moral law. Therefore, they are "inviolable" in the sense that they cannot properly be treated as if they were mere things or instruments—as means only rather than as ends in themselves. Furthermore, they would agree, all individual persons as "rational beings" possess rights to the recognition and protection not only of their lives and liberties but also of whatever property or possessions they have acquired without having violated any rights of others. That means that we have an "entitlement" to things that we may or may not have done something to deserve: rights possession does not derive from or depend upon justice or desert. We have an individual entitlement not only to goods we acquired by putting to productive use the talents we have but also to gifts of nature or inheritance given to us by others. Any attempt by others to take either from us constitutes theft. And that is so even if the taking comes through laws enacted by democratic majorities.[33]

Welfare State Rights Arguments

We will conclude this chapter by swinging back to the other side of the moral disputation between free-market liberals and liberal advocates of the welfare state and explaining how the latter have appropriated a similar logic and language of rights and entitlements to support their own position. The simplest and most straightforward way to understand this argument is to say that it accepts the most fundamental premises of the libertarian argument for property rights but draws from them very different conclusions. Recall that, when pushed to justify his account of natural rights, Rothbard bases his adoption of that position on what he calls "the natural law of man's needs." We have a right to liberty and property, he says, because having those things is necessary for us to be able to live and function as rational and spiritual beings. Just so, say some welfare state advocates. We are all rational beings, not just those of us who are relatively well off. So if there is some basic moral imperative on behalf of access to the most basic necessities for functioning as rational beings, then it follows that the members of a human society are under a moral obligation to find a way to place those necessities within the reach of all of their fellow citizens. In the concrete circumstances of the real world, that means that those members of society who are relatively well-off are subject to a moral obligation to give of their surplus enough to allow the less well-off members of their society to function as what Walt Whitman called "full grown men or women" or "separate and complete subjects for freedom."[34] This logic does not lead to strong claims of egalitarianism. But it does provide an argument based on what Rothbard termed a "natural law of man's needs" for some form of civic minimum, whether through guaranteed basic income or by in-kind provision.

There is also another, more historical account of an evolution of moral logic in Western societies that begins with charity and ends in a conception of economic rights. Call this the journey from "duties of beneficence" to the Universal Declaration of Human Rights. The central steps in this historical evolutionary pathway have been ably set out by Samuel Fleischacker in his book *A Short History of Distributive Justice*, and I will draw upon that account here.[35]

As Fleischacker observes, for most of its history the Western moral tradition did not see "poor relief"—provision for those in great need—as based upon considerations of justice or rights. Those struggling for subsistence were not seen as having any valid claim rights to greater equality or to relief from their poverty. And, correspondingly, those better off were not believed to have any obligations of justice to share their wealth with the needy. It was, however, widely believed by moral philosophers that people in dire need could be seen as having what were sometimes called "imperfect rights"—that is, not absolute or enforceable rights—to some form of assistance. And those who were wealthy or financially comfortable could properly be considered to be subject to what were termed "duties of beneficence." These were moral obligations but not properly legal ones. Imperatives to assist the poor were a real part of morality, but these were imperatives of charity (*caritas*, which is the kind of caring love celebrated by the Judaeo-Christian tradition as the sovereign moral virtue); and charity was seen as a discretionary sentiment, however essential it might be as part of living a good life.

Although the poor had only "imperfect" claims to any kind of financial assistance, it was held by many of the most important moral thinkers—including Thomas Aquinas, Hugo Grotius, Francis Hutcheson, and David Hume—that in cases of truly dire need, such as times of famine, people could properly be considered to have a "right of necessity" to appropriate what they needed to survive. As Aquinas wrote in the section of his magnum opus, *Summa Theologica*, that is devoted to property, when a need is "so urgent and blatant . . . that the immediate needs must be met out of whatever is available, . . . a person may legitimately supply his own needs out of another's property."[36]

It is interesting to note that it was Adam Smith who helped push the Western moral tradition another step toward seeing the state as playing a proper role in having a society fulfill its duties of beneficence—however surprising that might seem to those who see him as a champion of free-market purism. Smith—who, we need to remember, was a moral philosopher rather than an economist by trade—adhered to the traditional view that any claims for assistance based upon need were properly to be seen as "imperfect" rights. Such rights are not rights to which others have any "perfect" or absolute duty to respond; instead, they embody a morally compelling form of appeals to charity rather than to justice. And he follows the traditional view that trying to make it legally mandatory for people to comply with such appeals would be morally problematic and also could be "destructive of liberty, security, and justice."

Having said that, however, Smith goes on to qualify his stance against enforcing duties of beneficence. First, he tells us that the strength of our charitable duties varies in accord with the claimant's "character, situation, and . . . connection with ourselves" and that the strongest of these "approach . . . what is called a perfect and complete obligation." Second, he argues importantly that once institutions of civil government have been established in a society it can be legitimate for this government to *"impose"* such duties of beneficence.[37] As Fleischacker observes, Smith thereby "moves the jurisprudential tradition closer to . . . a recognition that people in certain circumstances have a strict, enforceable right to beneficence." Smith does not conclude, however, that the state is itself morally obligated to provide some form of an economic safety net for its members. Instead, he seems to have in mind the use of state power to compel its citizens to fulfill their particular duties of beneficence—with the most important of these being the familial obligations that parents, children, and other relatives have to each other.

In sum, then, Smith continues to endorse the traditional view that duties of beneficence are a species of charity rather than obligations of justice and that they are a subset of particular and private natural duties rather than general and public ones. He departs from the traditional view, however, by insisting that in exigent circumstances these duties—and the correlative rights of necessity—rise to approximate the imperative force of "perfect" duties and rights. And this insistence leads him in turn to adopt the view that it can be morally proper for the civil government to compel its citizens to fulfill their private and particular (e.g., familial) duties of this sort.

Upon reflection, however, this hybrid of old and new turns out to be an unstable one that results in both moral and practical difficulties if it is taken as a basis for law and social policy. Writing only a couple of decades after Smith, Immanuel Kant identified and emphasized the first of these problematic consequences, that of a kind of moral corruption. The basic problem here is a function of what Kant sees as the conceptual and moral impropriety and the tensions created by the elision of the moral vocabularies of charity on the one hand and duty on the other. Acts of charity are voluntary acts of generosity. As such, they are in effect morally "heroic" acts—what moral theorists would call acts of "supererogatory" virtue. Acting in accordance with imperatives of duty, in contrast, is not moral heroism worthy of special commendation. Strictly speaking, then, the whole notion of "duties of beneficence" is a contradiction in terms: performing one's duties is not an act of charity, and genuine acts of charity or beneficence are not morally mandatory. If those in serious need have a right of necessity to material assistance, as Smith insists and Kant agrees, then we are fulfilling our moral duty when we help them out. It is therefore, Kant insists, not only inaccurate but morally improper and corrupting for us to construe ourselves as benevolent moral heroes: that misconstruction implies that we are morally superior to those whose needs were met and that they are moral debtors. The consequence is the establishment in the eyes of society of a morally corrupting hierarchy of pride and debasement.

To avoid the destructive impact of this morally corrupting perception within a republican community of moral equals who are obligated to treat each other with the full respect due to rational beings, Kant says that the needs of the poor should be met by "some way other" than private alms. And this judgment leads him to conclude that it should be the role of the state to provide the necessary assistance. He thus follows upon Smith's suggestion that with the establishment of a civil society it is morally proper for the state to compel the performance of the duty to respond to "rights of necessity." But for Kant, that means not that the state should require particular citizens to meet their "natural" duties of assistance to other particular people to whom they are related. Instead, the state should enforce compliance with our affirmative duty to respond to rights of necessity more generally. It is part of the social contract of a republic of moral equals, he writes, that the government "constrain the wealthy to provide the means of sustenance to those who are unable to provide for their most necessary natural needs."[38]

In short, Kant presses upon us his conclusion that the best and most logical way to institutionalize the moral imperatives of duties and rights when it comes to the basic needs of life is the creation of what we commonly refer to today as a social safety net. The neediest members of society should be given access to the material resources required to save them from destitution. And all members of the society are under an obligation to support the costs of this safety net through their tax dollars. So institutionalizing the right of necessity and the duties of beneficence not only creates buffers against the corrosive moral dynamics of unwarranted pride and damaging debasement that distressed Kant so much. It also prevents the problem of the arbitrary inequalities that result from relying entirely on private sources and familial obligations to provide the necessary resources. On the recipient side, any system that relies solely upon private philanthropy will result in people who are similarly situated and equally deserving or needy coming out very differently—with many falling between the cracks almost entirely. And on the donor side, exclusive reliance upon private philanthropy would burden the generous and socially responsible while enabling the selfish and irresponsible to be free riders.

Coming closer to the present day, the most prominent contemporary document that bases welfare state entitlements upon the moral logic of individual rights is the United Nations Universal Declaration of Human Rights, which was adopted soon after the 1945 founding of the United Nations itself. That international agreement is composed of a preamble and thirty articles, most of which take the form of stating that "everyone has the right" to something. Most of the rights that appear in these articles are the kind of freedoms and democratic participation rights found within the constitutions and bills of rights of today's liberal democracies. A number of the articles, however, make claims about people's rights to important benefits of welfare state policies. For example, Article 22 asserts that everyone "has the right to social security." Article 23 asserts that everyone has "the right to work" and "protection against unemployment." Article 24 says that everyone has a right to "reasonable limitation of working hours and periodic holidays with pay." Article 25 is especially assertive about welfare state entitlements "to a standard of living adequate for the health and well-being of oneself and one's family, including food, clothing, housing and medical care and necessary social services, and the right to security in the event of unemployment, sickness, disability, widowhood, old age or other lack of livelihood in circumstances beyond one's control." And Article 26 asserts that "everyone has the right to education [which] shall be free, at least in the elementary and fundamental stages," and that "higher education shall be equally accessible to all on the basis of merit." It is important to note that the Declaration does not make the claim that these rights are legally actionable claim rights; and it does not provide or suggest the possibility of enforcement mechanisms to compel member countries to honor and to fund these entitlements. Instead, the content of the articles is stated to constitute "a common standard of achievement for all peoples and all nations," to the end that all of the signatories shall "strive . . . to promote respect for these rights and freedoms and . . . to secure their universal and effective observance."

IN THE PREVIOUS CHAPTER, we examined the major arguments on both sides of the question: Would a society that left all its economic transactions and distributions to be determined by the free marketplace achieve the greatest material prosperity possible for itself? In this chapter, we shifted from the domain of political economy to the domain of moral philosophy. The central questions at issue here between the various disputants have been: Are the distributive criteria and results of the free marketplace just? Are they deserved? Are they morally proper? If so, why? If not, why not?

Before moving on in the next chapter to consider different views about the relationship between capitalism and the larger ideals and purposes of liberal democratic societies, let me summarize briefly the competing arguments we have encountered here regarding the moral propriety—or lack thereof—of the distributive results of the capitalist marketplace.

As we have seen, the defenders of the moral propriety of free-market distributive outcomes offer several arguments on their behalf. Some argue that the judgments of the marketplace—like the judgments of a just but demanding deity—may be at times harsh and certainly unequal. But they are a morally valid form of proportional justice. People get what they deserve from a capitalist system, because what the market gives them is directly proportional to the value of the goods and services they produce for other participants in the marketplace. Furthermore, the actual and proper measure of the value of what they produce is the collective judgment of these other participants—whether consumers or employers—who render their judgment by putting their money where their mouth is. Some free-market moralists also add that those who fare well in the economic marketplace are being rewarded for certain moral virtues they possess and are putting to good use: hard work, deferred gratification, honest dealing, living up to their contractual commitments, and so on.

Other defenders of market distributive outcomes, as we have seen, are more concerned with the moral imperative to recognize and respect important natural rights or entitlements people should be seen as having. And they argue that interference with the freely consensual transactions of the marketplace violates some of these rights and entitlements. Forceable redistributions of the consensual allocations of the marketplace are said to violate people's right of self-ownership and their entitlement to whatever holdings they have legally acquired or received.

We have also found that some laissez-faire advocates are what we might call "justice and rights skeptics." They do not believe that there are any convincing arguments on behalf of certain patterns or criteria of resource distribution being fair and just—whether those arguments are for or against the allocations of the marketplace. In the face of what they see as our ultimate inability to adjudicate and resolve the multiple conflicting arguments about economic justice and entitlements, they argue that the logical and morally appropriate thing to do is to fall back upon the utilitarian standard of the greatest good for the greatest number. And they then argue that by that standard we should opt for the allocations that come from the "invisible hand" of the markets—both because these allocations are economically efficient and because they leave individuals with maximum freedom to use their money and productive energies as they wish.

On the other side of the debate, the critics of unfettered capitalism and advocates for welfare state programs begin by insisting that, whatever we may think in the abstract is just and fair when it comes to the distribution of wealth in a society, one thing we can say with certainty is that abiding by market allocations institutionalizes and gives legal force to enormous and unfair disparities. Any society with pretensions of justice surely cannot, for example, leave starving children with their noses pressed against the windows of restaurants where people are dining on quail and foie gras. They cannot let people die from tooth infections because they have no access to dental care. They cannot leave the children of impoverished parents without education or with no real opportunity to earn a decent living when they grow up.

When it comes to saying what the standard for fair distributions should be, these reform liberals and welfare state advocates, as we have seen, do not speak with one voice. Some argue that, because it is a democratic axiom that we are all moral equals, a society dedicated to justice will strive to make its citizens economically equal up to the point at which the absence of incentives to spur productivity would make everyone worse off. Some would settle for genuine equal opportunity—or the closest reasonable approximation to that—and then turn things over to the marketplace. All would insist upon the establishment of an economic "safety net" to keep children, the disabled, the aged, and the involuntarily unemployed from falling into destitution.

Finally, there are also "justice skeptics" among reform liberals and welfare state advocates. And, like their philosophical counterparts in the laissez-faire camp, they often fall back upon the utilitarian standard of the greatest good for the greatest number. However, on the basis of variance in the marginal utility of a dollar between the rich and the poor, they draw the inference that faithfulness to the utilitarian standard requires some degree of downward redistribution from what the markets would dictate on their own.

Having looked at the arguments over the policies and arrangements that would maximize prosperity and then having looked at the competing views about what economic distributions are just and fair, we shall turn in the next chapter to look at competing arguments about the role of the capitalist marketplace in a good society. And when we talk there about the good society, we shall confine ourselves to conceptions that abide by the core standards of liberal democracy, such as civil liberties, moral and political equality, government by consent, and the rule of law. So it is the relationship between market institutions and the purposes and ideals of democracy that will be at issue here. The arguments about prosperity took place on the terrain of political economics. The arguments about distributive justice took place on the turf of moral philosophy. The arguments to be canvassed in the next chapter take place in the domain of political philosophy in general and within democratic theory specifically.

One might think that the previous two chapters canvassed all there is to say about the good society: If you get maximum prosperity and distribute the proceeds in a way that is morally right, what else do you need? Brief reflection, however, should reveal that there is more to consider when thinking about a good society than prosperity and fairness alone. Certainly both economic success and social justice are critical and important components of a good society. But there are other goods we need to consider when deciding what kind of society would be the one we would be most happy to live in. Is the society stable? Is it harmonious? Do the citizens have the power to govern themselves—and to do that well? Does the society promote human flourishing? Does it produce good and happy people? These are all relevant questions. So in the next chapter we have to broaden the playing field, as it were, to consider some of these other democratic purposes and to ask how well they are served by the capitalist marketplace.

CHAPTER THREE

The Democratic Ideals Debate

Markets and the Good Society

Much of the debate about the relationship between capitalism and democracy turns on competing assessments of the economic performance and the fairness of a free-market economy. Does the capitalist marketplace produce optimal results in straightforward economic terms? Does capitalism maximize prosperity? What are the distributive consequences of relying entirely upon market outcomes? Do these outcomes conform to a persuasive conception of social justice? We have considered some of the major competing answers to these questions in the previous two chapters.

People often assume that a similar pattern characterizes the larger question about the compatibility of market institutions with the constitutive norms of democracy. We think that we know and generally agree about what democracy is and that what we disagree about is whether the capitalist marketplace is compatible with and conducive to this shared understanding of democracy. It turns out, however, that this is really not the case. The fact is that once we get beyond the most basic defining features of a liberal democracy—popular rule, majority vote, equal protection of the law, and civil liberties—we encounter some important disagreements about the defining goals, purposes, and ideals of democracy itself. So even if we were of one mind about what a society governed by laissez-faire policies would actually look like, we could still have quite different views about whether that kind of free-market society was compatible with and supportive of democracy, or whether it instead would be inconsistent with and even destructive of important democratic aspirations and ideals.

Contemporary liberal democracies are actually heir to several rather different conceptions of the animating purposes and ideals of democracy. These conceptions all share a commitment to government by consent and popular self-rule. They are all members of the democratic family, as it were. But they do not embody identical conceptions of what the ideal democratic society would look like. They instead offer overlapping but also divergent understandings of what Walt Whitman referred to in his "Democratic Vistas" as "the ulterior [we would say "ultimate"] object of political and all other government."[1] And these competing understandings of democratic purposes turn out to have a lot of impact upon their adherents' views about the proper role of capitalist institutions in a well-ordered democratic society.

With this in mind, the purposes of this chapter are: first, to identify some of the most important of the several democratic traditions that have shaped our understandings of democratic ideals; second, to provide a sketch of the main features of these traditions, with particular attention to their accounts of the ultimate goals and defining norms of the ideal democratic society; and third, to point out how these different conceptions of democratic ideals lead to divergent assessments of the relationship between capitalism and democracy. Because this review of the various conceptions of the good society represents a kind of genealogy of Western democracies—a look at our ancestors, as it were—we shall consider them more or less in chronological order. One of the conceptions is a premodern one, antedating both the rise of modern science and also the advent of modern individualism. That tradition is what political theorists commonly refer to as civic republicanism. The other conceptions are all versions of democratic liberalism, originating in the seventeenth, eighteenth, and nineteenth centuries. Political theorists have used terms such as *Reformation liberalism, Enlightenment liberalism, individualist liberalism,* and *perfectionist liberalism* to characterize them.

We shall now look at each of these "schools" of democratic liberalism in turn. As a necessary disclaimer: these will be somewhat rough-and-ready sketches, and other political historians and political theorists might opt for "ideal types" slightly different from the ones I present here.

Civic Republicanism

The premodern political tradition that has exerted a lasting influence over our ideals of democracy is what political theorists and intellectual historians refer to as civic republicanism. When Benjamin Constant made his famous distinction between what he called the "liberty of the ancients" and the "liberty of the moderns," it is fair to say that he was taking civic republicanism as the principal theoretical embodiment of the first of these archetypes.[2] The liberty of the moderns, on the other hand, is a core feature of democratic liberalism. And the central distinction between these two accounts of liberty is that the "ancient" conception sees freedom as consisting in popular self-rule while the "modern" conception sees it as consisting in individual freedom from state coercion.

The central political goal of civic republicanism is the creation of a *demos*—or a body of citizens—who are free from structural forms of elite domination and who are therefore free to govern themselves. A republic is contrasted with regimes ruled by monarchs, by tyrants, by wealthy oligarchs, or by a hereditary aristocracy. Republicanism is in a broad sense "populist": it centers on an ideal of a government "of the people, by the people, and for the people"—to borrow Abraham Lincoln's famous peroration from his Gettysburg Address.

Along with that most fundamental commitment to popular self-government, the civic republican ideal also incorporates a strong allegiance to norms of civic equality. The most important status or rank in a civic republican democracy is that of citizen—no dukes, earls, counts, lords, majesties, highnesses, or other designations of differential and higher status. There are, of course, those who govern and are entitled to their authority. But they attain that role and status by being selected to their offices by their peers. Sovereignty is vested not in the officeholders but in the whole body of citizens. Indeed, the ultimate and encompassing political status is precisely that of citizen. (In the years immediately following the French Revolution, the new French Republic made a point of this by using "Citizen" as a title. Thus the French ambassador to that other fledgling republic of the United States, someone who caused a famous contretemps regarding America's neutrality in a war between France and Britain, went by the name "Citizen Genet.")

The animating purpose of a political society in classic republicanism is to foster the welfare of the whole people—to achieve the common good. The civic republic is not merely a pact among self-interested individuals for mutual protection. It is instead a corporate enterprise dedicated to the success and well-being of all the members of that enterprise. The whole, in effect, is more than the sum of its parts and takes precedence over these parts. The agreement among the members of the society to form and participate in their common endeavor is not merely a bargain. It embodies their mutual dedication to a moral enterprise that transcends their own narrow interests. So when the "father of modern conservatism" Edmund Burke issued his famous protest against reducing the bonds of political society to an aggregation of economizing bargains, he was invoking a classical civic republican ideal: the state, he wrote, "ought not to be considered as nothing better than a partnership agreement in a trade of pepper and coffee, calico or tobacco, or some other such low concern, to be taken up for a little temporary interest, and to be dissolved by the fancy of the parties. It is to be looked on with other reverence. . . . It is a partnership in all science; a partnership in all art; a partnership in every virtue, and in all perfection."[3]

Conceiving a society as a moral enterprise among civic equals dedicated to achieving the common good, republican democracy places a high value on social solidarity. Aristotle's name for this good was "civic friendship." And he saw it as a very important good indeed, saying that the promotion of civic friendship was the "first business" of a good statesman. Aristotle's account of the structure and animating motivations of friendship, moreover, casts light on why and how the republican focus upon the common good and the republican prioritizing of civic friendship fit together and are mutually reinforcing. For the source of true friendship, he argues, is not merely that friends are very useful to each other—although they are—but instead their mutual dedication to the good life they are building together. So to the extent that a political society is understood as a mutual endeavor animated by a desire to achieve the morally worthy goal of the good human life in a good human community, the true citizens of such a community will consider themselves as friends of a high order.

This understanding of the bonds among the members of the republican community leads to another important feature of civic republicanism—to wit, its conception of the nature and importance of "civic virtue." For to civic republicans, the essence of civic virtue—of being a good citizen—is a willingness to subordinate, and even in some instances to sacrifice, one's personal welfare and self-interest on behalf of the common good. Such a commitment can take various forms—from volunteering to take up arms in defense of one's country, to voting for policies that might not be best for oneself but seem best for the general welfare, to taking the time and effort to join in community service efforts. From the civic republican perspective, these public-spirited actions are what civic virtue is all about.

Conversely, when members of a democratic republic habitually neglect the common good and always privilege and act on behalf of their own narrow self-interest, they—and their society—are seen by civic republicans as "corrupt." Such corruption not only is a moral failure in republican eyes. It also represents a potentially fatal malady—a mortal threat to the society's health and very existence.

Here then, in summary, are the core defining ideals and commitments of the civic republican version of democracy: popular self-rule, rule of law, civic equality, social solidarity, and civic virtue—all centered on the overarching goal of promoting the common good. What seems missing—or at least too subordinated from the vantage point of modern liberal democracy—is an express dedication to individual liberties. That dedication to providing a private space where individual citizens can live as they see fit without interference from other citizens is what Benjamin Constant called the "liberty of the moderns." For according protection to the independent functioning of subset spheres of society and of individual citizens as well is a hallmark of modern liberalism. And this concern for freedom from the controlling supervision of society as a whole—or a majority thereof—is an important later addition to what we now commonly think of as our democratic values. Classical republicans did extol liberty, but what that meant for them was nondomination rather than the right of individuals to a private sphere of unimpeded action.

Civic republican ideals have influenced the Western democratic tradition at least from the time of the ancient Greek city-states. Even though they differed from each other in important ways, for example, both of the most prominent and powerful of these city-states—Athens and Sparta—understood themselves in broadly republican terms. It should be noted up front, however, that both of these societies' celebrations of themselves as republics were marked by the same hypocrisy that the English man of letters Samuel Johnson saw in the rhetoric of the American colonists at the time of the American Revolution: namely, "They talk a lot about liberty—for slavers." For there were a significant number of slaves in both of these city-states who were not recognized as citizens and who had as a consequence no role in self-rule. Women, also, were largely sequestered within the defined realm of the household and usually did not play a direct role in the public forums or governance of the polis.

There were, moreover, differences of emphasis between the two societies in the specific ways that they understood and embodied republican ideals. Sparta was a militaristic society, and its civic ethos celebrated what would surely seem to us to be extreme and inappropriate forms of subordination of personal concerns to the interests of the state. A famous example was the veneration accorded the response of a Spartan woman to a messenger from the battlefront who told her that her sons had perished in battle: "Vile Slave! Tell me not whether my sons lived or died but whether Sparta was victorious." The Athenian ethos, in contrast, seems to have been less militantly solidaristic and to have been—if Pericles's account in his famed Funeral Oration is to be believed—willing to give each other some latitude in their life choices: "Far from exercising a jealous surveillance over each other," said Pericles, "we do not feel called upon to be angry with our neighbor for doing what he likes."

The other version of republicanism in ancient times that has exerted a significant influence upon modern democratic ideals and practices was provided by the celebrated Roman statesman Cicero, in his account of what he saw as the animating norms of Rome in its republican era. Cicero's republican ideals incorporated the core ideals of republicanism in the Greek city-states: nondomination of elites, popular representation and participation in governance, rule of law, focus on the common good, and the importance of civic virtue and the avoidance of corruption. In addition, he championed the central role of reason and natural law in the virtuous republic; he emphasized the importance of good oratory on behalf of the public interest; and he advocated a "mixed constitution," which accorded a role to both common citizens and a meritocratic aristocracy, as a valuable arrangement in achieving good governance. Centuries later, as part of their rediscovery and veneration of the ancient philosophy, leading thinkers of the Italian Renaissance retrieved and championed the Roman republicanism of which Cicero was the leading expositor. Machiavelli was one of these; and although it was mostly the political power and success of republican Rome that attracted his envy, his account of good governance in his *Discourses on Livy* incorporated many of the themes of classical republicanism.

Scholars have differed regarding the relative influence of Machiavelli and Cicero on early modern thinkers and political practitioners. In his influential book *The Machiavellian Moment*, for example, J. G. A. Pocock famously argued that the English "country party" and one of its principal theorists, James Harrington, were influenced by Machiavelli's republicanism.[4] Other intellectual historians have not been so persuaded that Machiavelli was a central channel for the republican ideas that found their way into the political ideals of such canonical early modern political theorists as Montesquieu and Adam Smith, noting that these figures, along with the founders of the American republic, were classically learned and more likely to have assimilated their republican themes directly from their reading of Cicero.

The civic republican tradition clearly had a significant influence on many of the French revolutionaries at the end of the eighteenth century and also upon central themes of Rousseau's *Social Contract*. Rousseau was, for example, effusive in his praise of the Spartans, lauding them as a "republic of demi-gods rather than men, so superior to humanity did their virtues seem."[5] His most famous political concept, the General Will, was a voluntarist version of the republican common good. Like the classical republicans, he emphasized the importance of civic virtue—the willingness to subordinate one's "partial will" to the General Will—to the good of the society as a whole. He saw the erosion of this virtuous disposition of the popular will as constituting the corruption that would ultimately cause the demise of the state. He advocated placing limits upon the extent of economic inequality among the citizenry. And his conception of liberty—reflected in his pronouncement that implementing the General Will on dissenters could be justified as "forcing them to be free"—was clearly more attuned to the ancient republican freedom to be collectively self-governing than to the modern liberal individual freedom from coercion by one's fellow citizens. Finally, Rousseau embraced the republican emphasis upon the rule of law—saying laws must take a "general object" and apply universally to all citizens equally.

What role has the civic republican tradition had in shaping American political beliefs and ideals? As it happens, this question has been the subject of significant historiographical investigation and controversy over the past several decades. We shall not pursue the specifics of the relevant literature in any detail here. But the snapshot version is that prior to 1970 the general consensus was that American political ideals, historically speaking, essentially represented a national endorsement of the form of liberalism found in John Locke's explanation and defense of England's Glorious Revolution in 1688—which we will examine in a moment. As the political theorist Louis Hartz expressed this view, the United States represents "a nationalist articulation of Locke" that runs so deep and is so taken for granted that it "usually does not know that Locke himself is involved."[6] This account of a Lockean ideological hegemony in American politics then received a strong challenge in the 1970s, when the colonial American historian Bernard Bailyn argued that eighteenth-century Americans were influenced more by civic republicanism than by Lockean liberalism.[7] More recently, a number of scholars have argued that the principles invoked by the American colonists in defense of their rejection of British rule and in founding their own regime were neither purely Lockean nor purely republican but an updated combination of both of these traditions.[8]

Whatever the outcome of these ongoing debates might be, one thing that is clear from the historical record and the texts these scholars have brought to light is that the core ideals of the civic republican tradition were unquestionably alive and influential at the formation of the American republic. The contents of the extensive political pamphlet literature—the equivalent of newspaper op-ed pieces and internet blogs today—make that quite evident. One after another, these pamphlets drew upon the republican conception of free and self-governing citizens, displaying the civic virtues of courage and devotion to the common good, while being threatened by the forces of oppression and corruption. These themes are also found in the postrevolutionary era, for example in the expressed worries of anti-Federalist critics of the proposed constitution that its Madisonian logic and institutions paid insufficient attention to the crucial task of fostering civic virtue.[9] Madison himself, it turns out, especially in his later writings, actually seemed to share this concern—even if he likely would have seen the promotion of civic virtue as supplementary to, rather than as a component of, the kind of institutional arrangements found in a constitution.[10]

Civic republicanism contains not only an account of the key elements of a well-ordered political society but also an account of how these societies tend to decline and die. Both of these, as Bailyn's research made clear, were on full display in the American pamphlet literature he examined. In this civic republican account, healthy republics are peopled by citizens who live simply and unostentatiously, who are honest and courageous, and who place the welfare of the whole above their own particular interests. They live by rules they establish for themselves that are fair in content and equitable in their application. But these republics are seen, in a narrative that stretches back to Plato and Polybius, to exhibit a characteristic pattern of decay in which the central causal force is the corruption of the people—their loss of civic virtue. In their early stages, their virtues make them happy, productive, and strong. But their success makes them increasingly wealthy and powerful. The citizens then are seduced by the lure of these goods. They become soft and lazy in their luxuries, venal in their pursuit of wealth, and prideful in their hunger for power. With the people thus corrupted, private interest trumps public good, internal divisions appear, the people lose their freedoms as new patterns of domination and subordination appear, and the republican regime effectively dissolves, possibly into an authoritarian regime of some sort or other. (Were our civic republican forebears able to walk among us today, it is pretty safe to say that they would be quite concerned about both the recent slide toward autocratic governance in some Western democracies and also what they would perceive as a slide toward what American intellectual historian Christopher Lasch famously termed a "culture of narcissism"—whether in the form of Donald Trump's mode of governance or in the self-preoccupation found in some forms of identity politics.)

Since the principal burden of the political broadsides leading up to the American Revolution was to challenge the legitimacy of British rule over the colonies, the pamphlet literature of that era devoted much of its attention to depicting the British crown and court as having succumbed to this cycle of corruption. And in doing so, they could avail themselves of the similar complaints levied against King George's regime from within England itself by adherents of what historians call the "country party." But since higher learning in the colonies included an emphasis on the classical literature of ancient Greece and Rome, the colonial pamphleteers also devoted considerable attention to the decay and demise of the Roman republic. For, to them, the illegitimate overreach of the British monarchical regime was the result of its own similar descent into corrupt and despotic rule.[11]

In contrast to what they saw as British corruption, the colonists presented themselves and their political institutions as exemplars of republicanism and its civic virtues. Undoubtedly there was here some self-congratulatory self-glorification. But there was also some justification in the facts of the matter. For, as Tocqueville marveled as he reflected upon the political phenomenon of America, the colonists had in fact created for themselves what appeared to him as precociously democratic institutions at a time when political absolutism dominated the European societies from which they came. As Tocqueville wrote, in colonial America "a democracy more perfect than any of which antiquity had dared to dream sprang full-grown and fully armed from the midst of the old feudal society." This was especially visible for him in the New England townships, where "each locality was already a lively republic."[12]

It was not only in New England that leaders of the founding era looked to these little republics as inspiration for their vision of America. Virginian Thomas Jefferson, in a letter to John Adams, described his own proposal to subdivide the American states into what he called "wards" of approximately twenty-five square miles. These wards would, he wrote, function as self-governing "little republics" that would take care of their roads, their poor, their police, their elections, courts of law, and primary education. And he repeatedly noted to Adams that he hoped these miniature republics would function "as your people have so often done, and with so much effect by their own town meetings."[13]

One final observation about civic republicanism and its influence on American political ideals: although civic republicanism itself is a secular doctrine that originated in years dated BCE, its ethos in many important ways parallels and overlaps with the Protestant and Puritan religious moral culture that has played—and continues to play—a significant role in American political culture. When the revolutionary-era leader Samuel Adams opined in a letter that he hoped that his beloved city of Boston would become "a Christian Sparta," this was more a piece of rhetorical excess than a serious proposal. But his invocation of this phrase was not accidental, and it embodied his recognition of the similarities between the political ideals of New England Puritanism and classical republicanism. For both of these traditions celebrated civic solidarity, dedication to the common good, and an insistence on the crucial importance of the civic virtues of simplicity, honesty, hard work, and self-sacrifice. As a correlate, moreover, both traditions worried greatly about the political destructiveness of moral corruption: pride, lust for power, sloth, self-seeking, personal debauchery, and so on. The jeremiads that came in profusion from New England pulpits and that have become American moral and political set pieces thus closely mimicked the classic republican narrative of political declension. The former were essentially biblical condemnations of the wages of sin, while the latter was a more secular account of societies' natural tendencies toward social decay. But the different vocabularies could speak easily to each other because their conceptions of the good society shared a strong family resemblance.

Liberal Conceptions of Democracy

The other political philosophical or ideological traditions that have most influenced American democratic ideals are all versions of what political theorists would term "liberalism." What political theorists mean by liberalism, it is important to note in order to forestall misunderstanding, is not what that term tends to mean in today's everyday political discourse. It does not, for example, mean the egalitarian Left of Bernie Sanders and others of his persuasion. Instead, it designates modern (i.e., post-seventeenth-century) political theories that hold (1) that people are created free and equal in the sense that none are born entitled to obey others or rule others; (2) that therefore all legitimate political authority must come from the consent of the governed; (3) that, because no rational person would consent to be subject to absolute or arbitrary power, all legitimate government is limited in scope; and (4) that all members of a society are entitled to protection of their lives, personal and civil liberties, and duly earned property. These core precepts distinguish liberalism in the generic sense from earlier political traditions that saw legitimate political authority as derived from divinity or from some natural order, saw society as an organism rather than as an agreement, and assigned differentiated social roles and political obligations to people accordingly.

By these definitions, then, both Left and Right in this country fall for the most part under the broad umbrella of "liberalism" because America was in effect born modern, was born free, and (apart from the important and fateful exception of the plantation South) never was a feudal society divided into different "estates."

The Several Liberal Traditions

It is standard in this country to characterize those who champion minimal government and "free-market solutions" in social policy as "conservatives." So it always is confusing to my students when I tell them that laissez-faire "conservatives" are more properly seen as one of several overlapping but competing versions of liberalism. I point out to them that prominent knowledgeable free-market "conservatives" actually understand and affirm this about themselves. Thus we find Milton Friedman, who served as an economic adviser to "Mister Conservative" Barry Goldwater, writing that "the right and proper name" for his free-market-oriented "political and economic viewpoint" is "liberalism."[14]

To distinguish themselves from those toward the left of the American political spectrum who are commonly referred to as liberals, Friedman and others often identify themselves as "classical liberals"— in their view what liberalism used to be before others claimed that name. We can also note that the term *liberal* is commonly used elsewhere to designate free-market orientations and policies. If you read the *Economist*, a British news magazine, for example, you realize that *liberalize* means for them to relax governmental constraints and regulations on the marketplace. And political parties in both Europe and Latin America that call themselves liberal stand for individual rights, free enterprise, and limited government. Perhaps the confusion understandably created by this multiplicity of those claiming the mantle of liberalism can be alleviated by the recognition that the name has been claimed by or applied to several influential political persuasions beginning as early as the seventeenth century and continuing to the present day. All of these endorse the core precepts mentioned earlier about individual rights, political equality, government by consent, and limited government; but they differ in other respects. Given the many social and economic changes that have taken place over the several centuries since the birth of liberalism and modernity, this should not be surprising. What is important to understand in the context of this book is, first, that we in this country are heirs to all of these versions of liberal ideals and, second, that the different ways these various versions of liberalism understand and prioritize the various liberal ideals have implications for our understanding of the proper role of the capitalist marketplace within a good democratic society.

To make this point—and also to flesh out its substance—let me identify here four archetypal versions of political liberalism and also show how they have influenced important conceptions of democratic ideals in this country. These archetypal models were articulated and championed by canonical political philosophers over the two centuries extending from the late seventeenth century to the late nineteenth century. The first of these is what the political theorist William Galston has called "Reformation liberalism."[15] But it also has been called Lockean liberalism after its seminal articulator, John Locke. The second model is widely referred to as "Enlightenment liberalism." It had numerous expositors, but none of them provided a more paradigmatic statement of its essential tenets than did a prominent French political philosopher and political activist at the time of the French Revolution: the Marquis de Condorcet. The third archetypal liberal conception of democratic ideals is sometimes called "perfectionist liberalism" by political theorists. The most famous of its defenders was one of the most prominent political intellectuals of the mid-nineteenth century, the British philosopher, political commentator, and member of Parliament John Stuart Mill. And the last of these archetypal models of liberal ideals is the "contractual individualist" model championed in the Anglo-American political universe by figures such as Sir Henry Maine, Herbert Spencer, and William Graham Sumner.

Lockean Liberalism, aka Reformation Liberalism

First, let us look at Reformation liberalism, also referred to by some as Lockean liberalism after one of its most important and influential expositors. Although the use of the term *liberal* as designating a particular political persuasion did not become common until well into the eighteenth century, it is as appropriate as it is common to cite John Locke as one of its seminal thinkers. That is because Locke's path-breaking account of the origins, purposes, and limits of legitimate political authority takes as its axiomatic starting point his forthright insistence that, politically speaking, we are all born free and equal. In fact, of course, we all are born into a condition of utter dependency and inequality. But what Locke wants to insist is that none of us comes into the world invested with any right or authority to rule over the rest of us. That may seem to be a no-brainer to almost everyone reading this book, but that negative claim was by no means the conventional wisdom of European thought in Locke's own day. For the more standard view, derived from Aristotle and Christian theology, was that legitimate political authority derived from God or nature—or some combination thereof. However, in his *First Treatise of Civil Government*, which no one bothers to read any more, Locke systematically dismantled the "divine right of kings" argument that God had conferred political authority upon certain specific individuals. And in his *Second Treatise of Civil Government*, which is the masterpiece that became canonical in England and America in the eighteenth century— and that we still read and cite to this day—Locke wrote that there is "nothing more evident than that creatures of the same species and rank, promiscuously born to all the same advantages of nature, and the use of all the same faculties, should all be equal, one amongst another, without subordination or subjection."[16] Although we certainly are born with different levels of talent and capacities, "yet all of this consists with the equality which all men are in, in respect of jurisdiction or dominion one over another" (6.54). And that claim leads in turn to the logical conclusion that "being, as has been said, by nature all free, equal, and independent, no one can be put out of this estate and subjected to the political power of another without his own consent" (8.95).

Since all legitimate powers of government are based upon the consent of the governed, the determinative question then becomes: What powers, if any, would rational people willingly agree to bestow upon a government to which they were subject? For what reasons would any rational person agree to "part with his freedom" in a world without any government "and subject himself to the dominion and control of any other power"? (9.123). Locke's answer is that it is rational for us to establish and subject ourselves to political governance in order "to supply those defects and imperfections which are in us, as living single and solely by ourselves" (2.15).[17] The foremost of these defects of our natural condition is the insecurity of our persons and possessions. So "the great and chief end of men uniting into commonwealths and putting themselves under government is the preservation of their lives, liberties, and estates" (9.23, 24). The ultimate purpose of and justification for government power is, then, "directed to no other end but the peace, safety, and public good of the people" (9.131).

The important corollary of this account of legitimate political authority is that the powers of government are in principle necessarily limited. As no rational person would consent to be subject to absolute or arbitrary rule, so no legitimate legislative authority can exercise absolute power over its citizens, nor can that authority be exercised in an arbitrary fashion. That means that legitimate government is necessarily limited both in its scope and in its modes of action—both in what it may control and how it must exercise that control. The most specific and important limits upon the scope of government power— its legitimate reach and extent—are three, according to Locke. First, in a legitimate regime no laws may be enacted that contravene "the law of Nature," which "stands as an external rule to all men, legislators as well as others" (11.135). (Locke is here invoking a standard claim of the Western moral tradition that there are certain basic moral precepts ascertainable by human reason.[18] Essentially, these are precepts that acknowledge the moral dignity and equal moral status of all human beings, recognize rules of reciprocity proper to such moral beings, restrain us "from invading others' rights," and impose upon us as obligation "to preserve the rest of mankind" whenever our own preservation is not at issue [2.67].) The second important limit upon the scope of legitimate government power is that it "cannot take from any man any part of his property without his own consent" (11.138). This restriction follows from Locke's claim that people acquire an entitlement to private property from their labor, prior to and apart from any government action, and that the preservation of this property right in their persons and possessions was the principal reason for their agreeing to join the society in the first place. (In order to avoid significant misunderstanding, however, it is important to note that requiring one's "own consent" for having any part of one's property to be taken by the state does not mean that individual people are free to refuse to pay their taxes. As Locke takes care to explain, "own consent" means "the consent of the majority, giving it either by themselves or by their representatives chosen by them" (11.140). So the American colonists protesting the British Stamp Tax got their rallying cry right: it was not "no taxes," but "no taxation without representation.")

The third crucial limitation on the scope of legitimate government power, finally, was the one Locke explained and justified in his *Letter concerning Toleration*: namely, government can have no legitimate authority to dictate to people what their religious beliefs or practices must be. The legitimate domain of the state extends only to the management of the external and secular goods of this world. For it was the protection and promotion of our bodies and possessions, insecure as these are in the state of nature, for which government was instituted in the first place. Moreover, those chosen to serve as political authorities possess no expertise in matters of religious belief. No rational people would consent of their own free will to have others tell them what to believe in their own hearts and minds. And no legislators or police could make us share their own beliefs even if they wanted to do so.

In addition to these limitations on the scope of legitimate political powers, Locke insisted upon certain constraints on the ways that legitimate governing authorities could exercise the powers they held. These limits are those we have come to think of as the requirements of rule of law, due process, and the equal protection of the law. Locke sets out these formal and procedural limits on the exercise of political power in this way. First, "Whosoever has the legislative or supreme power of any commonwealth is bound to govern by established standing laws, promulgated and known to the people and not by extemporary decrees" (9.131). And second, these "promulgated and established laws" are "not to be varied in particular cases, but to have one rule for rich and poor, for the favorite at court, and the countryman at plough" (11.142).

The profound and persistent influence upon America of Locke's seventeenth-century version of liberalism should be readily apparent from even this very cryptic thumbnail sketch of some of its basic features. One needs here to look no further than the Declaration of Independence and the American Constitution. The colonists' case against the Stamp Act, which precipitated the conflict that led to the Revolutionary War, was taken straight from Locke's account of property rights and the fundamental illegitimacy of absolute and/or arbitrary power. Locke had provided a prominent justification for the 1688 Glorious Revolution in England, and the colonists a century later deployed Locke's words against the British Parliament's claims of authority to levy taxes on them. They quoted again and again Locke's words from chapter 11 of his *Second Treatise* about property rights and the limits on any government power that did not come from the consent of the governed: "For I have truly no property in that which another can by right take from me when he pleases against my consent. . . . For if any one shall claim a power to lay and levy taxes on the people by his own authority, and without such consent of the people . . . that is, the consent of the majority, giving it either by themselves or by their representatives chosen by them . . . he thereby invades the fundamental law of property and subverts the end of government" (11.138, 140).

In a similar fashion, the Declaration of Independence follows almost to the letter Locke's justification for "the dissolution of government"—namely political rebellion. As Locke puts it: whenever ruling powers "endeavor to grasp themselves, or put into the hands of any other, an absolute power over the lives, liberties, and estates of people, by this breach of trust they forfeit the power the people had put into their hands for quite contrary ends, and it devolves to the people, who have a right to resume their original liberty" (19.222). To those who worry that by this argument he threatens the stability of government, Locke insists that such revolutions will "happen not upon every little mismanagement in public affairs" but only when "a long train of abuses, prevarications, and artifices, all tending the same way, make the design visible to the people" (19.225). Exactly so, states the Declaration of Independence. "Governments long established should not be changed for light and transient causes. . . . But when a long train of abuses and usurpations . . . evinces a design to reduce them under absolute Despotism, it is their right, it is their duty to throw off such Government, and to provide new Guards for their future security." Then follows a long itemized account, constituting the largest part of the document, of the specific "abuses and usurpations" visited upon the colonies by "the present King of Great Britain."

The Constitution of the United States also reflects the essential elements of Lockean liberalism. The first words of the document, "We the People," make clear that this is a government established by consent in order to accomplish what Locke designated as the fundamental purposes of a legitimate democratic government—to "promote the general welfare" and to "secure the blessings of liberty." The three branches of the government have as their respective charges making good what Locke identified as the crucial "things wanting"—that is, not present—within the prepolitical human condition: namely, the lack of "established, settled, known law," the lack of "a known and indifferent judge," and the lack of a power "to back and enforce" the law and to "give it execution" (9.124, 125, 126). And the crucial limits of both scope and mode of governance specified by Locke are given embodiment in the protections of the Bill of Rights, the separation of church and state, the requirements of due process and equal protection of the laws, and the prohibition of ex post facto laws. Most of these provisions, of course, were not entirely novel, as they reflected the carryover of British constitutional norms and practices. But those norms and practices, in turn, took their leave from the constitutional settlement of 1688, established by the English Bill of Rights and the Act of Toleration, whose logic and justification were set out in Locke's writings.

Enlightenment Liberalism

Another influential conception of liberal ideals and purposes came to prominence during the eighteenth century. Since its hopes and premises were a product of the European Enlightenment, we will refer to it here as Enlightenment liberalism. The Enlightenment was a broad movement, encompassing many philosophers who unsurprisingly differed in some respects regarding their political ideals and expectations. But the vision of what intellectual historian Carl Becker famously called "the heavenly city of the eighteenth century philosophers" was perhaps best captured by the Marquis de Condorcet in his

Essay on the Progress of the Human Mind.[19] Condorcet was both a brilliant mathematician and a political figure who served as secretary of the French Assembly (Parliament) at the time of the French Revolution. In that capacity, he also led the committee that wrote the constitution proposed by the moderate republican party known as the Girondins. When the Revolution radicalized and the Jacobins came to power, Condorcet was forced into hiding, where he wrote his famed *Essay*—which was intended to be the outline of a much larger work to come. That larger work never was completed, however, since he was captured while fleeing not long afterward and was thrown into prison, where he soon died, or possibly was poisoned.

Enlightenment liberals believed strongly in historical progress. Indeed, the "heavenly city" they hoped for was not located in some eternal otherworldly realm but was instead the future of humanity in this temporal world. Thus the English Enlightenment philosopher Joseph Priestly—a polymath who was the discoverer of oxygen, a founding Unitarian minister and theologian, and a prominent liberal political theorist—wrote in 1771 that "whatever the beginning of this world, the end will be glorious and paradisiacal, beyond what our imaginations can now conceive," and that this glorious future would "arise from the natural course of human affairs."[20] Some twenty years later, Condorcet concluded his epic essay on the progress of human knowledge, morality, and society with a similar vision of "the human race, emancipated from its shackles, released from the empire of fate and from that of the enemies of its progress, advancing with a firm and sure step along the path of truth, virtue and happiness! It is the contemplation of this prospect that rewards the philosopher for all his efforts to assist the progress of reason and the defense of liberty. He dares to regard these strivings as part of the eternal chain of human destiny."[21]

The driving force behind this progress toward the freedom and flourishing of all human beings was, according to Enlightenment liberals, the advancement of human reason—both scientific and philosophical. In his account of the progress of knowledge in the century or so following upon the Scientific Revolution, Condorcet cited the interlocking chain of discoveries in mathematics, physics, chemistry, biology, and even economics and sociology that had taken place in the preceding decades. This was, of course, the century of Newton, who was with reason seen as the exemplar of transformative scientific knowledge. As the English poet Alexander Pope wrote in a famous couplet: "Nature and Nature's laws lay hid in night. / God said, let Newton be! and all was light."

As Condorcet took pains to emphasize, moreover, it was not only the content of Newton's discoveries that was important. Even more important, perhaps, for the prospects of the future advance and dissemination of knowledge was the precision and simplicity of his mathematizing methodology. Newton's work seemed to open up a future vista of not only continued progress in knowledge but also its increasing availability to a wider public. For by use of his mathematizing method Newton was able to explain both the behavior of falling bodes and the movements of planets in their orbits by a single formula. In doing so, he demonstrated the capacity of science to "reduce the relations between various objects . . . to more general relations" and to do so with "a new precision." The captivating prospect opened up by the scientific method, then, is this: "Truths that were discovered only by great effort . . . by men capable of profound thought, are soon developed and provided by methods that are not beyond the reach of common intelligence" (185). Not only should the pace of scientific discovery become even faster ("The methods that lead genius to the discovery of truth increase at once the force and the speed of its operations"; 185), but all literate human beings should become able to achieve levels of understanding previously attainable only by a few people of genius: we can all, in terms of the content of our knowledge, be veritable philosophers.

Condorcet's political program, appropriately for a liberal, centered on freedom—not only the freedom of individuals but also the freedom of important social enterprises. The most important of those enterprises were scientific inquiry and economic activity: what we today would call academic freedom and free enterprise. France—and most of Europe in his time—were governed by regimes that exerted significant control over both of these enterprises: they censored ideas and controlled publications; and they practiced what economists call "mercantilist" controls upon economic activities, granting monopolies to firms in some areas and placing restraints on entry into various trades. So Condorcet's policy priorities were to minimize these state controls so that scientists and business people would be free to act in accord with the norms and institutional logic of their respective activities.

The realm of science for Condorcet and his fellow philosophers encompassed both the natural and the social sciences and also what they called "moral science." Politically speaking, the most important fruit of moral science was the recognition of human rights. As Condorcet put it: "After long periods of error, after being led astray by vague or incomplete theories, we have at last discovered the true rights of man." We also have seen, he continued, "that the maintenance of these rights was the sole object of men's coming together in political societies . . . and that in every society the means of assuring the rights of the individual should be submitted to certain common rules, but that the authority to . . . determine these rules could belong only to the majority of the members of the society itself" (128). In short, once liberated from Scholastic doctrines that justified the authority of princes and prelates, our free reason—what he also called our "simple common sense"—would clearly apprehend the self-evident validity of human rights, the rule of law, and the rule of the majority.

The advance of the natural sciences—and their handmaiden, technological progress—would also, he predicted, bring huge practical benefits to the human race. Writing on the cusp of the Industrial Revolution, Condorcet predicted that technological inventions made possible by science would vastly enhance economic productivity and increase the wealth of nations accordingly. Advances in biology, anatomy, chemistry, and physiology would in turn provide the basis for vast improvements in medical understanding and treatments. Agronomy would improve agriculture and the production of both more and better food. In short, thanks to the advance of the various sciences and the technological innovations based upon their findings, future generations could be expected steadily to become healthier, wealthier, and wiser. Regarding the first of these attributes, Condorcet wrote, "No one can doubt that, as preventive medicine improves and food and housing become healthier, as a way of life is established that develops our physical powers . . . the average length of human life will be increased and a stronger physical constitution will be insured. . . .

It is reasonable to hope that all other diseases may likewise disappear as their distant causes are discovered . . . [and] that the day will come when death will be due only to extraordinary accidents or to the decay of the vital forces" (199–200). As for increasing wealth, the combination of free enterprise and trade together with advances in scientific technology would have the results that "each successive generation will have larger possessions" because "new instruments, machines, and looms can add to man's strength and can improve at once the quality of his products, and can diminish the time and labor that has to be expended on them" (187–88). As for future generations becoming wiser, "By a suitable choice of syllabus and of methods of education, we can teach the citizen everything that he needs to know in order to be able to manage his household, administer his affairs . . . to know his rights and . . . duties; . . . to be no longer the dupe of those popular errors which torment man with superstitious fears and chimerical hopes; [and] to defend himself against prejudice by the strength of his reason alone" (182).

What, then, did this paradigmatic Enlightenment liberal see as the political values, the animating purposes and ideals, of liberal democracy? The answer is that he was a true son of the French Enlightenment's liberal republicanism, adhering to the multiple political goods captured by what became the official motto of France: *liberté, égalité, fraternité*. As we have already seen, liberty was central and crucial to him. It was not only a great good in itself but also the key to the realization of many other good things, both political and utilitarian. It encompassed not only economic liberty, both domestic and international, but also freedoms of speech, inquiry, and religion.

Condorcet was not, however, a simple and straightforward "libertarian" of the stripe we are familiar with today. He was interested in more than personal freedom and economic efficiency. When he contemplated the "future condition of the human race" in the final chapter of his most famous essay, for example, it was actually the goods of greater equality and personal development that took pride of place. As he wrote: "Our hopes for the future condition of the human race can be subsumed under three important heads: the abolition of inequality within each nation, the lessening of inequality between nations, and the true perfection of mankind" (173).

As for progress of equality within nations, Condorcet observed that there was historically and in his own day "a great difference . . . between the equality established by political codes and that which in fact exists among individuals." This gap between legal equality and actual social equality, he said, had "three main causes: inequality in wealth; inequality in status between those whose means of subsistence are hereditary and those whose means are dependent on [labor]; and inequality in education." These "three sorts of real inequality," he argued optimistically, "must constantly diminish without however disappearing altogether" (179). They would diminish in part as a consequence of the abandonment of mercantilism and the instantiation of free markets and free enterprise. And they could also diminish as the result of other appropriate social policies.

As for lessening the inequality of wealth, Condorcet—writing a bit before the onset of the Industrial Revolution—had the happy belief that "wealth has a natural tendency to equality, and that any excessive disproportion could not exist or at least would rapidly disappear if civil laws did not provide artificial ways of [creating, consolidating, and perpetuating inequalities]" (180). And, as we noted previously, he expected inequalities in education to diminish because of improvements in pedagogy, because of people's greater access to facts as a result of technological progress, because of an end to government censorship, and because of the way that scientific advancement made knowledge more precise and more intelligible to the wider public.

As for diminishing inequalities of class and states, Condorcet believed that the abolition of laws and traditional practices that discriminated among different categories of citizens in terms of taxation, admission to certain trades, inheritance, and so on would help reduce these social and economic gradations. But it is quite important to note here that he also proposed important government policies to address these inequalities directly. "There is a very real difference," he wrote, "between people [whose income derives solely from their labor] and those . . . who live either on revenue from land, or on the interest on capital." This difference, he continued, represented a crucial "cause of inequality, of dependence and even of misery, which ceaselessly threatens the most numerous and most active class in our society" (181). This serious barrier to greater social equality and source of economic dependency and misery, he argued, could and should be "in great part eradicated" by enacting measures that closely resemble today's social security provisions. Specifically, he proposed a system of social insurance that would "guarantee people in old age a means of livelihood produced partly by their own savings and partly by the savings of others who make the same outlay but who die before they need to reap the reward; or, again, on the same principle of compensation, by securing for widows and orphans [a decent income]" (181). He advocated in addition the kind of program that Bruce Ackerman and Ann Alstott recently proposed in their book *The Stakeholder Society*. Ackerman and Alstott there argue that to make equal opportunity more than an empty idea to which we pay lip service, every American citizen should be "entitled to a stake in his [or her] country: a one-time grant of eighty thousand dollars as [they] reach early adulthood, ... financed by an annual two percent tax levied on all the nation's wealth."[22] Condorcet's proposal was more cryptic and less specific about the amount in question, but it was quite similar. Society, he wrote, should "provide all children with the capital necessary for the full use of their labor, available at the age when they start work and found a family" (181).

In the context of our central concerns in this book, what is perhaps most important about the kind of Enlightenment liberalism exemplified by Condorcet is that it espouses a "both/and" account of the purposes and policies of the good society. In part because it appeared shortly before the Industrial Revolution, and also in part because of certain optimistic empirical beliefs about human nature and the social consequences of free markets, Condorcet's Enlightenment liberalism saw no incompatibility between economic liberty and social equality. It endorsed both as important features of the good democratic society. It also did not see any fundamental incompatibility between free markets and what we today would refer to as welfare state social policies. Its vision of the bright future of "enlightened" democratic societies was based in part upon a belief in free markets as the basic engine of economic prosperity. But most Enlightenment liberals did not believe that their enthusiasm for a free-market economy required them to champion a "minimal state." As the example of Condorcet demonstrates, Enlightenment liberals could also argue that the state should use its taxing power on behalf of public goods; and for them, preventing penury among the aged and giving working-class youth access to the capital resources necessary for their economic advancement definitely qualified as public goods.

"Perfectionist" Liberalism

Our third version of democratic liberalism is what some have called perfectionist liberalism. Around a half century after Condorcet set out his vision of what the ideal democracy of the future would look like, the great English philosopher and political theorist John Stuart Mill provided his contemporaries with his own famous and influential justification of democratic government and civil liberties. He wrote in the context of a time in which Great Britain was becoming more fully democratized through a series of suffrage acts that greatly expanded the British electorate. At the outset of the nineteenth century, only male property owners age twenty-one and over were eligible to vote. In 1832, the property requirement was lowered somewhat. In 1867, another reform act gave the vote to all men who paid property taxes, doubling the electorate to about 30 percent of male citizens. In 1884, the Third Reform Act further lowered the property qualification, again doubling the size of the electorate. In 1918, the property qualification was eliminated and women were given the vote for the first time—but only if they were over the age of thirty. Finally, in 1928, women were allowed to vote at the same age as men, and full universal suffrage was achieved. In the midst of this long process, John Stuart Mill championed universal suffrage and women's rights in general. (He did favor requirements that voters be literate and pay some form of tax, however.) He also provided an important and influential account of why democracy (or what he called "representative government") was the ideally best form of government. And he offered, in what is probably his most famous and widely read work, *On Liberty*, a classic defense of why representative governments should provide extensive civil liberties to their citizens.

Mill was a utilitarian. That meant that, for him, a question like "What's the best form of government?" should be answered by reference to the utilitarian maxim: choose whatever policies or institutions that will produce "the greatest good for the greatest number." By their results shall we judge them. Before that standard can be applied, however, there is an additional question to answer: What does "happiness" mean in concrete terms? What counts as "happiness"?

The founder of modern utilitarianism was Jeremy Bentham, a philosopher and social reformer who was a mentor and hero of Mill's father, James Mill. And Bentham's answer to the "What counts as happiness?" question was simple and straightforwardly hedonistic: pleasure. So, for Bentham, in order to know what to do we should add up the "utils" of pleasure that all possible courses of action would produce, subtract the negative "utils" of pain each would produce, and choose the option with the highest positive outcome. This was known as "the utilitarian calculus."

In John Stuart Mill's view, this conception of happiness as pleasure is too crude to apply to human beings. As he once wrote, Bentham saw only "what the one-eyed could see." Surely influenced in part by the classical philosophers his father made him read as a child, Mill insisted that people are not simple pleasure/pain machines. Instead, we are highly complex and sophisticated conscious organisms endowed not only with physical sensations but also with cognitive powers and moral sensibilities. Happiness for creatures like us, then, comes not from simple bovine contentment and absence of pain but from the successful development and exercise of these higher human capacities. This kind of quintessentially human satisfaction was what the ancient Greek philosophers called *eudaemonia*. This term is often translated as "happiness," but moral philosophers these days prefer to translate it as "flourishing," precisely to characterize what that word meant more accurately—and to avoid mistakenly identifying it with pleasure simpliciter.

When Mill says that he "regards utility as the ultimate appeal on all ethical questions," then, he immediately adds that "it must be utility in the largest sense, grounded on the permanent interests of man as a progressive being."[23] And he offers further evidence of the meaning and importance of this understanding of utility by choosing for the epigram of *On Liberty* these words of the German philosopher Wilhelm von Humboldt: "The grand, leading principle towards which every argument in these pages directly converges, is the absolute and essential importance of human development in its richest diversity." Mill's democratic theory, therefore, consists in his explanation of why liberal democracy is the form of government that best serves this ultimate goal of promoting the human flourishing of its citizens in their richest diversity—and in specifying some of the particular rules and institutions that seem most conducive to producing this desired result.

Mill begins his argument on behalf of representative government by explaining why a different possible answer to the question "What is the ideal best form of government?" would be unacceptable. It might seem reasonable to believe, he notes, that the ideally best regime would be one in which a perfectly wise and benevolent ruler would exercise absolute power. Assuming such a person could be identified, it might seem logical to endow that paragon of wisdom and virtue with total control of the government. But the seemingly logical conclusion that this kind of benevolent despotism would be the ideally best form of government begins to unravel, he writes, if we ask what consequences such a regime would have for the nature and lives of its citizens. Assuming that we accept Mill's insistence that the ultimate purpose of any regime type is not efficiency or some other technical measure of good governance but the improvement of the people themselves, we have to ask, Mill writes: "What sort of human beings can be formed under such a regime? What development can either their thinking or their active faculties attain under it?" Given that people can develop and exercise their faculties only if there is some reason or practical effect for doing so, the answer would clearly seem to be that the inhabitants of such a regime would become a very passive flock. Mill writes that not "only in their intelligence would they suffer. Their moral capacities would be equally stunted. Whenever the sphere of action of human beings is artificially circumscribed, their sentiments are narrowed and dwarfed in the same proportion."[24]

The same reasons that lead Mill to dismiss benevolent despotism as a good form of government, then, serve to justify his conclusion that the "ideally best form of government will be found in some one or other variety of the Representative System."[25] Since the criterion for assessing "the merits of forms of government" is their tendency to "favor and promote not some one improvement" in the moral and intellectual capacities of its citizens "but all forms and degrees of it," Mill's case for the superiority of democratic government is based on his claim that representative government is the best form for promoting human development.[26] That's what "the greatest good for the greatest number" properly means, he says, and representative government—aka democracy—is the form of government most likely to achieve that goal.

That is so, he argues, for several reasons. In the first place, the utilitarian standard of "the greatest good for the greatest number" is intrinsically democratic and egalitarian, for it assumes the equal worth of the welfare and interests of every member of the society. Practically speaking, Mill argues, that means that all the competent adult members of a society should have some direct say in choosing those who serve in political office. "The interest of the excluded," he writes, "is always in danger of being excluded." Even were we to assume that the members of a parliament elected solely by the propertied class would be wholly devoted to the general welfare rather than to their class interests, that would not be good enough, Mill writes. For "Does Parliament, or almost any of its members composing it, even for an instant look at any questions with the eyes of a working man? When a subject arises in which the labourers as such have an interest, is it regarded from any point of view but that of the employers?"[27] Mill says the answer is "no." And the necessary and proper conclusion is that all competent adults should have the right to vote.[28]

As important as popular sovereignty is for achieving a legitimate measure of the general welfare, a system of self-governance with broad participation also has for Mill an even more important benefit. Active participation in the practice of self-governance, Mill argues, is a powerful way of promoting the most important purpose of a human society: the improvement of the people themselves. To perform their duties in a representative system, the people have to develop and exercise both their intellectual abilities and their moral sensibilities. And it is precisely those abilities and sensibilities whose development constitutes their improvement. As Mill writes, "Among the foremost benefits of free government is that the education of the intelligence and of the sentiments is carried down to the very lowest ranks of the people when they are called to take a part in acts which directly affect the great interests of the country . . . and it is from political discussion, and collective political action, that one whose daily occupations concentrate his interests in a small circle round himself, learns to feel for and with his fellow citizens, and becomes consciously a member of a great community."[29]

Democracy, or representative government, is therefore the ideally best form of government because the active participation in democratic decision-making and governance is important to developing the mental and moral capacities of the people. It is equally important for Mill, moreover, that the democracy be liberal. That is, it must allow its citizens the widest possible freedom to form and pursue their own conceptions of the humanly good life. "The human faculties of perception, judgement, discriminative feeling, mental activity, and even moral preference are exercised only in making a choice," Mill writes. "The mental and moral, like the muscular, powers are improved only by being used. . . . He who lets the world, or his own portion of it, choose his plan of life for him has no need of any other faculty than the ape-like one of imitation. He who chooses his plan for himself employs all his faculties." Therefore, "It is essential that different persons should be allowed to lead different lives. . . . Individuality is the same thing with development, and it is only the cultivation of individuality which produces, or can produce, well developed human beings."[30]

If the ultimate test and purpose of a good society is the fullest possible development of the mental and moral capacities of its citizens, then, the best society is a democratic one that accords its members "absolute freedom of opinion and sentiment on all subjects," freedom of speech, freedom of association, and also the freedom of action to "do as we like . . . without impediment from our fellow creatures, so long as what we do does not harm them, even though they should think our conduct foolish, perverse, or wrong."[31] This, then, is Mill's famous "harm principle": "The only purpose for which power can be rightfully exercised over any member of a civilized community, against his will, is to prevent harm to others." When it comes to the part of an individual's conduct "which merely concerns himself, his independence is, of right, absolute. Over himself, over his own body and mind, the individual is sovereign."[32]

At its heart, then, John Stuart Mill's case for representative government with extensive civil liberties rests upon two central claims, one of them normative and the other empirical. The normative claim is his belief that the ultimate purpose and measure of a political society is its ability to produce people who can and do reach their full potential as human beings—people who develop and exercise their hearts and minds, their moral and intellectual capacities. The empirical claim is that the kind of political societies best able to achieve this aim of human development are those that are both liberal and democratic. His political philosophy thus combined something old with something new. The normative belief that the ultimate purpose of politics is to produce good people was old: he found it, for example, in the classical texts of Plato, Aristotle, and Cicero that he had read as a child. The empirical belief was a newer one, based on the hopeful Enlightenment belief that—on the basis of the great advances in human knowledge since the Scientific Revolution—even the average person on the street might achieve what the ancients generally had thought was possible only for the few, for the aristocrats: namely, a level of mental and moral development sufficient for self-governance.

This was a conception of the meaning, the purposes, and the possibilities of democracy that found a welcome reception across the Atlantic Ocean in an America that entertained a belief in its own moral purpose and destiny, its mission to serve as a "City upon a hill" (John Winthrop) and its status as "the last best hope of earth" (Abraham Lincoln). One of the most prominent early examples of the impact of Mill's account of democracy's purposes and promise on these shores can be found in Walt Whitman's "Democratic Vistas." Whitman is often celebrated as the poetic bard of American democracy; and it was Mill to whom he accorded pride of place as his primary philosophical inspiration in the opening paragraph of this work. He tells us in its opening paragraph that the deeper meaning of "New World politics and progress" might best be found "in John Stuart Mill's profound essay on Liberty . . . where he demands two main constituents, or substrata, for a truly grand nationality—first, a large variety of character—and second, full play for human nature to expand itself in numberless and even conflicting directions."[33]

For Whitman, Mill's account of representative government as animated by the overarching goal of "human development in its richest diversity" captured the deeper meaning of Lincoln's famous phrase "government of the people, by the people, for the people." The ultimate purpose of government, he wrote, is "not merely to rule, to repress disorder, etc., but to develop, to open up to cultivation, to encourage the possibilities . . . of that aspiration for independence, and the pride and self-respect latent in all characters." Democracy, then, is to be understood as "the grand experiment of development, whose end . . . may be the forming of a full-grown man or woman—that *is* something." And, again, "Political democracy, as it exists and practically works in America, with all its threatening evils, supplies a training-school for making first-class men. It is life's gymnasium, not of good only, but of all."[34]

Finally, he notes, these fully developed characters it is democracy's goal to produce are not to be the self-absorbed individuals that both Mill and his mentor Tocqueville feared. They are instead to be members of a self-governing community. "I say the mission of government, henceforth, in civilized lands, is . . . to train communities through all their grades, beginning with individuals and ending there again, to rule themselves." "Topping democracy," he writes, is "that it alone can bind, and ever seeks to bind . . . all men . . . into a brotherhood, a family." Today's "liberalist," he says, "seeks not only to individualize but to universalize. The great word Solidarity has arisen." Moreover, this importantly must be a community of civic equals: "Of all dangers to a nation . . . there can be no greater one than having certain portions of the people set off from the rest by a line drawn—they not privileged as others, but degraded, humiliated, made of no account."[35]

In sum, then, this is Walt Whitman's visionary elaboration for the New World of what he saw in John Stuart Mill's account of democracy as the realization of the grand project of human development: we should understand the ultimate purpose of democracy as building a society where all its members can participate in communal self-rule, where by doing so—and by taking advantage of their civic freedoms—they can develop their human capacities, both mental and moral, to their fullest extent, and where none are left out or left behind. This is a conception of democratic ideals that perhaps can be captured best by a striking phrase of the contemporary political philosopher Benjamin Barber: democracy hopes to create "an aristocracy of everyone."[36]

Libertarianism, aka "Classical Liberalism"

The final conception of democratic ideals relevant to our central question about the relationship between capitalism and democracy that we need to review here is sometimes called "classical liberalism" by its academic champions but is also often referred to these days as "libertarianism."

For libertarians, the central purpose of democracy is to maximize what Benjamin Constant called "the liberty of the moderns": that is, the freedom of individuals from collective constraint—especially constraint imposed by the state. All the other ideals and values endorsed by other conceptions of democracy—such as equality, fraternity, civic virtue, and social justice—are construed narrowly and are either subordinated to individual liberty or denied the status of public goods. Democratic equality is, on this view, simply equality before the law. All citizens should have equal legal rights, and there should be no invidious distinctions of political rank, such as the feudal ranks of duke, earl, count, prince, and so on. But democracy, say libertarians, does not require and need not aspire to equality of power, or social status, or wealth. Inequalities of power, social status, and wealth are considered to be entirely acceptable and compatible with democratic standards so long as they are products of the free actions and judgments of free democratic citizens.

As for the third ideal in the motto *liberté, égalité, fraternité*, that is considered by libertarians to be entirely a private matter. Aristotle, in their view, was wrong to have insisted that promoting civic friendship needs to be the "first concern" of political leadership. Friendship may indeed be a human good, but it is for them not a matter of public concern. Friendship is a happy relationship among individuals that may—or may not—be essential to a good life. But citizens who do not know each other personally cannot really be friends. Given Aristotle's account of the genesis of friendship as having a good in common, civic friendship might conceivably have been relevant to the ancient polis—where there was, or was alleged to be, universal devotion to a specific conception of "the good life in common"—but it is not a possibility in today's morally pluralistic democracies. In these contemporary pluralist societies, in fact, most libertarians would contend that there is no such thing as "the common good," unless that term is understood to be the aggregated sum of individual goods.

It also follows from this individualistic conception of a democratic society that attaching any real significance to traditional notions of civic virtue is unnecessary and perhaps even improper. This traditional notion—central to classical republicanism and clearly important to America's founding generation—centers on the willingness of citizens to subordinate and at times to sacrifice their personal welfare on behalf of the commonweal. Such was the implicit understanding that informed the Spartan celebration of the woman who denounced the messenger who told her first about the fate of her sons instead of whether Sparta had been victorious. More contemporaneously, a similar understanding informs a standard expression of commendation often offered to members of the military: "Thank you for your service/sacrifice."

It is impossible to know for sure whether such thanks to our troops are deemed by libertarians to be gratuitous in the context of today's volunteer army: the troops signed up voluntarily, after all, and are being paid for what they are doing. But, in any case, most libertarians consider admonitions to people that they are subject to altruistic obligations to their fellow citizens to be misguided. They consider such admonitions misguided for two reasons: because they are politically unnecessary, and because they are arguably also improper. Most, although not all, libertarians deem them unnecessary because they broadly share the view expressed by Immanuel Kant in his treatise *Perpetual Peace* that "even a race of devils" can be well governed if they have properly designed institutions.[37] The institutional contrivances that are capable of accomplishing this feat are essentially two: laws that enact and effectively enforce penalties on those who violate others' rights to life, liberty, and property; and the organization of economic activity by the discipline of the marketplace. The first of these is precisely the task of the minimal state. And the purpose and effect of market discipline, recall, is precisely to incentivize individuals who want to further their own self-interest to act in a way that ultimately benefits the community as a whole.

In the opening lines of his book *Capitalism and Freedom*, Friedman explains why moral admonitions on behalf of personal sacrifice in the service of society as a whole should be seen not only as unnecessary but also as morally improper. He there chastises President John Kennedy for his widely celebrated appeal to his listeners in his inaugural speech to "ask not what your country can do for you—ask what you can do for your country." Such an appeal to the traditional civic republican conception of civic virtue, Friedman argues, is inappropriate because

> neither half of the statement expresses a relation between the citizen and his government that is worthy of the ideals of free men in a free society. The paternalistic "what your country can do for you" implies the government is the patron, the citizen the ward, a view that is at odds with the free man's belief in his own responsibility for his own destiny. The organismic "what you can do for your country" implies that government is the master or the deity, the citizen the servant or the votary. To the free man, the country is the collection of the individuals who compose it, not something over and above them.[38]

For libertarians, then, the ideal democratic society is one where individuals are maximally free to pursue their own self-interests and where the allocation of economic goods and resources is governed entirely by individual actions and decisions in a free and unfettered marketplace. That ideal leads, in turn, to the insistence that a good democracy is one in which the public sector is small and the functions of government are few and specific. Those functions are limited to the protection of life, liberty, and property against threats from abroad and from within—against both foreign imperialists and domestic predators. This is the "minimal state" or the "night watchman state."

The libertarian conception of the ideal democracy thus stands at the opposite end of the spectrum of democratic theories from civic republicanism, for civic republicanism places great importance upon civic equality, civic friendship/fraternity/solidarity, and the fostering of public-spirited and potentially self-abnegating civic virtues. And it correspondingly sees individual liberty as properly subject to constraints on behalf of the general welfare. Libertarianism flips that hierarchy of democratic goods on its head, according primacy to individual freedom while minimizing or even rejecting altogether the obligatory force or value of civic equality that goes beyond straightforward legal equality, of civic friendship, and of the need for civic virtues that extend beyond respect for the rights of others.

As for their historical lineage and inspiration, libertarians often give homage to late eighteenth-century figures such as Adam Smith and the French physiocrats, including Condorcet. The similarities here are somewhat limited, however, for Smith and Condorcet both accorded more powers and responsibilities to the state than do libertarians—and some of the economic theories of the physiocrats were dated and idiosyncratic.[39] A more appropriate French political economist to cite as an early precursor of today's libertarian persuasion was Frederic Bastiat, who wrote toward the middle of the nineteenth century at a time when socialist economic policies were gaining advocates. Bastiat's arguments against these socialist policies rested upon his strong endorsement of unrestricted (except for "extraordinary" and "urgent" circumstances) free markets. He also provided a defense of the justice of market distributions and the minimal state, while characterizing redistributionist government programs as "legalized plunder." Moving further into the latter part of the nineteenth century, other critics of attempts to rein in some of the allegedly disruptive consequences of industrial capitalism gained prominence—people such as the Social Darwinist Herbert Spencer and the "Protestant ethic"–oriented William Graham Sumner, whom we discussed in the previous chapter. And in the twentieth century, the market-affirming critiques of welfare state policies by Austrian-school political economists such as Friedrich von Hayek and Ludwig von Mises have given further inspiration to those who champion laissez-faire economics and the minimal state.

So what do minimal-government free-market libertarians believe that the good society would look like? What is their positive vision of the good society? What would and should be the actual social institutions and arrangements that libertarians want and expect to see once the welfare state has been "reduced to the size where we can drown it in the bathtub," as the minimal-state activist Grover Norquist once famously said? Libertarian thinkers have provided a variety of answers to these questions.

The first answer is one that, in principle, all libertarians could subscribe to. Call this the "agnostic" open-ended vison—if we could call that a vision. This answer is the one that Robert Nozick gives to the question "What exactly will [your utopia] turn out to be like?" His response is, "I do not know, and you should not be interested in my guesses about what would occur."[40] We could also add that he does not really care what will happen in any specific way. His answer, then, is that the actual concrete libertarian "best of all possible worlds" will be whatever its citizens want it to be: in the sense, not of what a majority vote would produce, but rather of the aggregate of what all the individual citizens want—in a political system that grants them complete freedom to do as they wish, so long as they are self-financed and do not infringe upon the rights of others. The two good features of whatever the result turns out to be that we can know in advance, libertarians argue, are that (1) the individuals living there would enjoy the maximum possible freedom, and (2) the aggregate wealth of the society would, thanks to the market's invisible hand, be the highest possible.

If pushed to offer more concrete depictions of their ideal society, libertarian theorists provide a range of overlapping but somewhat divergent answers. Any attempt to characterize and categorize these (often rather sketchy) concepts will be somewhat contestable. But let me attempt here a rough and cryptic survey to provide some sense of the family of libertarian "utopias."

One group of libertarians seem to envision their ideal society as essentially akin to an omnibus economic marketplace. The good society is simply an aggregate of self-interested individuals whose relationships are purely transactional. The citizens of this society, if we can call them that, have no obligations or enforceable connections with each other except through mutually consensual agreements or bargains. There is no overarching social contract—except for the constitutional agreement to establish a governing authority to protect its members' lives, liberty, and property. The ideal democracy is composed entirely of contractual agreements among individuals (or corporate entities), which the government is authorized to enforce.

These hyperindividualists, if we may so call them, in effect carry to their logical conclusion the core claims of social theorists such as Henry Maine, who wrote that "the movement of progressive societies has hitherto been a movement from status to contract," or William Graham Sumner, who wrote that "a society based on contract is a society of free and independent men, who form ties without favor or obligation, and cooperate without fear or intrigue . . . and . . . the only social improvements which are now conceivable lie in the direction of more complete realization of a society of free men united by contract."[41] Or, more contemporaneously, these libertarians might embrace the individualist manifesto of Ayn Rand's fictional hero in *Atlas Shrugged*, who declaims: "The symbol of all relationships among rational men, the moral symbol of respect for human beings, is *the trader*. Do you ask what moral obligation I owe to my fellow men? None—except rationality. . . . I seek or desire nothing from them except such relations as they care to enter of their own voluntary choice."[42]

Another utopian vision carries this hyperindividualist ideal even further. It imagines and celebrates a "society" composed not of self-interested individuals who relate to each other entirely through consensual contracts for specific purposes but of individuals or families who hardly relate to each other at all. I have in mind here libertarians such as the minimal-state activist Grover Norquist, who famously said that his "ideal citizen is the self-employed, home schooling, IRA owning guy with a concealed-carry permit—because that person doesn't need the goddamn government for anything." Or take Hank Williams Jr.—who campaigned for Sarah Palin and sings about the same self-sufficiency in his song "A Country Boy Can Survive." Or consider a feature article in *Time* magazine written by an economics professor at the libertarian-oriented George Mason University entitled, "The United States of Texas: Why the Lone Star State Is America's Future." The article concedes that in Texas, "The states' social services are thin. Welfare benefits are skimpy. Roughly a quarter of residents have no health insurance. Many of its schools are less than stellar. Property-crime rates are high. Rates of murder and other violent crimes are hardly sterling either." But he points out that, nevertheless, "more Americans are moving to Texas than to any other state." That fact, he argues, is because of the "search by many Americans for a radically cheaper way to live and do business." And, in keeping with the self-sufficient semihermit theme, the article features a couple who moved from New York and established their home site "some eighty miles from the nearest town." As the author notes: "The Americans heading to Texas and other cheap-living states are a bit like the mythical cowboys of our past—self-reliant, for better or worse."[43]

These visions of libertarian utopia celebrate a kind of society whose possible appearance was viewed with alarm by earlier social theorists such as Edmund Burke and Alexis de Tocqueville: a world of social isolates who relate to each other only intermittently and transactionally. For its libertarian champions, this represents the utmost realization of personal independence, a place where people are not bound by obligations to anyone else unless they assume them entirely freely in pursuit of their own freely chosen purposes. But Burke objected, you may recall, that a political society "ought not to be considered as nothing better than a partnership agreement in a trade of pepper and coffee, calico or tobacco, or some other such low concern, to be taken up for a little temporary interest, and to be dissolved by the fancy of the parties."[44] In a similar vein, Tocqueville worried about the dangers of a new form of self-centeredness born of democratic times. "Our fathers," he writes in *Democracy in America*, "were only acquainted with egoism . . . , a passionate and exaggerated sense of self. . . . Individualism is a mature and calm feeling, which disposes each member of the community to sever himself from the mass of his fellows, and to draw apart with his family and friends; so that, after he has thus formed a little circle of his own, he willingly leaves society at large to itself. . . . Egoism blights the germ of all virtue: individualism, at first, only saps the virtues of public life; but, in the long run, it attacks and destroys all others, and is at length absorbed in downright egoism."[45]

Ardent libertarian individualists would simply dismiss objections and worries like these as the result of a failure to appreciate the transcendent importance of freedom and a misguided moralistic deprecation of self-assertion. But there is another response to such concerns that has been offered by adherents of a somewhat different vision of libertarian hopes. Let's call this the "romantic anarchist" wing of libertarianism. I have in mind here libertarian-leaning academics who characterize themselves as "Aristotelian" libertarians, some followers of Friedrich von Hayek who draw upon his Humean pragmatic conventionalism and an expansive interpretation of his notion of "spontaneous order," and advocates of the "Jeffersonian" version of libertarian goals found in Charles Murray's *In Pursuit of Happiness and Good Government*.[46]

The crucial defining feature of those I am calling romantic anarchists is their hopeful belief that the dynamics of what Hayek characterizes as "spontaneous order" can be relied upon to produce benign outcomes not only in economics but in social relations as well. The "spontaneous" (i.e., not the result of mandates or arrangements imposed by some overarching authority but the result of the freely chosen actions of the participants) good order of the economic marketplace is mediated by Adam Smith's "invisible hand." All act freely in their own behalf, and the "spontaneously" generated incentives and rewards of the marketplace will push the sum of these actions toward optimum efficiency and productivity. In a similar fashion, libertarian "romantics" argue, when rational human beings are faced with tasks demanding some form of cooperative social endeavor, they will organize themselves "spontaneously" (i.e., voluntarily) to perform these tasks. They do not require some superintending power above them to decide what to do and to order them to do it.

Now, in the case of economics, individual actors are motivated by their own personal self-interest. And they are pushed into doing things that contribute to the general good of a prosperous society by the discipline of the invisible hand. In the larger domain of politics and social action, however, the invisible hand does not rule. The market discipline that in economics transforms self-seeking behavior into common good ("private vice, public virtue") is not in force. So the crucial question for these "romantic" libertarians becomes: What are the substitutes for the profit motive and market discipline that can be expected to produce voluntary social cooperation in the service of communal goods? Romantic anarchists for the most part give remarkably little attention to these crucial questions. (Ironically, although they would surely be horrified by the analogy, they resemble here Marx and his followers, whose faith in the socialist utopia depended upon their own parallel optimistic assumption that its inhabitants would happily and spontaneously work diligently for the general welfare instead of for their own personal benefit.) There are possible answers they might offer, of course. They could, for example, invoke the classic Aristotelian belief that human beings are by nature social animals and that this "natural sociability" can be counted upon to motivate us all to pitch in our efforts and resources for the good of the whole. Or they could be relying upon what Tocqueville called "self-interest rightly understood" or "enlightened self-interest"—the idea that people who act on behalf of the group to which they belong are ultimately working for their own best interests—and are innately capable of understanding this. And certainly there are examples of such behavior and motivations that make this optimism somewhat plausible. Think, for example, of communal barn-raisings in the Amish farming community, or volunteer fire departments, or the Posse Comitatus in the Old West. Tocqueville himself was impressed by what he saw as the propensity of early Americans to form such communal endeavors and associations. "If a stoppage occurs in a thoroughfare," he wrote, "and the circulation of vehicles is hindered, the neighbors immediately form themselves into a deliberative body; and this extemporaneous assembly gives rise to an executive power, which remedies the inconvenience before anybody has thought of recurring to a pre-existing authority superior to that of the persons immediately concerned."[47]

So some logic and some experience can lend credence to the optimism of "romantic anarchist" libertarians—and to their counterparts on the political left who believe in the "withering away of the state." On the other hand, however, it seems that market-oriented libertarians—especially those who rely upon public choice theory—would be keenly aware of the problem of free riders whenever it comes to collective action endeavors. They surely should understand how reliance upon spontaneous effort on the behalf of collective goods was a major cause of the disastrous failures of agricultural policies in the Soviet Union and China. And how could any serious student of

American politics and history forget the disastrous failure of voluntary collective action among the states that quickly undermined our newly independent country under the Articles of Confederation? As Hamilton concluded his trenchant dissection of why the Articles' reliance upon voluntary contributions by the several states to the federal government was doomed from the outset: "It has happened as was to have been foreseen. The measures of the Union have not been executed; the delinquencies of the states have, step by step, matured themselves to an extreme, which has, at length, arrested all the wheels of the national government, and brought them to an awful stand. . . . Each state, yielding to the persuasive voice of immediate interest or convenience, has successively withdrawn its support, till the frail and tottering edifice seems ready to fall upon our heads, and to crush us beneath its ruins."[48] Perhaps it is the force of Hamilton's logic that explains why the attempts of libertarians who pin their hopes upon the voluntary cooperation of individuals for the achievement of collective goods wind up offering highly localistic visions of small communities essentially unrelated to each other.[49]

A final subset of self-described "classical liberal" libertarians might be termed the "relentless privatizers." These libertarians are neither quasi-anarchists, nor hyperindividualists, nor localists in their visions of the ideal liberal democratic society. They simply want to rely as much as possible upon private enterprises and voluntary private action both in the conduct of the economy and in social arrangements more generally. They recognize that government has an essential role. But they want that role to be limited to (1) protecting life, liberty, and property; (2) pursuing "indivisible" social goods, such as natural defense; and (3) dealing with technical monopolies and the "externalities" of "neighborhood effects" that private transactions might cause. Any governing activities beyond these, in their view, are unwise or illicit. They may concede that democratic governments have a legitimate role to play when it comes to things like public health, education, and even the alleviation of extreme economic need. But they believe that many current government activities should be left to private hands.

Milton Friedman is a good representative of this subset of libertarians. Friedman recognizes that there are many positive neighborhood effects of having an educated populace. Therefore, public investment in providing education is appropriate and desirable. He argues, however, that public subsidy is proper only for primary and secondary schooling. And public schools should wherever possible have to compete with private schools funded by taxpayer-supported vouchers. Higher education and vocational education, he says, represent an investment in one's own human capital—and therefore should for the most part be paid for by the recipient. Because, however, "an imperfection in the capital market" has arguably led to "underinvestment in human capital," there is a case for a government role in making funds for such investments in oneself available; but these subsidies should be loans rather than grants. He also recognizes that the alleviation of poverty provides positive neighborhood effects and that relying entirely on private charity to do this would almost surely be inadequate and subject to extensive free-rider problems. Some government action in this area may therefore be justifiable. The right way to do this, he argues, for reasons of efficiency and minimizing government paternalism, would be through a negative income tax (a form of a guaranteed basic income) funded by the elimination of existing income support programs such as social security, aid to dependent children, farm price supports, food stamps, and public housing subsidies. Friedman would also end a long list of other current government activities: for example, (1) all tariffs on imports and restrictions on exports, (2) rent control, (3) minimum-wage laws, (4) government regulation of radio and television, (5) conscription in peacetime, and (6) vocational licensing laws. And he also argues that neighborhood effects "do not justify a national park, like Yellowstone National Park or the Grand Canyon," where entry can be controlled.

The Implications for Political Economy of These Different Models of Democratic Ideals

We could consider here still more extant models of what an ideal democracy would look like. In recent decades, for example, political theorists have described and defended models of democracy such as interest-group liberalism, pluralist democracy, agonistic democracy, participatory democracy, social justice democracy, deliberative democracy, and liberal realism—to cite some examples. The five conceptions of democracy we have reviewed here, however—civic republicanism, Lockean or Reformation liberalism, Enlightenment liberalism, perfectionist liberalism, and the libertarian interpretation of "classical liberalism"—are arguably sufficient for the purposes of this book. That is so for three reasons. First, these democratic traditions are those that historically have had the widest influence on America's political institutions and political imagination. Second, even the rather basic and cryptic accounts of these several democratic models make it quite evident that there is no single and universally accepted definition of "democracy" as a normative ideal. Third, our review of them has, I hope, provided the basis for us to understand how these different conceptions of democratic ideals can and do lead to divergent views about the proper role of the capitalist marketplace in a democratic society.

In the context of this book, this last point is the most important for our purposes. So let us conclude this chapter by looking a bit more fully and specifically at the ways that these different models of the good democratic society lead their adherents to endorse competing accounts of the appropriate relationship between capitalism and democracy.

Of the several conceptions of democratic ideals we have reviewed in this chapter, the polar positions on the relationship between capitalism and democracy would be occupied by civic republicanism on one end and "classical liberalism"/libertarianism on the other—with the remaining three traditions falling somewhere in between.

On one end of the spectrum, those who adhere to what they call "classical liberalism" see the norms and institutions of the free marketplace and the norms and institutions of the good democratic society as unproblematically compatible. Indeed, one could say that these appear from the libertarian perspective to be virtually coterminous. For the capitalist marketplace is populated by separate, free, and unencumbered economic actors who relate to each other solely through the contractual rights and obligations they create by formalizing the results of self-interested bargaining. The arrangements and procedures of the marketplace can therefore be said to be optimally liberal—in the sense of according all individuals complete freedom to make bargains with others. And these arrangements and procedures can be said to be democratic in the sense that they create economic governance by consent of the governed via their choices in the marketplace. It is true that reducing the relationship among democratic citizens to the relationship between buyers and sellers in the marketplace makes our relations with our fellow citizens entirely transactional—or, as conservatives like Thomas Carlyle and socialists like Marx complained, reduces these relations to nothing more than a "cash nexus." But from the libertarian perspective, that attenuation of the bonds among society's citizens is entirely appropriate and not something to be mourned. It merely represents the supplanting of relations of status by relations through contract that classical liberals see as the heart and soul of social progress.

At the opposite end of the spectrum of democratic ideals, civic republicanism would see this libertarian reduction of the bonds of citizenship to the self-interested transactions of the marketplace with alarm. Instead of viewing such a society as the acme of personal freedom, civic republicans would consider it to represent a triumph of political corruption, the demise of civic virtue, and the pathway to the disintegration and ultimate demise of the democratic republic. That is because civic republicanism was, in the words of Barry Shain, "particularly concerned with the standing of the public good and the priority it was to enjoy."[50] Where laissez-faire liberals rely upon the magic of the markets' invisible hand to produce "public virtue" out of "private vice," civic republicans believe that when private self-seeking begins to pervade the citizenry and supplant public-spiritedness this will cause a republic to descend into a cycle of increasing factional conflict that can tear it apart.

Since civic republicanism antedated the emergence of both modern-day capitalism and modern-day liberal democracy, we cannot really say exactly what its stance would be in response to our central question about the relationship between capitalism and democracy. We can, however, draw some reliable inferences from the core tenets of their political perspective and social values. Given the priority civic republicans placed upon social solidarity, for example, it is quite clear that they would not have endorsed the capitalist/libertarian ethos of self-seeking or its ethic of distribution. Given also their insistence upon the priority of the public good over private interest, they would almost surely have insisted that a healthy commonwealth would need to have a strong public sphere, both to make provision for the economic viability and the health of its members and also to instill in its citizens a willingness to make sacrifices for their fellow citizens. In contemporary terms, this account of democratic vitality and success would seem to translate logically into support for a fairly strong and somewhat redistributive state that would keep moneymaking in its place and keep it from undermining the social cohesion upon which it depended. Members of contemporary America's Republican Party would likely condemn the ideal civic republican regime as a nefarious form of socialism. And civil libertarians in both of our major parties would surely consider it to be too authoritarian.

As for the other premodern, or nearly so, conception of democracy that has shaped the American polity, it is also not easy to specify the stance of Lockean liberalism with respect to the proper relationship between (modern) capitalism and (modern) democracy. Locke, after all, also did not experience either of these.

Those who explicitly invoke John Locke as inspiration for their political views usually self-identify as free-market conservatives. There is in my home state of North Carolina, for example, an organization that has named itself the John Locke Foundation. Created and financed by businessman Art Pope, this organization engages in lobbying for free-market policies. It states on its website that it "believes in free markets, limited constitutional government, and personal responsibility." And it also states there that the "problems" it seeks to remedy include "crushing tax burdens on families and businesses; the costly, immoral, and destructive welfare state; and oppressive rules and regulations on business." "In the modern American context," they write, their principles "are labeled conservative. . . . Some observers also consider these principles libertarian." Accordingly, "If someone asks whether the John Locke Foundation is conservative, (classically) liberal, or libertarian, the appropriate answer is 'yes.'"[51]

Presumably this organization adopts the mantle of John Locke because he is known as an apostle of "limited government," because he provided a famous moral justification for private property, because he said that "the great and chief end of men uniting into commonwealths . . . is the preservation of their property," and because he wrote that "I have truly no property in that which another can by right take from me when he pleases against my consent."[52]

It is not at all clear, however, that Locke—were he to be resuscitated and living among us—would fully endorse this foundation's views. Indeed, I think that would be quite unlikely for several reasons. In the first place, what Locke meant by "limited government" was not the same thing as the "minimal government" championed by laissez-faire liberals. As political theorists well know, in order to understand the concrete meaning of terms describing what a political thinker is for, you have to know the antonyms of those terms. You have to know what they are against. And when Locke argued for limited government, he was not arguing against the welfare state or socialism of some sort: he was arguing against autocracy and theocracy. Affirming limited government meant rejecting the legitimacy of a hereditary monarchy that claimed to hold absolute power over its subjects. And it meant rejecting the claim of any government that it was entitled to dictate the religious beliefs and affiliations of its citizens. So by his standards, the British acquired a limited government by the enactment of the Bill of Rights and the Act of Toleration after the Glorious Revolution. And Americans, by this definition, were guaranteed limited government by the explicit grants and limitations of government power found in our constitution and the Bill of Rights.

Second, although Locke wrote that "every man has a 'property' in his own 'person,'" that did not mean the same thing as the libertarian notion of total "self-ownership." For Locke believed that while no other human being had ownership rights over our person, the God who made us certainly held a lien on us and our efforts. "Being all the workmanship of one omnipotent and infinitely wise Maker, all the servants of one sovereign Master, sent into the world by His order and about His business," he wrote, we are "His property." This is a version of the Christian notion of stewardship: we may have a right to the integrity of our person and to the fruits of our labor. But we also are under an obligation to use our talents for God's purposes. And, among other things, this means, according to Locke, that "when our own preservation comes not in competition, ought we as much as we can to preserve the rest of mankind."[53]

Finally, when Locke stipulates that no one's property can legitimately be taken from him or her without consent, he makes it clear that this does not mean that contributions to the public good—the pursuit of which he repeatedly says is the ultimate purpose of legitimate government—must come from an individual's freely granted philanthropic beneficence. Instead it means that mandatory contributions—namely taxes—both must and may be enacted by our designated representatives: "It must be with his own consent—i.e. the consent of the majority, giving it either by themselves or their representatives chosen by them."[54] In short, for Locke, only democratically elected governments are entitled to impose taxes. But taxes imposed by laws consented to by the people's elected representatives and applied to all citizens (i.e., equal protection of the laws) are entirely legitimate. There are no set limits. If the people are unhappy, they can elect new representatives. But until then, they are morally as well as legally under an obligation to pay.

If we ask, then, what the implications of Lockean liberalism are for adjudicating our question about the proper relationship between capitalism and democracy, the best answer is that it is very hard to say. Partly this is simply because Locke never saw either a full-fledged democracy or a modern industrialized free-market capitalist system. But he also said things that, taken alone and out of context, could be cited in support of a pretty minimal state and other things that could be cited as providing grounds for the affirmative obligation of a good society to act on behalf of the larger public interest and the welfare of needy citizens. So partisans on various sides of our central debate can pick out particular parts of Locke's arguments to invoke in their own behalf. The truth is that those claiming to say with definitude that Locke would, if living today, support their favored viewpoint are pretty much talking through their hat.

Moving to our next model of liberalism, it is probably safe to say that those who see the purposes and ideals of democracy in the way that most Enlightenment liberals did would almost surely fall in the middle of the spectrum when it comes to the relationship between capitalism and democracy. For, generally speaking, the values and social aspirations of Enlightenment liberals led them to be keenly appreciative of the virtues of a free-market economy. But the same values and aspirations led them to envision a role for state-governed fiscal enterprises as well. They treasured personal freedoms—not only of economic pursuits but also of religious persuasion and intellectual inquiry. They would have found a society that fully embraced the civic republican insistence upon political unity and the subordination of individuals to collective views and goals to be somewhat stifling. They did, nonetheless, specifically value civic equality and fraternity as well as liberty. They held the happy and important belief that extensive civil and economic liberty would bring greater social equality along with it. And they were not averse to envisioning certain government programs as legitimate and even necessary to achieving their goals.

We saw this "both-and" view of liberty/equality and private/public enterprise in Condorcet's vision of the social progress that he expected scientific advances, political democratization, and social liberalization would bring. He rhapsodized with the fervor of a contemporary advocate of laissez-faire about the benign magic of the markets' invisible hand. But he also clearly took for granted a collective effort to support the broad and inclusive educational programs needed to advance and spread the explosion in knowledge that would be the central driver of social progress. He explained the logic and benefits of social insurance programs like social security and proposed financial grants to give those entering adulthood the means to succeed economically. And so on. So, to put this into a contemporary context, the Enlightenment liberals of whom Condorcet was an archetypical representative could speak like a Cato Institute spokesperson one minute and more like Bernie Sanders the next. They did not see extensive reliance upon free markets and the creation of government programs for important public goods as antithetical or irreconcilable. You cannot build a house—much less a cathedral—with only a single tool in your toolbox. In like fashion, Condorcet and others who shared his perspective seemed to take for granted that a variety of institutional tools—some private, some governmental—would be needed to build the free, equal, peaceful, and prosperous democratic society of their dreams and expectations.

Since the most prominent American political figure who broadly shared the hopes and convictions of the Enlightenment was Thomas Jefferson, it is possibly useful to say a few words about him here. That is because some small-government advocates like to claim him as one of their own, attributing to him the maxim "That government governs best which governs least." (In fact, there seems to be general agreement among those who have researched this quote that Jefferson may never had said this. And he certainly was not its originator. Instead, it appears that the American journalist John O'Sullivan used a variant of that phrase as the motto for a journal he edited in 1837 and that Henry David Thoreau appropriated and popularized it in his essay "Civil Disobedience" a few years thereafter.) Jefferson was, in any case, not a partisan of minimal government. He was instead—not unreasonably in the context of a largely agrarian society with little of the interconnectedness of today's America—what we might call a "localist." His vision of American national governance was that it had to deal with such intrinsically national concerns as foreign affairs, national defense, regulating relations between the different states, regulating trade, imposing tariffs, and so on. The other tasks of governance, however, he believed were best conducted at the local level. (This is essentially a version of a principle of Catholic social thought known as "subsidiarity." This principle essentially asserts that political decisions should be made at the most decentralized site of competent authority.) Jefferson did believe that, in the context of a far-flung and largely agricultural society composed of multiple state jurisdictions, the functions of the national government should be as few as possible. But that did not mean that everything else would fall into the hands of private enterprises. On the contrary, he sought a system of vigorous and accessible local governing institutions that would perform important public functions such as building infrastructure, providing relief for the indigent, and offering that most important Enlightenment public good of all—namely, access to quality education for all citizens of the republic.

The "perfectionist" democrats among us, those whose political ideals resemble those of John Stuart Mill and Walt Whitman, also tend to support some version of a mixed economy—that is, to endorse a market system but also to see a legitimate role for government regulation and provision of certain goods. That assessment can be seen to follow from their conception of the ultimate justification and purposes of liberal democracy. And that logical inference also receives validation from Mill's own explicit judgments regarding the proper role and limits of a democratic government in economic matters. (We have these to look at because he alone of our archetypal theorists lived after the Industrial Revolution.)

When it comes to the moral justification and central purposes of democracy, we can recall that Mill saw these as the attainment of the greatest good for the greatest number—and that "good" here meant the fullest possible development of our human moral and intellectual capacities. Success in this democratic project—what Whitman called this "grand experiment of development"—also required allowing its participants a wide range of freedom in both thought and action. Moreover, success in this project of human development was essential if democratic citizens were going to become capable of self-rule. (As Whitman wrote: "The mission of government, henceforth, in civilized lands is . . . to train communities, through all their grades, . . . to rule themselves." And, in Mill's words: "The first element of good government, therefore, being the virtue and intelligence of the human beings composing the community, the most important point of excellence which any form of government can possess is to promote the virtue and intelligence of the people themselves. . . . It is on these qualities, so far as they exist in the people, that all possibility of goodness in the practical operations of the government depends.")[55]

When it comes to the scope of government action, then, Mill argued that the proper rule of thumb should be this: "A government cannot have too much of the kind of activity which does not impede, but aids and stimulates, individual exertion and development. The mischief begins when, instead of calling forth the activity and powers of individuals and bodies, it substitutes its own activities for theirs."[56] Consistent with his qualitative utilitarianism, then, Mill's standard for legitimate government activity is all about its consequences. If the activity in question develops and improves the mental and moral capacities of the people, it is good and proper. But, here influenced by Tocqueville's musings about the possible emergence of a new form of benign despotism that would reduce its citizens "to nothing more than a flock of timid and hardworking animals with the government as shepherd."[57] Mill worried about the dangers of what today is sometimes called "the nanny state"—government as an overzealous guardian that would wind up "dwarfing" its people. So, for him, the maxim that should determine the scope of legitimate government activity is—at least in the abstract—quite straightforward: if such activity enables and promotes the project of development of the people's capacities, then it is good and proper. If it does not so enhance the people's capacities for self-rule, then the government should leave the people to act upon their own initiative.

What, then, are the implications of this maxim for the relationship between democratic governments and free markets? Mill sees it this way. First, there is no a priori principle that prevents a democratic government from regulating or engaging in economic activities—nothing like individual property rights that are absolute and imprescriptible, for example. Mill writes: "Trade is a social act. Whoever undertakes to sell any description of goods to the public does what affects the interest of other persons, and of society in general; and thus his conduct, in principle, comes within the jurisdiction of society."[58] The operation and distributions of free markets, however, have in his view prima facie legitimacy by the utilitarian standard of the greatest good for the greatest number. "It is recognized," he writes, "that both the cheapness and the good quality of commodities are most effectively provided by leaving the producers and sellers perfectly free, under the sole check of equal freedom to the buyers for supplying themselves elsewhere."[59] So unless there are overriding considerations to the contrary, Mill would counsel reliance on the free marketplace for the allocation of economic resources in his democratic society.

That said, Mill recognizes a significant number of areas in which important considerations require the government to fund and operate certain enterprises on its own, and also some parts of the economy that require government regulation of the marketplace. We can quickly review some of the more important of these instances here.

First, Mill recognized that the necessary conditions for markets to perform as advertised are not always there: the real world does not always reflect the enabling assumptions on the economists' blackboard. For example, the market discipline that serves to optimize the price of economic goods depends upon the competition of multiple buyers and sellers. So when the circumstances of production or distribution create a "practical monopoly" (what we today usually call a "natural monopoly"), as in the case of gas, water, or electric utilities, the relevant government jurisdiction is justified in either providing those services itself or "exercise[ing] the right of fixing a maximum of fares and charges."[60] In short, municipal monopoly of water and sewer provision and state utility commissions that regulate the price of gas and electricity are both rational and justified.

Second, considering how essential a decent education is both for the well-being of the individual and for creating citizens who possess the competence to perform their civic duties, Mill considers it to be "almost a self-evident axiom that the State should require and compel the education . . . of every human being who is born its citizen." Parents with means, in his view, can properly be required to provide their children with a good education. And the government should "help to pay the school fees of the poorer classes of children and defray the entire school expenses of those who have no one else to pay for them."[61]

Third, Mill argues that the government has a responsibility to provide the economic resources needed to prevent destitution. He believed it mandatory, for both moral and practical reasons, for any sensible and decent society to have what the British of his time called Poor Laws or something like today's food stamps program, Temporary Aid to Needy Families, and public housing subsidies where needed. "I conceive it to be highly desirable," he wrote, "that the certainty of subsistence should be held out by law to the destitute able-bodied, rather than that their relief should depend on voluntary charity. In the first place, charity almost always does too much or too little: it lavishes its bounty in one place and leaves people to starve one another. Secondly, since the state must necessarily provide subsistence for the criminal poor while undergoing punishment, not to do the same for the poor who have not offended is to give a premium on crime."[62] He argues, moreover, that the basic rules and regulations regarding such subsistence provision should be the same "throughout the country," even if administered locally. That is because, he says, "no locality has a moral right to make itself by mismanagement a nest of pauperism, necessarily overflowing into other localities and impairing the moral and physical condition of the whole laboring community."[63]

Mill also says that the principle of individual liberty and the general reliance upon freedom of contract in matters economic can properly be constrained by government regulations to protect salaried employees—that is, by provisions in what we refer to as labor law. First, "It is right that children, and young persons not yet arrived at maturity, should be protected, so far as the eye and the hand of the state can reach, from being over-worked. Laboring for too many hours in the day, or on work beyond their strength, should not be permitted to them, for if permitted it may always be compelled."[64] Second, Mill argues that it is permissible in principle for the state to impose upon employers "sanitary precautions or arrangements to protect workpeople employed in dangerous occupations."[65] And he also lays out the case for what we now refer to as maximum-hours legislation.[66]

Finally, Mill says that government enterprises—or government-funded enterprises—are justifiable and probably even necessary in cases where important positive externalities are at stake. These are "cases in which important public services are to be performed, while yet there is no individual specially interested in performing them, nor would any adequate remuneration naturally or spontaneously attend their performance." For example, he writes, "it is a proper office of government to build and maintain lighthouses, establish buoys, etc. for the security of navigation" because "no one would build lighthouses from motives of personal interest." Scientific research is another example of such enterprises. The results of some such research can in fact be profitable—as in the development of pharmaceuticals. But private profits are often not found in the case of more general basic scientific research that can produce immense public good. So this too is an enterprise that may require government support. The general principle here, Mill writes, is "that anything which is desirable should be done for the general interests of mankind or of future generations . . . but which is not of a nature to remunerate individuals or associations for undertaking it, is in itself a suitable thing to be undertaken by government."[67]

THE CENTRAL AND IMPORTANT lesson of this chapter is that if you want to make any claims about the role of free markets in a democratic society, you must first establish what you mean by *democracy*—for there is no single universally accepted definition of that term. Instead, the term *democracy*—if we are speaking of a normative ideal rather than about certain bare-bones arrangements such as majority rule and popular sovereignty—is used to describe a number of overlapping but sometimes quite different models of the good society.

Our review of the several major conceptions of democratic ideals that have shaped today's democratic societies has also, I hope, been sufficient to make it clear that these different conceptions lead us to see the proper role of the capitalist marketplace in significantly different ways. At one extreme, the self-described "classical liberal" or libertarian conception of a rightly ordered democracy is virtually identical with the institutionalized arrangements of the capitalist marketplace. The civic republican conception of a well-ordered democracy, in sharp contrast, would see that kind of a society as one that is both morally corrupt and doomed to decline and failure. Somewhere between these quite divergent accounts of the good society are other models that do not share the civic republican hostility to what they see as the corrupting and inevitably politically disintegrative effects of a market economy. But these more "centrist" models, if we can call them that, are also less universally and unequivocally celebratory of free markets than are libertarians. Their adherents appreciate the value of free-market arrangements while also believing that these arrangements must be constrained and supplemented by certain kinds of collective action if a democratic society is to prosper and to be true to its core values.

I hope, then, that this chapter has demonstrated that the judgments we as citizens must make about the role and limits of capitalism in a democratic society depend not only upon our understanding of political economy and upon our moral judgments about fairness and justice but also very importantly upon our views about the governing values and the ultimate purposes of democracy—our visions of what an ideal democracy would look like. In the chapter that follows, I will shift gears somewhat and try to explain why, for somewhat different reasons in each case, no definitive judgments are available to us in any of these three areas. Having conceded there that no perfect answers are to be had, I hope in my final chapter to persuade you that some judgments about the role of markets in a democratic society are nonetheless more reasonable than others.

CHAPTER FOUR

Why No Slam-Dunk Answers

In my introduction to this book, I said that the dispute over the proper relationship between capitalism and democracy actually consists of three distinct arguments: one about the relationship between free markets and the achievement of economic prosperity, another about the relationship between market outcomes and the moral imperatives of justice and fairness, and a third about whether the ideals of a good democratic society are best achieved by market transactions plus the minimal state.

In the preceding three chapters, we have looked at some of the best and most relevant arguments on both sides of these three disputes. On one side are the claims of those who argue that free-market capitalism will maximize prosperity, will distribute resources in a morally defensible way, and will create a society that comports with democratic ideals. On the other side are those who argue that some collective actions are necessary to constrain and supplement the functions and results of the marketplace on each of these fronts. Their claim is that democratic government has a necessary role to play in achieving economic well-being, in achieving a morally acceptable distribution of material resources, and in achieving the larger ideals of democracy.

My principal goal to this point, then, has been to clarify and explain the issues and competing arguments rather than to assess and adjudicate them. It would seem remiss of me to leave it at that, however. The fact is that it is our responsibility as democratic citizens to make informed and reasonable judgments about the proper relationship between capitalism and the kind of democratic society we want to live in. The answers we give to the questions at hand will govern the policies we advocate and whom we vote for.

In my final chapter, therefore, I will move from analysis to assessment. I will share there some of my own considered judgments about the relationship between capitalism and democracy—for you, in turn, to consider in making your own judgments. Before I do that, however, I have in this chapter a preliminary task that seems to me equally important: to explain why there are no slam-dunk answers to any of our three central questions. Even if I believe that some views are more reasonable than others, we all need to recognize and acknowledge that the complexity and conundrums regarding the causes of economic prosperity, the canons of social justice, and the ideals of the good society are such that no one can credibly claim to have perfect or incontestable answers to these questions. So, before offering my own conclusions, let me here say a few words about why those conclusions—and any of yours, as well—have to be acknowledged as vulnerable to reasonable disagreement.

Prosperity and the Limits of Economic Knowledge

Claims about the best way for a society to achieve maximum prosperity are not based upon moral judgments. They are instead claims about cause and effect based upon the empirical science of economics. The primary goal at stake here is not at issue: it is the attainment of the highest possible GNP (Gross National Product). The debate here, in short, is not about ends but about means. The question is: What economic arrangements and policies will produce the highest aggregate wealth for society at large? Can we expect reliance upon completely free and unfettered market transactions to produce the greatest wealth possible for our society? Or must we also take collective action at times to supplement or adjust the work of the capitalist market-place? And if such actions are needed, what exactly are they?

To provide credible answers to questions like these about the consequences (prosperity levels) of certain causes (policies and arrangements), we can look for evidence and we can also use logic. We can work empirically or theoretically, or both. For example, if I want to explain the cause of a sudden and excruciating pain in my jaw, both evidence and logic sustain the proposition that it was the effect of you hitting me with your clenched fist. The empirical evidence for this conclusion includes the temporal simultaneity between the blow and my pain and also the similar unhappy consequences of other hard collisions my jaw has suffered in the past. And logical inferences based in theory can be invoked to support that conclusion: we can use our knowledge of biology (pressure on the nerve tissue causes pain), and put 2 and 2 together. In short, both logic and evidence point to the same explanation about the cause of the pain in my jaw. So I am justified in having great confidence in reaching that conclusion about a cause-and-effect relationship.

So far, so good. But what happens to the reliability of our judgments about cause and effect when we move from a simple event like this to much more complicated and complex interactions among a whole host of variables? Clearly, our inferences about the causal impact of these many relevant variables upon the outcome we want to achieve become much more difficult to make and much less certain. Moreover, suppose that all of these potentially causal variables do not simply influence the result we are concerned about (i.e., economic prosperity) severally and directly but also exert causal influence on each other? And suppose that these causal influences are not only one-directional but reciprocal? In dealing with very complex phenomena like this, reaching reliable and definitive answers to questions about cause and effect becomes considerably more difficult and problematic.

Some of the changes in medical and dietary advice offered to the public over recent years provide pertinent—and often frustrating—examples of these difficulties. Our bodies are very complex biological systems with many interrelated forces and causal variables at work in them. As a result, ascertaining the causes and origins of diseases can be a hazardous undertaking. Equally hazardous are attempts to specify and develop ways to prevent illness, whether by diet, activity, or pharmacological intervention. Let me offer a few examples. Several decades ago, it was found that a cause of many heart attacks was unstable plaque in the arteries—and that the steroid alcohol cholesterol seemed to be a central component of these plaques. So the medical decree came out: lower your serum cholesterol. And that meant: avoid or minimize the consumption of food items containing high levels of cholesterol. Egg yolks are high in cholesterol, so those at risk of heart disease were admonished to delete them from their diet. One of those so admonished was the father of a friend of mine. He loved egg dishes, so he only very unhappily complied with this medical advice. Indeed, he instructed his family that if he were to be struck by a car and was dying in the street they should bring him an omelet. Some years later, it was decided that dietary cholesterol was not as major an issue as had been thought, because much of that was excreted. The principal problem was the cholesterol produced by our own bodies. I'm sure my friend's father rolled over in his grave at the news. So the pharmaceutical industry developed drugs—statins—that inhibited the production of cholesterol by the liver. The decree went out: everyone with cholesterol levels above a certain point should take these drugs. More recently, however, some studies have suggested that these drugs have minimal bearing on heart-related death rates—especially among certain populations such as women and people over a certain age. We were also informed some years ago that dietary fat should be avoided and that we should therefore use oleomargarine instead of butter. More recently the changed advice is that fat consumption within normal levels is not a problem but that the problem items are carbohydrates and sugars. Oh, and butter may be less problematic than margarine. We were also told a few years ago that red wine in modest amounts could improve heart health. Very recently however, a couple of studies found little support for that claim. Similarly, taking omega-3 oil was found in some studies to be valuable in maintaining heart health. Very recently, other studies have called that hopeful claim somewhat into question. The latest wisdom seems to be that the best predictors—and hence likely important contributing causes—of heart incidents are stress and recent infectious episodes. So if you have been stressed out by all this changing advice, you may be in trouble.

Another problem caused to the healing arts by the great complexity of causes and effects in human physiology is the danger of producing unanticipated negative effects on the body by interventions intended to be therapeutic. Drug prescriptions are not the only example of such potentially adverse interventions, but they are illustrative. Back around 1950, for example, a drug was developed to alleviate the malady of "morning sickness" that afflicts many women in the early stages of pregnancy. That drug was thalidomide. As it turned out, one unanticipated effect of the drug was to inhibit some important developmental processes in the fetus. I have a relative who, like many others, has had as a result to spend his life in a wheelchair.

I say these things not to demean the medical profession, which is dedicated to keeping its patients alive and as healthy as possible. My purpose instead is to illustrate how very difficult it can be to arrive at clear and reliable accounts of cause-and-effect relationships within complex systems with many forces and components that affect each other in multiple ways. The relevant point here is that political and economic systems are also extremely complicated systems with many variables that impinge upon each other in multifarious ways—and that it is therefore an extremely challenging task to determine exactly what mix of circumstances, institutions, and policies is most likely to maximize the economic performance of a particular society. If we are talking about relatively primitive economies—for example, a society that is small, relatively isolated, and composed very largely of yeoman farmers—we can do pretty well in depicting the casual patterns in play. On the other hand, when we are talking about large modern economies in a globalized world that features a panoply of economic actors including massive and complex corporate entities, millions of stockholders, huge financial institutions, rapid technological changes, nearly instantaneous transmission of economic data and consummation of property exchanges, government rules and institutions that affect and participate in the conduct of the economy, and so on, reliable explanation and prediction become exponentially difficult.

Moreover, social scientists—including economists—do not have the ability to set up approximations of "critical experiments" (also called "crucial experiments"). In such experiments, the idea is to create two sets of circumstances in which everything is the same except for the single variable whose causal effect you are interested in establishing. The drug tests required by the Food and Drug Administration before it will approve a new drug for sale, for example, take that form. The testers take two groups of patients who are as similar as possible in terms of age, gender, ethnicity, medical history, and so on. Then they treat one group with the drug in question while treating the other group either with the best current medication or with no medication at all. Then they monitor the outcome in both groups in order to see if there are divergent outcomes—and this logically provides good evidence for the value (or relative value, if the control group is given a different drug) of the drug being tested.

Economists do not have the luxury of doing anything of the sort. They can, of course, look for similar cases to compare; but such comparisons are rough at best, since other relevant causes that may be in play cannot be controlled. Suppose, for example, that we want to run an experiment to assess the relative validity of competing accounts of the most important cause, or causes, of the Great Depression of the 1930s. Was it liquidity preference and discrepancies between planned savings and planned investment, as John Maynard Keynes argued? Or was it bad decisions by those who were responsible for monetary policies at the crucial time? We can't replicate the Depression and change the monetary policies to see what the effects were. The best we can do is to assess the plausibility of competing explanations that seem to have some basis in theory. But we have no method or algorithm to adjudicate these competing explorations in any definitive way.

Or, to get closer to home in a temporal sense, consider the attempts to explain the dramatic plunge of the American economy into the "Great Recession" of 2008–9. The sequence of events, although not foreseen by most economists and policy makers, is pretty clear. A housing market that had been booming started to come under downward pressure. Homes lost value. Mortgage payment failures multiplied, and mortgage-backed securities then became problematic. The financial markets began to freeze up. And large financial firms that were highly exposed to the problematic securities fell into crisis. Some of these firms were forced to sell themselves to stronger competitors.

Lehman Brothers, a prominent global financial services firm founded in 1850 and the fourth-largest investment bank in the United States, was forced to declare bankruptcy. AIG, a huge insurance company that was left holding the bag of the collapsing mortgage-based securities, was saved from bankruptcy only by an $85 billion bailout package provided by the Federal Reserve because it was considered "too big to fail." Congress was compelled to authorize $700 billion for a bailout fund to loan to other troubled financial firms. The stock market cratered: by March 2009 it had lost over half of its value. And these huge financial pressures pushed the US economy into a damaging recession that took years to recover from.

The crucial political economy questions then, are: Why did this happen? What were the economic causes or policy failures that caused these very damaging events? And what could be done to prevent or mitigate similarly destructive events in the future? As one might reasonably expect, a major economic event in a large and complex corporate economy is almost inevitably the result of many causal variables. That was certainly true of the Great Recession of 2008–9. Among the logically relevant contributing factors that caused this dramatic economic downturn were the bursting of the bubble of an overpriced housing market; the encouragement and acceptance of falsified data on mortgage applications by mortgage originating firms; incentives offered by federal laws and housing agencies such as Fannie Mae and Freddie Mac to encourage mortgage lending to lower-income families; the practice of slicing and dicing mortgage loans and packaging them into "collateral debt obligations" that were then sold to investors; lax oversight of the financial industry by the US Securities and Exchange Commission; faulty calculations of risk by quantitative analysts; conflicts of interest within the most prominent bond-rating accounting firms; and several other possible contributing factors.

What we would like to do, of course, is to establish the precise casual role of all these variables in creating the recession. That would give us the kind of explanatory certainty we would like to have, not only for theoretical purposes, but also to help us prevent the occurrence of similar unfortunate events down the road. But the only sure way to achieve that kind of explanatory certitude empirically would be to perform tests that could isolate the relative effect of each of the potentially relevant causal variables. And doing that is, quite obviously, not a possibility.

In the absence of certitude about the causes of the Great Recession—and of similar important economic events—must we admit defeat in our quest for explanations in the service of prudent future policy? No. But in cases such as these the best we can do is to provide our partially conjectural judgments. The conjectures involved must not be groundless. They have to be situated within theoretical models that have logical plausibility, and they must also be consistent with observable events. That said, there often remain more than one line of explanation and counsel based upon it that satisfy these criteria. Such is the origin of what we think of as the contending "schools" of macroeconomics more generally. And these theories and explanations are to some extent shaped by our preconceptions, by our ideological inclinations, and possibly by our values and interests.

In the context of our quest for reliable casual explanation of the Great Recession, then, Richard Posner—who wrote perhaps the best contemporary book about this event—sums up our situation quite ably. "When competing hypotheses cannot be subjected to rigorous empirical testing," he writes, "the choice between them will be heavily influenced by preconceptions about depressions, and the preconceptions are likely to be influenced by ideology. . . . Left-leaning economists tend to see depressions as evidence of the failure of unregulated capitalism, and right-leaning ones to blame depressions on misguided government policies, without which, they believe, there would be at worst mild recessions."[1]

So, stepping back from particular cases like these, what does all this mean for attempts to answer one of the central questions examined in this book—whether an entirely unencumbered and unregulated capitalist marketplace is the most reliable way to maximize economic prosperity. It means that it is impossible for us to provide a slam-dunk answer to that question. A dispositive answer to questions of this sort about causes and effects would require us to perform head-to-head comparisons of the results of a completely free-market society with every other possible set of economic policies and arrangements. And that is obviously not possible for us to do. For one thing, there has never been an advanced industrial economy that had no regulations or other interventions on the past of government. The result is that we have on the one side no extant test case. And on the other side, it would be quite impossible for us to construct societies with every plausible set of alternative economic institutions to use for comparative purposes.

Where then does this recognition of the unattainability of a definitive empirical answer to our empirical question leave us? Must we simply throw up our hands in surrender, say that anything goes—that any claim about the relationship between the free market and prosperity is as good as any other? No, not at all. Some claims about this empirical relationship are to any knowledgeable observer clearly more credible than others. What it does mean, however, is (1) that anyone who claims to have a certain and demonstrably true answer to our central question about the relationship between laissez-faire policies and maximum prosperity is talking through his or her hat, and (2) that the best we can do is to offer careful and informed judgments that are somewhat conjectural.[2]

I shall try to offer some of my own considered judgments about the relationship between markets and prosperity in the following chapter. But for the moment we are looking at the reasons that none of the three debates about the merits and limitations of free markets canvassed in this book can be answered in some incontestable way. So let us turn now to see why that is true of arguments about social justice.

Social Justice and Moral Tragedy

Debates about the policies most conducive to economic prosperity are not definitively resolvable debates because of our epistemic frailty—the limits of our casual and predictive understanding. Debates about whether free markets produce fair and just distributive outcomes are also not definitively resolvable. But here the cause of uncertainty is not epistemic. Instead, it is the impossibility of finding morally unobjectionable ways to deal with certain inescapable tragedies in the human condition.

The closing words of the Pledge of Allegiance to the American flag are "with liberty and justice for all." That phrase embodies a noble aspiration: not justice only for the strong, not justice only for the politically well connected, and not allocation of the good things in life to such favored groups at the expense of the weaker and less favored members of society. We embody that commitment in the iconography of Lady Justice, with her blindfold and evenly weighted scales. To some extent, this is an aspiration we can achieve. We can, for example, accord everyone a fair hearing in court. We can provide equal protection of the laws. We can establish—and to some degree enforce—prohibitions of discrimination on the basis of race, gender, or creed with respect to voting, public accommodations, and the like. Upon further examination, however, certain irrevocable facts of the human condition make it quite impossible for even the most well-intentioned society to allocate the resources at its disposal in an unequivocally fair and just way.

Before elaborating on why it isn't possible for any society to achieve perfect justice, let us back up a step to ask: What are the standards for perfect justice? What would it take for us to say that a particular distribution of goods—or some particular set of criteria for distribution—was fully and truly just? We would likely and properly say that such distributions or distributive arrangements would have to be fair both absolutely and relatively. Absolute fairness would mean that people received in proportion to some reasonable measure of what they deserved. Relative fairness would require that there were no arbitrary inequities involved. Recall here Edmond Cahn's admonition, cited in an earlier chapter, that it is precisely violation of our "notion of desert" and revulsion "against whatever is unequal by caprice" that arouses our sense of injustice. Cahn goes on to say, then, that what "justice" means in practice is "the active process of remedying or preventing" outcomes or arrangements that we see as violating what people deserve or as creating capricious inequalities.[3]

Our central question here therefore becomes: Is it possible for a political society to prevent or remedy distributions that are either undeserved or capriciously unequal? If so, how can a society achieve such a perfectly just outcome? Is it sufficient for a society to afford its citizens the "equal protection of the laws" and to accept and defend economic assets that its citizens acquire through their free and willing exchange in the marketplace? If not, what else can and must it do to achieve social justice—that is, to produce distributive outcomes that both give people what they deserve and also are not influenced by capricious inequities?

The short and sobering answer to these questions is that it is simply impossible for any political society to achieve such perfectly just outcomes. If social justice is taken to mean the attainment of fully and unqualifiedly fair distributive outcomes, then we need to recognize that this is a noble aspiration beyond the capability of any human society to achieve. To say this is not to say that social justice is a "mirage," for we can say in the abstract what it would consist in. It is instead to appreciate that social justice may be a meaningful concept but that it is an unattainable goal in the real world we live in. The reason it is unattainable is that, as President Kennedy—and presumably many others—once said, "Life is unfair." Prior to any action—or even the creation—of an organized society, people enjoy great benefits and suffer great injuries they did nothing to deserve. Moreover, although political societies may be able to mitigate or compensate for arbitrary inequities, many of these inequities lie beyond anyone's power to ameliorate. And when efforts of mitigation and/or compensation are undertaken, these may require the imposition of costs and burdens upon others that they did nothing to deserve.

These unfortunate facts of life place limits upon what any society can achieve in the way of social justice—of producing outcomes that are both absolutely and relatively fair for all its members. We can certainly demand of our governing institutions that they do nothing to create injustices by treating their citizens in inequitable or arbitrary ways. Things get a whole lot messier, however, when we as members of an organized political society consider how we should deal with the morally arbitrary inequities produced either by natural causes, or by the free and morally unproblematic actions of families and voluntary social affiliations, or by the actions of people long dead.

Consider first the problem of the gross inequalities in people's natural endowments. Some of us are given, by no human choice or action, a robust constitution and great good health, while others have to deal with serious and debilitating health issues from birth. Some of us are endowed with exceptional talents and abilities of various sorts, while others lack that good fortune: some are musical and graceful while their fellows are tone-deaf and clumsy; some have great cognitive gifts while others are slow to learn; some have a noble countenance while most are plain or unattractive; some are sunny and charming while others are anxious and timid by nature. And so on. Moreover, those better endowed by nature can draw upon these desirable traits to do well in the marketplace or in the public forum—to acquire wealth and power and fame and friends. So how should a society that aspires to be fair and just deal with all this natural injustice? Do those of us well endowed by nature with fungible assets owe some form of recompense to those of us whom nature cheated? Why would it be fair to force that burden or deprivation upon them when they bear no responsibility whatever for the randomly inequitable rolls of our genetic dice? And what would be the measure and extent of that obligation?

There are, to put it mildly, no easy answers to these questions. Instead, we can imagine—and can see in the moral disputations found in any society—a number of quite reasonable arguments here that are sharply at odds with each other. Those less well endowed with natural assets that provide the wherewithal to attain fame and fortune—and their champions who sympathize with their plight—have a quite reasonable argument to make on their behalf. They can reasonably say: "Those among us with less in the way of natural assets are clearly disadvantaged in their quest for many of the good things of life. And that was through no fault of their own. They did nothing to deserve their disadvantage. They simply lost out in nature's capriciously unfair lottery that governs the allocation of natural assets and abilities. This unfortunate fact of life places a profound injustice at the very foundation of any society's social and economic relations, its hierarchies, and its inequalities. It is a form of natural unfairness for which—at least at the outset—no one is causally responsible and hence blamable. However, if a society simply shrugs at this profoundly unfair random and capricious inequality among its citizens, and does nothing to compensate for it, the society in effect becomes complicit in this morally indefensible state of affairs. Indeed, the dynamics of the society's allocation of wealth, power, and the other good things of life that money can buy will surely compound the unfairness. Reasonable people may disagree with the claim that justice requires the closest approximation of equality consistent with the incentives needed to create economic prosperity and foster the general interest. But all reasonable and morally sensitive members of a society that aspires to fairness and justice must support some kind of affirmative measures to diminish the social consequences of the deep and capricious inequities produced by the genetic lottery."

In response to this kind of argument, however, Mr. and Ms. Well Endowed by Nature might protest such claims that they are morally obligated—and should be legally required—to sacrifice some of the good things they have acquired in the economic marketplace as a dictate of justice. They might reasonably say: "It is not within my power, or within anyone else's power for that matter, to alter someone else's genetic composition to make them smarter, healthier, handsomer, or more industrious. So what would you have me do? It seems that you would require me to hand over to those less well endowed by nature some of the alienable assets that my genetic endowment might have helped me acquire. But why is it fair and proper to take from me by force of law assets I have earned by my labor in order to give those goods to others who did nothing to earn them—simply because they are not as attractive, or charming, or intelligent, or energetic as I am?"

Mr. and Ms. Well Endowed by Nature might even up the ante and argue that if any compensatory transfers were to be required these should go in the other direction. "Actually," they might say, "the genetically less well endowed should in all fairness compensate me and others who are similarly well endowed by nature. That is because the ordinary run of humanity enjoy significant collateral benefits from the work and achievements of more talented and intelligent fellow members of society such as we. With all due respect to those of lesser intelligence and ambition, it was not people of their stature, but instead some of those of us better endowed by nature, who were responsible for discoveries and inventions that have benefited all of us, including autos, airplanes, antibiotics, vaccines, minimally invasive surgery, television, the internet, organized legal systems and governing institutions, fertilizers and pesticides, and on and on."[4]

So when it comes to the question of the fair and just way for an organized society to deal with the great disparity of natural endowments among its members, it turns out that there are respectable arguments on behalf of quite different answers. Those on one side are entirely justified in their insistence that disparities in the gifts of nature are clear instances of the capricious inequities that moral philosophers cite as a paradigmatic example of things that should arouse our sense of injustice. These underserved disparities are obviously unfair. And their consequences can be profound. Surely people committed to fair and just social arrangements are under an obligation to do something to minimize the effects of this unfairness, even if they cannot for obvious reasons eliminate them. But the only way to take measures to reduce these disparities is to inflict costs or sacrifices on people who were in no way responsible for these unfortunate disparities and who have done nothing wrong. And to do that violates strong moral intuitions that stand at the heart of almost all systems of both civil and criminal justice. For people to be liable to penalties under civil law, for example, they must be credibly deemed to have done something wrong. That's what "tort" law is all about—indeed, that is what *tort* means. For the law to require some form of payment to extract "damages" from someone because of some injury suffered by another party, the court must establish that the person or persons being forced to pay were responsible for the injury. If the result of a surgery you undergo is not the one you had reason to hope for, you cannot receive a judgment for recompense from your surgeon for that reason alone. You have to demonstrate that the surgeon was negligent in some way. And the law of torts has consistently held that no one can be subject to legal penalty for their failure to provide assistance to someone in trouble unless it was some action of their own that created the trouble.[5] Similarly, it is a requirement of imposing criminal penalties on anyone that they must be shown to have had "mens rea"— that is, to have had criminal intent.[6]

In short, the moral intuitions that lie at the heart of both civil and criminal law provide clear and reasonable grounds for those well endowed by nature to reject the claim that they should be forced in the name of justice and fairness to hand over some form of compensation to others less well endowed than they. They can quite credibly, if rather callously, reject demands from the less endowed by saying:

Sorry, old chap, for your admittedly undeserved paucity of natural assets. Sorry you are a homely and clumsy dim bulb of a human being. But, you know, that's just the way the cookie crumbled. I did not create the reality that people are unequally endowed. Nor was I responsible in any way for the specific distributions that came from nature or the hand of God. Moreover, the economic resources you are demanding from me did not appear like manna from heaven: I had to take the effort—perhaps a considerable effort—to develop my talents and put them to work in a productive way. So I will perhaps help you out a bit out of the goodness of my heart. But please don't try to tell me that I'm morally obligated to do that. Instead, I am perfectly entitled to say that having to do so is actually unfair to me—because it is a burden I did nothing to deserve—to be forcibly required to hand over resources that I received in return from my labor, from gifts of nature, or from the beneficence of others—none of which violated any rightful claims of others.

These challenges visited upon political societies by the randomly discriminatory vagaries of nature are compounded by two other sources of injustice: the important role of families in human life, and the burdens of history. Let's look briefly at each of these.

First, the role of families. None of us get to choose our parents. And none of us do anything to deserve the parents we get. But nothing—perhaps not even our natural abilities—determines our prospects in life more than the quality of the adults who provide for us, supervise us, and guide us while we are growing up. Most of us are fortunate enough to live in a home with adults who care for our well-being and are reasonably competent. Some of us have the extravagant good fortune to grow to adulthood with the help of people who have the resources and determination to provide us with every possible advantage on behalf of our future success in life. And some of us have the very bad fortune to get stuck under the charge of incompetent, negligent, or abusive adults who leave us psychologically damaged and devoid of the capacities needed to perform well as adults.

What then does justice require of a society in the face of such grossly inequitable circumstances enjoyed—or suffered—by its children? That's very hard to say. Obviously, those children who suffer from the neglect or abuse of the adults in their life have been treated very unfairly. They need—and could be said to deserve—some form of recompense for their misfortune. But how is that to be done? And how can it be accomplished in a manner fair to all parties? Full restitution for disadvantaged children is close to an impossibility. Abused children can be placed in foster homes or in an orphanage. But, absent enormous good fortune, these options cannot fully substitute for a loving home with one's parents. Moreover, the damage from the circumstances that led to removal of the children from their situations cannot always be completely undone. And while visits from assiduous social workers can help children who live with incompetent or indifferent parenting, such measures are never an adequate substitute for living with talented and dedicated parents.

Some social reformers have in the past proposed the creation of more far-reaching institutional ways of equalizing the prospects of children, despite the disparities in their parents' competence and dedication. The educational reforms championed in the mid-1800s by the egalitarian social reformer Frances Wright provide one example of such schemes. Her proposal was to establish a universal system of public boarding schools that children would attend from the age of three years onward. Her hope was not only to achieve greater social equality but also to create a community devoted more to the public good than to promoting individual interests. But schemes of this sort, including hers, have never received a warm reception from the public. Most people value the close bonds of family affiliation too much. And most, especially in a morally pluralist society, want to socialize their children within the context of their own values and beliefs rather than outsourcing these tasks to public functionaries.

Any decent society will, I believe, realize that it has a responsibility to provide some form of assistance to the children of negligent or incompetent parents. Partly, such assistance is for practical reasons: neglected or abused or ill-provided-for children will likely not enter adulthood prepared to fulfill the tasks incumbent upon productive citizens. But taking such action involves imperatives of justice as well: no child deserves bad parents, and the widely variant fate of children in this respect is a paradigmatic case of the capricious inequality that arouses our sense of injustice. So considerations of distributive justice with respect to a society's children clearly beg for remedial measures requiring social and economic resources. But the measures necessary to satisfy this call of justice create in turn an element of injustice with regard to the adults from whom the necessary resources must be extracted. Why should you, who work diligently to provide and sacrifice for your own children—thereby fulfilling your natural obligations to them as well as your civic obligations to the larger society—be required to work and sacrifice even more in order to provide for my children, whom I neglect, abuse, or fail to care for? That's not fair, either—even if it seems a morally and practically necessary thing to do.[7]

A third and last set of cases we should note under the heading of why perfect justice is beyond the capabilities of even the best-intentioned political society are those created by historical injustices. With few exceptions, political societies are not writing on a clean slate. They are not starting from scratch. Instead, they are working within the context of social arrangements and conditions bequeathed to them by others who are now dead and gone. These arrangements and conditions may well represent a valuable legacy. Those of us who live today in the United States, for example, have to be grateful for the rule of law, the democratic institutions, the civil liberties, and the economic resources that the efforts of our forebears have provided for us. On the other hand, many societies—including our own—also find themselves having to deal with arrangements and conditions marked and disfigured by historical injustices. And when a society dutifully attempts to overcome that dubious legacy and deal fairly with its lingering effects, it will once again find perfect justice to be systematically elusive. Injuries and disadvantages inherited from the past cannot be easily repaired. And the efforts to do so may unavoidably result in visiting new forms of unfairness upon people who bore no responsibility whatever for the previous injustice—and who also perhaps cannot credibly be said to have been a beneficiary of the misdeeds.

The efforts in this country to confront and make appropriate amends for the injuries, exclusions, and economic exploitation visited upon African Americans by legalized slavery and Jim Crow discrimination provide an instructive example of the dilemmas encountered in such cases. The Emancipation Proclamation and the passage of the Thirteenth, Fourteenth, and Fifteenth Amendments to the Constitution ended legalized slavery long ago. And the landmark civil rights legislation enacted in the mid-twentieth century dismantled Jim Crow practices in the public realm. So far, so good. But enacting legislation to prevent racial discrimination going forward did not indemnify those who suffered its effects over the years. Nor does it make good the damage or disadvantage that some people currently suffer partly as a consequence of past injustices. If your parents and grandparents and their families were denied economic and educational opportunities because of unjustly discriminatory social practices and institutions, your own starting point in life is quite likely to have been unjustly compromised as well.

Therefore, it seems reasonable to argue that justice requires something more to be done to counteract the current effects of past injustices. How that can be done successfully and without creating other forms of injustice, however, turns out once again to be a very difficult task at best. The measures most commonly advocated in the service of this restitution are reparations and affirmative action. Reparations would consist of some kind of economic redistribution to those disadvantaged by the effects of past discrimination. Affirmative action consists in according to presumed victims of past injustice some degree of preference when it comes to competition for jobs or admission to selective institutions. In the abstract, such policies seem to be defensible—perhaps even mandatory—as a morally appropriate means of restitution for the legacy of past injustice. When such policies are put into practice, however, new moral conundrums rear their head; and those particular people who are required to put up money or to sacrifice an opportunity they otherwise would have had may very well have legitimate grounds to argue that they have themselves been treated unfairly.

To illustrate the complexities and dilemmas here, consider different versions of a simple scenario. Let us suppose that it is proven that your grandfather embezzled thousands of dollars from my grandfather and got away with his crime. Would justice require that you give me that amount of money? On the one hand, that seems only fair: your family cheated mine. Shouldn't you have to make that moral indebtedness good? On the other hand, you did nothing wrong. Why, then, would it be fair for you to suffer such a loss? Would what your grandfather did with the embezzled funds make a difference in your answer? Suppose, for example, that your grandfather used the funds he stole to buy a property that he passed on to one of your parents, who in return passed it on to you. Or, alternatively, suppose that your grandfather instead blew all the money in riotous living or gambled it away in Las Vegas. Would the difference between these divergent scenarios require us to give different answers to the question about what you owed me? If so, what happens when, in the service of reparations, a society has to establish policies that would apply to a vast set of cases that encompassed both of these alternative scenarios? What if most of those required to pay reparations had no larcenous grandparents at all? And suppose that many of the reparation recipients in a society-wide program of this sort were better off than many of those taxed to provide them. Taking it as a given that black Americans were systematically subordinated and exploited economically by many white Americans for generations, should a white American working at a minimum-wage job have to write a check to a wealthy African American hedge fund manager? Also, would it make any difference if either of these were a recent immigrant?

Similarly vexing questions pop up in the context of attempts to employ affirmative action when it comes to jobs and school admissions. (Before proceeding any further, however, I should say up front that to my mind the strongest arguments on behalf of what goes under the heading of affirmative action are often not justice based. They are instead practical arguments grounded in the mission of the institutions in question. College admissions are not simply a prize awarded for past academic performance or high scores on aptitude tests. Instead, one important purpose of college admission decisions is the creation of a student body best constituted to function as a community of learning. Among other things, that requires the presence within that community of students and faculty of people from a variety of backgrounds that reflect and represent at least to some extent the diversity that the university's graduates will encounter upon graduation. It is also similarly essentially mandatory for practical reasons for a police department to include officers who are not wholly unrepresentative of the communities they serve. Otherwise, the police force in question could understandably come to be seen by some as an army of occupation, thereby greatly complicating and impairing its functioning. Armies similarly need an officer corps that bears some degree of ethnic resemblance to the enlisted troops. Private firms need a sales force that can connect with their customer base. Hospitals need their patients to see their ethnic communities represented among the doctors and nurses treating them. And so on. These important practical considerations, which are not justice related, may require some element of "affirmative action" in the staffing decisions of all these institutions.)

To the extent that affirmative action policies are motivated by considerations of justice, however, the same kind of awkward moral dilemmas presented by any possible monetary reparation policy appear in this context also. The logic behind giving some degree of preference to those of specific ethnicities as an imperative of justice presupposes that students from the groups to be favored have been disadvantaged in their preparation. The underlying casual sequence is presumed to run: ethnic-based discrimination leads to subpar elementary and secondary preparation, which in turn results in weaker academic credentials and lower scores on standardized tests. The problem from the standpoint of justice is that the links in this alleged causal chain are not all that reliable. The result is that the applicants most benefited by race- or ethnicity-based affirmative action tend disproportionately to be students or job applicants from the group or groups favored by the policy who come from relatively well-off families and better schools. Perhaps this outcome serves the educational purposes of the institution and perhaps also works in the service of building a society with greater diversity among its professional classes. But as an instrument of justice, affirmative action in hiring or in college admissions is a very imperfect tool. And applicants who are passed over as a consequence of such policies will understandably experience the requisite double standards as positively unfair to them regardless of the good intentions behind them.

We can summarize the central lesson of our look at the conundrums encountered in the quest for a just society in the following manner: the unavoidable hard truth we have to face up to is that it is simply not possible for any society to achieve social justice in any definitive sense. At least, it is not possible to achieve that feat in the context of the imperfect world we live in. The profound inequities that all societies inherit from nature, from the role of families, and from history have the unhappy result of trapping them in a kind of moral impossibility theorem: the unfairness so inherited can be reallocated to some extent, but it cannot be fully expunged. It can only be passed around. Because we never can begin with a clean slate, even the most well-intentioned society finds itself in a real-world version of a card game many of us played while growing up. In that game—a version of the game of Spades—the player holding the queen of spades at game's end lost big time. So everyone kept passing that card around like a hot potato; but someone had to lose, because there was no way to get rid of it entirely. Similarly, in the very imperfect world we live in, if being treated fairly means not to suffer from any morally capricious inequity, and also not to have costs or penalties imposed upon you for something you did not do, someone has to lose. We might conceivably be able to establish what perfect social justice would look like—especially if we lived in a world unafflicted by inequities beyond human control. But establishing a definitive and unobjectionable standard of perfect justice for the real world we have to live in—much less actually being able to achieve it—is beyond our grasp. We can only choose among demonstrably imperfect options.

Achieving the Good Society and the Problem of Moral Pluralism

Just as our attempts to fashion a truly just society are afflicted by a form of moral tragedy visited upon us by an imperfect world, so our attempts to achieve the ideally good society—a society in which all important social goods are attained—are afflicted by a different kind of moral tragedy. The quest to build a perfectly just society is frustrated by the natural injustices inherent in the human condition. The quest to build the good society—in a similar but also contrasting fashion—finds itself faced by dilemmas arising from what the moral philosopher Isaiah Berlin has called "moral pluralism."

I invoke the term *moral pluralism* here with some trepidation, for people have used it to refer to somewhat different things. So let me be clear about what it meant to Berlin and what it will mean here. *Moral pluralism* will here mean three things about human goods. First, there is not just one human good; instead there are several—even many—things that human beings find conductive to their flourishing and satisfaction. Second, all of these particular goods turn out not to be fully reconcilable with each other: neither individuals nor societies can attain all of these goods entirely or simultaneously. Third, there is no neutral or definitive algorithm that can adjudicate the relative value of or the proper balance among these multiple goods.

First, the plurality of human goods. Quick reflection will show that having a good life requires a number of particular goods. A standard form of wishing someone well wishes for them that they be healthy, wealthy, and wise. Are those three desirable things sufficient? Probably not. Suppose you had no friends, no leisure, no privacy, no music or beauty, no recreation? It's very doubtful that your health, wealth, and wisdom would then suffice to make you happy. And there may be other goods that some of us consider essential to having a good life.

The same is true when it comes to the attributes required for a good society—the features you would think essential for a society you would truly and fully be happy to live in. No single social good would by itself suffice, however crucial it might be. Even if you believe with John Rawls that "justice is the first virtue of social institutions," you likely would not find that virtue sufficient to guarantee your willingness to live in a society if all you knew about it was that it was just. As another democratic theorist once wrote: "Would I want to live where democratic justice has been legitimately achieved? I have no idea!"[8] In similar fashion, I feel sure that a devout libertarian would upon careful reflection not be willing to commit in advance to living in a society if all he or she knew about it was that it had a minimal state. It might turn out to be a place that resembled what Thomas Hobbes famously termed a "war of all against all." Or a passionate egalitarian would be foolish to pledge to live in a society if all he or she knew about it was that the inhabitants were completely equal. It might turn out to be a place that felt like a prison.

The important point here is this: any society we would happily choose to live in would have to encompass a number of social goods. Which of the following virtues of a good society, for example, would you be entirely willing to live without: personal safety and security, a healthy environment, the rule of law, freedom of religion, the right to own property, civic equality, the right of the citizens to choose those who govern, a spirit of community, economic prosperity, access to education, a right to privacy, or the opportunity for personal growth and development of your abilities? If you are like me, you would not really be content to sacrifice any of these things. Which is to say that you have to concede the truth of the first tenet of moral pluralism: there are a significant number of social goods that have great value.

The second tenet of moral pluralism is that these multiple goods are not entirely reconcilable. We cannot really have it all—either in our personal lives or in our social arrangements. Sometimes the reason we cannot have everything we want to acquire or to achieve is simply that we lack the resources of time, energy, and money to get it all done. At other times, the problem is more structural and intrinsic: the goods exist in some tension with each other. To get something we want, we may have to sacrifice some of another good that we also want. We have to make choices and trade-offs, however much it may pain us.

In our personal lives we want to be healthy, and wealthy, and wise—and also perhaps to have children, and to be good parents, and to enjoy leisure and music and time with our friends, and travel and adventure and other good times and things I won't try to enumerate. But as logic would suggest—and our hard experience amply confirms—we don't have the ability to have or accomplish all these good things to the extent we would like. We have to choose among them to some degree, possibly sacrificing some altogether and making trade-offs among the others. And sometimes the goods or goals actually war with each other. We want our children to become independent and adventurous and strong and resilient. For that to happen, we have to give them freedom and let them fail from time to time. But we then quite reasonably worry that by doing that we might expose them to danger and great damage. We have to choose, and balance, and keep our fingers crossed, and then worry about whether we made the right trade-offs. The realities of the world and the dynamics of causes and effects put us in a bind we cannot escape; we just have to suck it up and deal with it.

The same is true of our social institutions, arrangements, and allocation of resources. Public budgets, just like personal budgets, are finite. And they acquire their resources by depriving us of funds we would otherwise use for our own wants and needs—that is, from the imposition of taxes. In the abstract, all of us would presumably be happy to live in a society where we all had access to all the health care and assistance we might need or want, where we all would receive all the education we might need or want, where the environment was pristine and protected, where fast and pleasant transportation was universally available, where everyone was protected from catastrophic weather events, where we were perfectly secure from foreign attacks, where we all had access to either private or public space to use in whatever ways brought us pleasure, and on and on. But even the wealthiest of today's societies don't have the resources to accomplish all these good things to the level we would like.

And social goods, just like personal goods, sometimes are in tension with each other. We like both security and freedom, but we have to sacrifice some of one of those to have the other. I would love to drive faster than the speed limit at times. But if all of us could drive as fast as we wanted, we would pay the price in carnage on the highways. We would like our phone conversations to be entirely private and protected. But we also want our security agencies to be able to discover and prevent acts of terrorism. We want our country to be more prosperous; but we want to protect our environment, and we cast envious eyes on other countries where month-long summer vacations from work are standard. We prize privacy and independence, but we value strong communities where "everyone knows your name" and stands ready to offer help when we need it. These are the kinds of tensions and conflicts among the various social goods people value that have led to a recurrent phrase among democratic theorists in recent years: "nothing without loss."

The final core claim that forms a part of moral pluralism is that there is no incontestable way to adjudicate or to ascertain the right or best balance among these multiple and contending goods. There is no common measure that can establish in some definitive way how much security is equivalent to how much freedom, or where exactly to set the balance between the free exercise of religion and the prohibition of religious establishment, and so on. Part of the problem is that all the various social goods are not entirely compatible with each other. And part of the problem is that, as economists would put it, people have divergent "preference schedules." We may all be human beings. But we have different belief systems, different tastes, and different situations—all of which can incline us to make different trade-offs among competing goods.

One last and important point to make under this heading is this: these varying preference schedules that incline us toward divergent ways of prioritizing social goods also incline us toward embracing one or another of the different conceptions of the ideal democratic society that we canvassed in the previous chapter. We saw there that the two major democratic traditions that have provided inspiration to this country from the founding era until today are the civic republican and the liberal ones. And these traditions clearly prioritize some of the most important social goods differently. The civic republican tradition places great value upon civic equality and social solidarity, and it tends to prioritize the public realm above the private. Liberalism, in contrast, accords preeminent value to personal freedoms, and it values private enterprise above the public realm. So the way that we and our fellow citizens prioritize the several constitutive goods of liberal democracy will tend to push us toward favoring one of these democratic orientations over the other. As we champion our own favored version of democratic ideals, however, as we are entitled to do, we all need to recognize and concede that we cannot claim to possess some definitive grounds for subordinating alternative versions of morally legitimate democratic ideas to our own. We have to make some compromises among the various social goods we value. And we have to make some compromises with our fellow citizens who prioritize the multiple social goods differently than we do.

CHAPTER FIVE

Conclusion

Toward Reasonable Judgments

The burden of the previous chapter was to explain why there are no slam-dunk arguments when it comes to determining the best way to maximize a country's prosperity, the morally correct way to allocate a society's resources, or what the ideal democratic society looks like. We cannot say for certain exactly what policies and arrangements maximize prosperity because of the frailty of our knowledge when it comes to determining all the cause-and-effect relationships that determine economic outcomes in today's complex advanced economies. We cannot establish with certitude the most just distribution of social resources because of our entrapment in a world where perfect fairness is an impossibility. And we cannot say with certainty that one particular hierarchy of social goods constitutes the ideally best form of society, because not all good things are fully reconcilable with each other and because there is no way to establish the ideal balance among them.

So where does this acknowledgment of the moral tragedies and scientific limitations that thwart our quest for the right and best way to achieve prosperity, justice, and the good society leave us? Must we simply throw in the towel and say that anything goes, that all answers are as good as any others, or that it all is just a matter of personal taste? That we are all relieved of any obligation to provide arguments for our political judgments, and that we are free to support whatever policies and arrangements we might prefer for our own interests?

The answer is no. Acknowledging the moral and epistemic constraints that make perfect answers to questions about prosperity, justice, and the good society unattainable need not be a counsel of despair or license for unconstrained self-serving. Instead, it is a reminder that we need to have a measure of humility when we make judgments about these important policies and goals that determine how we are to live together. With full recognition of our inability to make incontestable arguments about these important matters, we nonetheless have as democratic citizens a responsibility to arrive at our considered judgments and to be willing to explain them to our fellow citizens in the public forum.

We must do that because these are not purely theoretical questions. They are practical questions of great moment, because our collective judgments about prosperity, justice, and the good society will be the basis for shaping the institutions, social arrangements, and policies we all will have to live with. And we can produce considered judgments on these determinative issues because, even though there are no perfect answers, some answers are more reasonable than others. The answers we give to the central questions regarding the best way for us to achieve a prosperous, just, and good democratic society are a function of two things: our ascertainment of the relevant facts, and our recognition of and respect for the relevant moral considerations. Insisting upon these requirements will not provide us one single and perfect answer, but it will narrow the field significantly.

The principal purpose of this book has been to provide a "guide for the perplexed" by identifying and elucidating the major lines of argument on the different sides of the question about the proper relationship between free markets and a democratic society committed to fairness and human flourishing. Having done that, however, I would be remiss if I did not provide at least a brief account of my own considered judgments about the issues we have examined here. So, in this closing chapter of the book, let me offer some of my own views regarding the central topics we have covered. My hope, of course, is that many of you will find my assessments to be broadly convincing. And for those readers who are not so persuaded, my hope is that you will rise to the challenge of having to provide and defend your own views where you believe I have gone wrong.

My general conviction is that reliance upon robust free markets as the principal mechanism for the allocation of a society's economic efforts and resources is wise and proper. But I also believe, because of real-world complications of the market's functioning and because there are important democratic goods markets cannot provide, that governments need to regulate and supplement the distributive consequences of markets in a number of significant ways. So let's begin by taking a look at the important benefits that free markets provide to democratic societies. Then, after doing that, we will look at the reasons why healthy liberal democracies need to constrain and supplement market outcomes through collective actions.

How Capitalism Benefits Democratic Societies

A strong and robust free marketplace provides democratic societies with many important benefits. Some of these benefits are economic: free markets play a crucial and irreplaceable role in making democracies prosperous. Some of these benefits are political: free markets protect us against certain forms of political domination and authoritarianism. And some of these benefits are moral: free markets motivate and reward people who contribute to their society's welfare.

A good way to appreciate the social benefits of markets is to consider the difficulties manifest in societies that try to abandon them in favor of a command economy—that is, an economic system in which a society's productive efforts and resource allocations are determined and mandated by a governing authority. Karl Marx's core argument was that free-market capitalism was an effective way to turn an agrarian feudal society into an industrial liberal society but that it suffered from internal structural flaws (or "contradictions") that made it incapable of managing a successful advanced economy. In retrospect, however, the actual historical trajectory of the world's largest and most important officially Marxist countries, the Soviet Union and China, suggests that he got it backwards.

Over the first two or three decades following the terrible destruction of the Second World War, the Soviet Union proved that a highly authoritarian regime with a government-controlled command economy could successfully build the necessary infrastructure for an industrial society. By dragooning industrial armies, as it were, and extracting necessary capital from forced labor, the Soviet Union built huge dams, electrified almost the entire country, created agricultural communes, and built many factories. The collective farm system never worked well: the standing joke was that Soviet agriculture—according to the regime—had suffered decades of unusually bad weather. But rapid industrialization had in fact been achieved. In fact, during the sixties and seventies authorities in the United States looked on with real concern and trepidation as the economic growth rate of the Soviet Union continually exceeded our own. In the late seventies and eighties, however, the Soviet Union economy seemed to hit a wall; and by the late eighties and nineties its apparent inability to deal with the demands of running an advanced consumer economy contributed greatly to the dissolution of the Soviet Union regime.

Despite important differences between the two countries, the Chinese economy under Mao Tse-Tung followed a somewhat similar trajectory. Adopting the Soviet model of centrally controlled Five Year Plans, China built the rudiments of an industrial society. Their progress seemed to stall after a while, however; and Mao's regime decided to reclaim forward momentum by a combination of unsustainable changes and heroic effort. These reforms, embodied in the Great Leap Forward and the Cultural Revolution, proved to be disastrous. And Mao's successors have found it necessary to institute some significant market-based arrangements—including allowing private farming—to move their economy forward.

Neither Russia nor China could today be called democracies in our sense of that word—regimes governed by popular sovereignty and protective of extensive civil liberties. Russia has elections, but these are tightly constrained. It remains a significantly authoritarian regime with ties to and sustenance from an oligarchic kleptocracy. And China is also an authoritarian regime governed by a centrally controlled communist party. In both cases, however, these still ostensibly communist regimes have found themselves forced to allow and take advantage of "capitalist" market incentives and mechanisms to make their economies productive.

So, what are these features of a capitalist marketplace that seem to make it an essential component of a successful advanced industrial economy?

First, market economies create wealth by providing incentives that are necessary to induce people to engage in productive labor. There are basically four sources of work incentives. The first, and most onerous, is outright force. Labor extracted by force, whether slavery or some form of conscription, is something found in many societies ever since the beginning of recorded history. Slaves built the pyramids in Egypt. The ancient Greeks and Romans had slaves, usually people who had been taken in battle. The British Navy—the one that "ruled the seas" a few centuries ago—was manned by young men who were forcibly conscripted off the streets. African slaves performed much of the hard agricultural labor in North and South America and the Caribbean in the eighteenth and nineteenth centuries. And much of the agricultural labor in European countries was performed by people who were effectively permanently indentured to large landowners.

The second, and most benign, incentive for productive labor is the intrinsic pleasure some people are able to find in their work. Artists, musicians, skilled craftspeople, and mission-driven professionals may have the good fortune to be so motivated, for example. A third motivation for labor might be a sense of being a participant in and a contributor to some higher cause—whether that cause be a collective human endeavor or service to a divine purpose. Volunteering to serve as a combatant in what you believe to be a just war is one example. Serving one's religion as a priest or as a minister or as a nun would be another. And Soviet communism—inspired by the Marxist claim that a new form of altruistic human beings created by socialism would happily labor for the general good—tried to induce and benefit from that kind of public spirit as well.

All three of these sources of work incentives, however, have their serious difficulties or limitations. Slavery is, quite obviously, morally opprobrious. It is certain that no contemporary civilized society would countenance it as a morally acceptable arrangement. Indentured servitude is similarly morally problematic—at least if it is not a time-limited version of job training. And conscription is justifiable only in cases of necessity or emergency. Work for the pure pleasure and satisfaction in its craftsmanship is available only to a certain few. Most productive labor involves some element of drudgery—indeed, often a lot of it. And even the most dedicated people who enjoy their work usually would happily practice their craft for fewer hours in favor of having more leisure time.

The third motivation for incentivizing work, devotion to public service or to what is believed to be a higher cause, suffers from two significant weaknesses or vulnerabilities. In the first place, fostering the necessary level of devotion to some allegedly higher purpose is quite difficult to maintain. The Soviet Union was able to trade for a while on its efforts to cultivate and heap public praise and status upon its especially productive workers—those it called "Stakhanovites." But as the conviction that the socialist utopia was on its way gradually lost credibility among the populace, this form of motivation lost its power as well. The other central difficulty with trying to motivate work effort by selling it as a contribution to the general welfare of a larger collective is this: it is logically apparent, and will become empirically obvious as well, that any benefits from one person's labor in a collectivity of any significant size will have negligible effect on anyone's welfare. Suppose, for example, that you are a worker in a commune composed of one thousand persons. You ponder whether you should serve the general welfare of your commune by working overtime—by working ten hours a day instead of the requisite of eight hours. It dawns upon you that if you work this 25 percent more, it will increase the welfare of both you and every one of your coworkers by only .025 percent. (Assume for the sake of argument that the return to each member of the collective from the proceeds of their work is $50,000.00. In that case, your working two extra hours or 25 percent more every day will be worth exactly $12.50 annually to each member of the commune—about $1 per month.) So you realize that (1) your voluntarily working an extra two hours every day will be both onerous and possibly damaging to your health, and (2) no one will be better off in any discernible way. And therefore you will almost certainly—and quite reasonably—decide that you would be crazy to undertake the hundreds of hours of extra labor you were contemplating.

On the other hand, if the value of your extra work were to be returned entirely to you and your family, you would be financially better off by a full 25 percent. If we assume that half of your original income has gone to necessities—food, shelter, and clothing—then your two extra hours of labor would raise your discretionary income by 50 percent. And if 75 percent of your original income has been required for necessities, your discretionary income would go up a full 100 percent as a consequence of your extra work. And for that much improvement in your family's life and fortunes, putting in the extra couple of hours each day would likely look very good to you.

So that brings us to the fourth incentive for work: self-interest, or the welfare of oneself and one's family. And that is the motivation relied upon and put in force by the free marketplace. Every participant receives the value (or, more technically, the marginal value) of his or her labor, as assessed by the other actors in the marketplace. This incentive—the promotion of the welfare of oneself and one's family—is quite powerful, unlike the more attenuated desire to add incrementally to the general welfare. This incentive may not be morally elevated, but it does not depend upon an immoral arrangement such as slavery or other forms of servitude. And it is not dependent upon some intrinsic pleasure or personal satisfaction in one's labor—a luxury unavailable to many.

Second, the "invisible hand" of the marketplace, which itself works automatically and for free, produces an "optimal" distribution of the currently available economic resources of a society—ceteris paribus. Note here the two qualifications to this general claim. I put optimal in quotation marks because the market's allocation of wealth would satisfy the utilitarian goal of the greatest good for the greatest number only if everyone's purchasing power permitted him or her the same level of "happiness" as everyone else. And the qualification of "ceteris paribus"—all else being equal—embodies the counterfactual assumption that all the enabling conditions of the ideal marketplace are met. But if we assume that the existing distribution of purchasing power is morally acceptable and that the enabling conditions of properly functioning markets are reasonably well satisfied, then market outcomes will at least approximate the maximum aggregate satisfaction of the material needs and desires of the populace.

This represents no small achievement. And it is an achievement that—in the context of any advanced industrial society—is beyond the capacities of a command economy run from the top down by some centralized authority. That is because central managers have very limited ability to access the information necessary to make the right allocations: namely, they cannot identify and take into account the "preference schedules"—all the desires and assessments of their relative value—of all the members of their society. Markets, on the other hand, are driven by the immediate consequences of all these consumer preferences. And they must adjust accordingly. Indeed, private enterprises may need to do more than adjust to changing consumer desires: they need to anticipate them, as best they can. That is what market research is all about. The managers of the auto production industry in a command economy may well have little need and few incentives to ascertain and react to a shift in consumer preference for SUVs instead of sedans. But private enterprise automobile companies have every incentive to be very much on top of such changes—and to adjust their product lines accordingly. That's what consumer sovereignty is all about, and what it accomplishes.

A third important economic benefit of free markets is that they exert pressure on producers/sellers of goods to keep their prices low. Their desire, of course, would be to sell at a high price. The higher their profit margin, the better off they are. If the conditions of a properly functioning market for their product are met, however, sellers are compelled to price their products at a reasonable level. Among the conditions of a properly functioning marketplace, remember, are a significant number of buyers and sellers. So each seller has to contend with many other firms who are working hard to attract the same customers they want to have as their own. Given these competitive pressures, sellers have to do a number of things—all of which work to the advantage of the consumer. To keep their prices competitive, they have to produce their product efficiently. They have to develop ways to keep their costs as low as they can, and that means figuring out the most economical way to grow their wheat, or build their cars, or make their television sets, or whatever. They also have to strive to make their products high in quality. If their product performs better, lasts longer, is more attractive, and is easier to use than those of the competition, businesses will be successful. If not, they struggle and fail. And if we assume that some of their competitors also can produce high-quality products in an efficient manner, then none of them will be free to sell at prices that would yield exorbitant profits. In short, under "normal" conditions, the competitive dynamics of free markets should deliver exactly what consumers want to have: quality goods, efficiently produced and reasonably priced. And if the marketplace is of sufficient size, consumers are also likely to enjoy having the ability to choose among a variety of products—because producers can also succeed by finding and satisfying a certain "niche" in their marketplace. Think here of the astonishing array of food options that are presented to their customers by today's supermarket grocery stores, or the range of options available to those who need to buy an automobile.

A last very important economic benefit of a free-market system is that it provides both powerful incentives and also the availability of capital to motivate and finance the technological and entrepreneurial innovation that drives economic development. In command economies, where the state-owned industries are run by salaried managers, those managers have very little in the way of incentives that would motivate them to conceive and carry out significant changes in product design—much less to create entirely new products. Indeed, they would likely incur substantial risks in doing so. Free markets, on the other hand, can munificently reward those who figure out how to "build a better mousetrap," as the old adage has it. And they can award extraordinary wealth to those clever enough and driven enough to come up with pathbreaking new products that meet the needs or capture the fancy of millions of people. Think here of the vast fortunes quickly generated by technological innovators such as Bill Gates, Steve Jobs, Jeff Bezos, and Mark Zuckerberg. And whereas government technocrats placed in charge of state-funded "five-year plans" would have no easy way to acquire funding for risky new ventures that might or might not pan out, developed economies with free markets are filled with "venture capitalists"—people who have accumulated some wealth and are eager to invest their capital in promising new products or services that seem to have a real chance of generating large profits when they come to fruition—not to mention hedge funds and mutual funds eager to find places to invest the accumulated savings in their customers' retirement accounts.

Political Benefits of Free Markets

In addition to the specifically economic benefits of a free-market system, there are a number of social and political benefits it bestows upon the society that it inhabits.

The first of these benefits is the right and ability of those in the society to own and control economic resources. We tend to take this power for granted. But a moment's reflection should make it clear that having some ability to control a certain amount of economic resources is almost essential to having control over one's life—to being a self-governing adult. Imagine for a moment that the state—or some other person—had the power to dictate where you lived, what you ate, and all other aspects of your life that required resources. It would in those circumstances be almost impossible to experience yourself as a free and independent adult.

A market system also affords its participants the right and opportunity to enter contracts with other members of society regarding exchanges of goods and services for their mutual benefit. These exchanges are economically advantageous to both parties. But the ability to make such choices and enter into such transactions also represents an important aspect of the personal freedom and self-governance that characterize the lives of competent democratic citizens. In the aggregate, all of these free exchanges among individuals add up to "consumer sovereignty"—which arguably embodies one dimension of governance "of, by, and for the people." It is we the people who, through our individual free choices, decide what goods are going to be produced in our society.

A final and very important personal freedom that a free-market economy affords its participants is the power to choose one's own vocation. It's not like being drafted into the army, say, where someone else has the power to order you to go dig a latrine. People have the right and power to survey the economic landscape, see what types of economic vocation are available, ascertain the demands and rewards of the different possible options, and decide which of the available ways to make a living works best for them. Decisions about what job to take, what career to pursue, can be very difficult. Many of us get it wrong and have to back up and start over or switch occupations mid-career. But having the freedom to choose our occupation is one that people rightfully prize. As we noted in an earlier chapter, when the Labour Party in England soon after the end of World War II decided that it needed to establish a "control of engagements" policy that gave the government the authority to assign people to particular jobs, that infringement upon people's ability to choose their own occupation was so unpopular that the government was quickly forced to rescind it—and also to back off from some of the central planning policies that had led to its enactment.[1]

In addition to providing people with these several important personal freedoms, free markets play a large role in the creation and protection of a private sphere that constitutes an important area of a good society. In addition to the privacy rights granted by provisions in the constitutions of most liberal democracies—think here of our own Bill of Rights—the economic power held by individuals in a market economy almost automatically results in the creation of private spaces, where private groups and individuals have the ability to pursue their own ends without intrusions by the state or by other people. The most obvious and widespread example here is the widespread private ownership of one's own personal or family domicile. As the saying goes: people's homes are their castles. They are a private domain where people have—apart from prohibitions of certain abusive practices—sovereignty over their land, their arrangements, and their activities. This sphere of society also encompasses private economic enterprises that—again within certain limits to protect other people's rights or the public good—exercise sovereignty over their land, their facilities, and their operations. And then there are the many private groups and associations—from religious denominations to country clubs—that own and control their sanctuaries or golf courses in pursuit of their private purposes and activities.

Above and beyond the private purposes these organizations pursue and the individual freedom of those participating in the activities they conduct, the presence and functions of these private enterprises provide another more public and valuable function for a democratic society. Taken altogether, these private enterprises constitute an important component of the countervailing power arrangements that serve to keep one subset of democratic society from dominating the rest. We are accustomed to thinking about the institutionalization of countervailing political power in our society in terms of the separation of powers and its checks and balances in our constitutional system. But the fact is that a democratic supermajority is capable at times of overcoming these checks and balances to—in Madisonian terms—"tyrannize" over the rest of us. And the social discipline exerted by a dominant supermajority of the larger society can also be experienced as quite repressive by minority groups in the public domain. So in this context the presence of a robust private sphere that is facilitated and protected by the functioning of private enterprises can serve as an important buffer against an unhealthy overconcentration of social power in the state.

Another important political service of the reliance on free markets is that it helps political stability. It has that benign effect by preventing conflicts that would arise if all our economic allocative decisions were made by some political authority. Think of it this way. Suppose that some government body had to decide what kind of automobiles would be manufactured, and you really wanted a particular kind of vehicle. And suppose that you were denied that opportunity because the governing agency believed that this kind of car would be too expensive to build or that not enough people would buy it. You then would likely be hostile toward both the governing authority that made this decision and also your fellow citizens who had lobbied hard and successfully for building other kinds of vehicles.

We see the same kind of conflicts break out when it comes time to establish the budgets for all levels of government—at city councils, in statehouses, and in the finance committees of the US Senate and House of Representatives. There are, of course, very good reasons that any organized society or social groups have to decide collectively how to raise and appropriate funds for their common needs and purposes. But whenever these reasons are not important, both social peace and people's sense of agency are best served by leaving allocative decisions to individuals to make in the context of the impersonal constraints and incentives of the marketplace. We all can be upset at times by what the free marketplace dictates. But it's hard to pick an argument with the invisible hand.

These examples all bear upon the benign effect that reliance on markets can have by preventing conflict and thereby promoting stability domestically. But the same dynamics have international applications as well. The benefits of division of labor and free trade are not confined within national borders. International free trade is economically advantageous to countries engaged in it. As a result, countries that have extensive trade relations with each other are thereby discouraged from political conflict more generally. Mutual economic dependency makes warfare more costly. When businesses in one country have millions of customers and also have important suppliers in another country, the last thing they want to see is some kind of international conflict or outright warfare that would cost them these crucial parts of their businesses.[2]

Markets also deliver a form of rough justice for a society. They reward individuals according to what other members of society consider to be the worth of those individuals' contribution to their welfare. The people "vote" on the value of someone's contribution not directly but with their dollars. And, although we all make mistakes at times about what uses of our money will maximize our happiness, we all are not only entitled to make those judgments but also best situated to make them. So when others freely pay me something for providing them some good or service, it is fair to say that to some extent I deserve what I have received—and that the sum total of all my receipts is a somewhat fair measure of my (economic) value to the world.

The market's allocations amount to only "rough" justice, however, for two main reasons. First, the price of a good or service not only depends on its intrinsic value to the consumer or possessor but also varies with its availability. It's not just what good something does for me but also what the supply of the good is. Having air to breathe is a whole lot more valuable to me than having the Hope Diamond or a baseball signed by Babe Ruth. But the latter items will cost me a whole lot more. In like fashion, good teachers and brave soldiers are more valuable to society as a whole than are movie stars or advertising executives, but the latter are better paid. Second, as was canvassed in our previous discussion of social justice, the talents that we bring to the marketplace vary greatly in value. And while these talents may partly be the product of long study or practice, they are to a considerable extent the product of one's random luck in the genetic lottery and the quality of the parenting we were fortunate—or unfortunate—to have received. Nonetheless, with these important reservations duly acknowledged, it is undeniable that the invisible hand of the capitalist marketplace produces a rough-and-ready form of proportional justice. It allocates shares of a society's wealth to its members in proportion to the value of their economic contribution to it—as assessed by what the other members are willing to pay for it.

To summarize, then, it seems clear that any advanced industrial society stands to benefit greatly from the presence within it of a robust capitalist marketplace. Economically, the marketplace creates strong incentives for its members to be economically productive. It strongly encourages economic efficiency and good management. It promotes economic progress through innovation in both technology and entrepreneurship. It protects a whole range of important personal liberties. It plays a significant role in the checks and balances that prevent the concentration of power in the state. It mitigates social conflict by its radical decentralization of decisions about the allocation of economic resources. And it provides a rough form of proportional distributive justice.

In light of all these virtues of a free-market system, and with due cognizance of the evidence gleaned from the performance of various modern economies around the world, it seems almost undeniable that the starting point and fundamental institution of a successful advanced economy should be the capitalist marketplace. No form of a centrally controlled command economy is capable of matching the results of a free-market system when it comes to productivity, efficiency, economic innovation, and personal freedom.

That said, it seems equally clear that collective action through government agency is an essential complement to the free-market system. Laissez-faire partisans want to insist that the only problem with a completely laissez-faire society is that it has never been tried. But there are in fact very good reasons that no democratic society has ever chosen to leave free markets totally unconstrained and supplemented. So let us now turn our attention to identifying the most important of these good reasons. They fall broadly under three basic headings. First, government actions are necessary to correct or manage the failure of the real world to provide the necessary enabling conditions of properly functioning markets. Second, governments need to prevent or buffer certain economically and socially destructive consequences that can be created by unconstrained market dynamics. And third, democratic governments need to act on behalf of important public goods that markets are incapable of providing.

Managing Real-World Deviations from Enabling Conditions
of Market Performance

Free markets perform as advertised only in the presence of certain enabling conditions. They perform optimally only when those conditions are perfectly met. That happens on economists' blackboards. But it doesn't often happen that way in the real world. Markets can often perform very well in less-than-perfect conditions. It doesn't take an infinite number of buyers and sellers, for example, for markets to price goods quite well. But there do have to be enough buyers and sellers for them to exert significant competitive pressure upon each other. Without market competition, free markets don't perform the way they are supposed to. So when real-world conditions deviate in a significant way from those necessary to make markets perform well, some form of government action may become necessary.

Occasionally, the technical requisites of providing a certain good or service will make it almost inevitable that there will be one single provider of the good in question. The result is a monopoly—one seller. In this case of maximal deviation from the necessary enabling conditions of proper market performance, some form of government intervention becomes a virtual necessity. The government could itself function as the monopoly provider. Recall here the desperate plea of the Populist Party in the late nineteenth century for the government to take over the railroads and the banks. Or, alternatively, the relevant government authority might exert regulatory supervision over the monopoly's pricing—as is often the case when it comes to utility companies that are the sole provider of essential services.

Even where there are only a very few producers of a good, what economists refer to as oligopoly, some government intervention may also be necessary to protect consumers. This is especially likely in cases where there are high barriers to entry on the producer side, because it then is quite easy for the producers to charge considerably more than what a competitive marketplace would have allowed. In some cases, the several producers might actively conspire not to compete in their pricing so that all of them can enjoy monopoly-level profits. As Adam Smith, the patron saint of free-market advocates, observed over two centuries ago: "People of the same trade seldom meet together . . . but the conversation ends in a conspiracy against the public or in some contrivance to raise prices."[3] Or the anticompetitive pricing may occur by a kind of de facto collusion, in which the several producers agree, either explicitly or tacitly, to engage in noncompetitive pricing or to cede specific geographic markets to each other. These are the dangers that prompted the passage of the Sherman Act in 1890 and the Clayton Act of 1914 that gave the federal government the power to prevent and/or penalize such anticompetitive activities and/or the conditions that allow them to happen.

Another necessary condition for proper market functioning is that all of the costs and benefits of a market transaction must be borne by the parties to the contract. In the real world, however, economic transactions may very well impose costs upon third parties or the public at large. When these costs—"negative externalities" in the economist's lexicon—are at all significant, once again some government institution has to step in, either to force the controlling parties to compensate those who have been damaged or to prevent the infliction of such third-party damage altogether. An obvious and important case in point is that of environmental pollution. Industrial producers cannot be allowed to dump dangerous waste into rivers, for example. Nor can municipalities be allowed to do the same with their sewage. Constraints or prohibitions also may need to be imposed upon the disposal of hog waste or coal ash or poisonous or radioactive industrial products in ways that would damage or endanger the health of third parties. In like manner, governing authorities arguably have a moral obligation to constrain their citizens from actions that threaten to impose serious costs upon future generations, who for obvious reasons are not in a position to protect themselves. The serious threats from global warming are the most obvious example here, but not the only one.

Properly functioning markets also require fully informed consumers. But in many cases in the real world, consumers are not able on their own to acquire important information relevant to their decisions. And those trying to sell their goods or services often have every incentive to misinform or to withhold important information from potential customers. Think here about the iconic "snake-oil salesmen" who made all sorts of fictional claims about the healing power of their elixirs. Consumers are also hardly in a position to know whether medications they buy actually contain the ingredients listed on the label or to confirm the accuracy of claims about complicated financial products. It is threats like these to the ability of consumers to make rational choices that have appropriately led to establishing certain agencies of government to provide the reliable information necessary for markets to perform properly. That is why, for example, we have a Consumer Product Safety Commission to establish and enforce product safety standards, a Federal Trade Commission to prevent palpably false advertising claims, a Food and Drug Administration to test and approve drugs and food products for safety, a Securities and Exchange Commission to provide investors with relevant data and to protect them against various forms of security fraud, and so on.

Another legitimate role for government intervention in the operation of the marketplace that at least partly fits under the heading of correcting real-world deviations from the enabling conditions of good market performances is the imposition of constraints upon what can be seen as contracts of desperation. One important assumption that informs and enables the benign depiction of market functioning is that the contractual agreements that produce the market's distributive outcomes are freely entered into by both parties. But this is in some respects a quite misleading depiction of an important subset of these contractual agreements in the real world. The tacit assumption that informs and justifies the notion of "freely entering into" a contract is that both parties have other reasonable options. In real life, that is not always the case. Suppose, to take an extreme example, a robber pulls a gun on you and says, "Your money or your life." When you hand over your wallet or purse, you probably would not be happy with me if I told you that this had been a voluntary transaction because you had the option of refusing and taking your chances.

The problem here is that the alleged voluntariness of both consenting parties to a contractual agreement can be compromised by a power imbalance between them. Think, for example, of the marriage vows of a woman in the context of a highly patriarchal society. She may be entering the marriage of her own "free will." But can we really say that she has freely consented to an arrangement that gives her husband full control of her property, the right to take other wives in the future, the right to inflict physical punishment upon her, and the right to divorce her without cause or compensation? The fact is that she had no real choice here if she wanted to be married—because the terms of the agreement were dictated by social forces over which she had no control. The ostensibly free contract between employers and employees can similarly be constrained by the power imbalance between the parties. In some cases the employee may bargain from a position of real strength. Think here of megastar performers like Paul McCartney and superstars like Mike Trout and Tom Brady, who can pretty much write their own ticket when it comes time for a new contract. In the much more common case of job seekers with no rare or distinctive skills, however, the employer usually holds most of the cards. Unless there exists a real shortage of labor, the employee may have no choice but to settle for a wage that may be considerably less than the value he or she adds to the company's product.

These are the circumstances that arguably necessitate and in fact have given rise to government intervention into the marketplace for labor. That intervention can take—and has taken—several forms. One way to correct for the proven imbalances in these cases is to stipulate a minimum level for hourly wages. Chief Justice Charles Evan Hughes invoked the distorting influence of the relevant power imbalance in his 1937 opinion in support of the Supreme Court decision upholding minimum-wage laws, writing that in many instances workers' "bargaining power is relatively weak, and . . . they are the ready victims of those who would take advantage of their necessitous circumstances."[4] Other legislation that has been enacted in order to protect workers from unsafe, abusive, or exploitative employer demands includes maximum-hours laws, work safety regulations, constraints on the use of child labor, and prohibition of various forms of harassment. And the same concerns about power imbalances in the marketplace for labor were what led to the provision in the National Labor Relations Act of 1935 that guaranteed workers the right to bargain collectively with their employer.

These laws and regulations designed to protect workers from being forced into contracts of desperation, I would argue, have played an important role in preserving the legitimacy and political support for the free-market system. And they are also justified by considerations of equity. Any free-market enthusiast who wants to complain that these interventions into the marketplace are inappropriate should be directed to the words of the patron saint of free markets, Adam Smith, who wrote: "No society can surely be flourishing and happy, of which the far greater part of the members are poor and miserable. It is but equity, besides, that they who feed, clothe, and lodge the whole body of the people, should have a share of the produce of their own labor as to be themselves tolerably well fed, clothed and lodged."[5]

Preventing or Moderating Dangers Created by Market Dynamics and Incentives

In addition to needing to correct for the failure of the real world to provide the necessary enabling conditions for free markets to perform as advertised, some form of government action can be required to cope with a number of potentially damaging consequences of market dynamics and incentives. Without any pretense of being comprehensive here, let's look at some important examples of how the visible hand of the government may need to keep the invisible hand of the market from causing economic or social damage.

A first and important example is "countercyclical policy." Advanced economic systems are composed of many interrelated parts and actions: financing, investing, hiring, producing, marketing, purchasing, consuming, and saving. On the economist's blackboard, these interrelated actions adjust to each other simultaneously. In the real world, the chain of causally related actions occurs sequentially over time. Notice also that each item on my list of the components of an economic system exerts a significant causal force upon the next component on the list. Moreover, the final item—savings—has a causal influence on the first two components—finance and investment: someone has to accumulate capital before it can be put to work. So the sequential list is actually a circular one, causally speaking. And the causal relationships among the various moving parts of a functioning economy are what produces the phenomenon commonly referred to as the "business cycle."

This cycle can go both upward and downward. Let's say that consumer confidence goes up and people start loosening their pocketbooks and are buying more. Companies see their goods flying off their shelves and place more orders with their manufacturers, who then ramp up production. That leads to more hiring, possibly to higher wages if the labor supply becomes tighter, and also to more borrowing from financial institutions in order for growing firms to acquire needed investment capital. That improves bank profits and puts more money into workers' hands, which increases "effective demand"—the will and ability to buy and consume more goods. And the business cycle continues its upward climb.

At some point, some adverse event or events occur that bring the upward motion to an end. Perhaps investment capital becomes scarcer, interest rates go up, and consumer demand cools off. Businesses sell less and their inventories pile up. As a consequence, they cut back their orders from manufacturers, who then decide to lay off part of their workforce because they have less demand for their products. The result is less money in the hands of the buying public, who have to cut back on spending, and now a downward cycle is under way. In the absence of some stabilizing forces, this downward cycle can pick up momentum and become a vicious cycle, forcing some businesses into bankruptcy, causing weaker financial institutions to fail, and consigning increasing numbers of the labor force into unemployment.

The economic damage and human suffering that result from sharp or protracted downward business cycles can be very substantial. And these damaging downturns were regular occurrences in capitalist economies in the years following the Industrial Revolution. The history of the American economy, for example, includes the following: (1) the Panic of 1837, when a bubble in the speculative real estate market burst, producing numerous bank failures and a five-year depression; (2) the Financial Crisis of 1857, which caused virtually every commercial bank in New York City to suspend payments, and which spread across the Atlantic to create banking crises and financial panic in multiple European countries; (3) the Panic of 1873, when the bankruptcy of a large American financial company, caused in part by a financial crash in Austria, led to a long and harsh depression; (4) the Depression of 1893, a serious downturn that caused double-digit unemployment that lasted for six years; (5) the Panic of 1907, which caused a series of bank failures and a stock market crash of around 50 percent; (6) the Depression of 1920, which was relatively short; (7) the Great Depression of 1929, which lasted for an entire decade, created unemployment levels as high as 25 percent, and saw at one point a nearly 50 percent drop in the country's GDP; (8) recessions in 1973 and 1981; and (9) the financial crisis and Great Recession of 2008–9.

This demonstrated propensity of industrialized capitalist economies to plunge into painful and destructive downturns every decade or two was one of the principal reasons that led to Marx and Engels's conviction that the capitalist system contained structural flaws that would bring about its demise. Not only would the human suffering produced by capitalism's recurrent depressions come to be seen as intolerable. In addition, another consequence of the downturns would be the increasing concentration of the control of a society's wealth into the hands of an increasingly few large and powerful corporations and their owners. Marx and Engels expected this to occur because smaller businesses would lack the resources to survive deep economic downturns and would get gobbled up by those wealthy enough to weather the storm. To use a more contemporary way of putting this: they anticipated Bernie Sanders's "1 percent" coming to control most of the wealth in a capitalist society—and with it to control the capitalist state as well. This situation would eventually become so intolerable and morally offensive, they surmised, that the "99 percent" would throw out their oppressors and take possession of the means of production and the control of the state.

A major reason that this implosion of free-market based economies did not take place in western Europe and the United States, which by Marxist logic would have been the logical places for it to happen first, was government intervention to moderate and control the ups and downs of the business cycle. This intervention took three principal forms: government control of the money supply, strategic use of government spending, and the creation of social insurance programs. Contrary to the beliefs and expectations of both laissez-faire economists and socialist advocates of government ownership of the means of production, it was the pragmatic interventions of the New Deal and the welfare state that "saved" capitalist economies by contrivances that have not done away with the business cycle but have greatly moderated and buffered its destructive consequences.

First, monetary policy. In this country it is set by the Federal Reserve Board, a government-authorized and -appointed group of financial managers charged with the task of moderating the swings of the business cycle by exercising control over the supply of money available to participants in the economy. The Fed, as this agency is commonly called, exerts its control of the money supply by setting the rate of interest it will charge banks who want to borrow funds from the central bank, by conducting "open-market operations" in which it buys or sells government securities, and by (within certain limits set by law) adjusting the required amount of funds banks must hold in reserve against their financial liabilities. By adjustments in these areas, the Federal Reserve can tighten the money supply if it believes that the economy is running too hot and creating dangerous speculative bubbles in certain assets or creating problematic inflationary trends. Or, conversely, it can make lending and investment easier and more attractive when it believes that the economy is in danger of a destructive contraction.

Second, fiscal policy: the timing and extent of government spending, investment, and taxation. Properly executed, astute management of government spending and investment can exert a helpful moderating force on swings in the business cycle. When business activity in the private sector weakens and a recessionary decline threatens the economy, timely government investment in the country's infrastructure or in defense can fill the gap, create jobs, maintain purchasing power, and prevent the downturn from getting out of hand. The government can also promote investment and effective demand by cutting taxes. When the economy reaches full employment and inflationary pressures and speculative bubbles threaten to get out of hand, government authorities can reduce public spending and let higher taxes exert a moderating influence on these potentially damaging trends.

That is the way government can and should execute its fiscal activities in the interest of a healthy economy. The omnipresent danger, of course, is that public pressure and the political interest of office-holders can push public economic policy into counterproductive directions. The voting public understandably enjoys having lower taxes and more government benefits, and elected officials want to remain in office. So there are strong incentives in a democracy to pursue imprudent fiscal policies that provide short-run benefits involving long-term costs. As I write, a Congress controlled by what used to be considered the more fiscally prudent party in this country has approved very large tax cuts in the context of an economy already at full employment. Not only are those tax cuts projected to add over $2 trillion to the national debt over the next decade, they also will make it extremely difficult for the government "pump priming" needed to pull the country out of a future recession. Party now, and let the kids pay later. So while fiscal policy can be a useful tool for controlling the business cycle in a capitalist economy, there is no guarantee that it will be used properly.

The third form of government intervention in the economy that helps prevent downturns in the business cycle from turning into painful recessions or depressions is to create social insurance programs that exert a stabilizing influence on the economy. Two of the most important of these programs are unemployment insurance and the insurance of bank deposits.

The first unemployment insurance program in the modern era was created in England as part of the National Insurance Act of 1911, which also included a system of health insurance for industrial workers in that country. In the United States, the first government unemployment insurance program was created by the state of Wisconsin in 1932 in the wake of the Great Depression. Three years later, the Social Security Act of 1935 created a joint federal and state system of unemployment insurance, funded by a relatively modest tax imposed upon employers. Through this program, employees who lose their job through no fault of their own receive payments that vary in size from state to state. The current usual time limit is six months, but Congress can extend these time limits at their discretion during serious economic downturns. Unemployment insurance payments help allay the human suffering that comes with being laid off from one's job. But in addition, they exert an important buffering force against the severity of macroeconomic downturns. During the Great Depression, vast numbers of the unemployed wound up in bread lines and became homeless. In that situation, they had no purchasing power to contribute to the economy's effective demand. And that was in turn a significant cause of the inability of the national economy to rebound after the stock market crash of 1929. Unemployment benefits provide the useful function for the larger economy during economic downturns, then, of mitigating the loss of purchasing power that keeps dragging it down.

Also in the wake of the Great Depression, Congress established the Federal Deposit Insurance Corporation in 1933. One of the standard causes of catastrophic plunges in capitalist economies had been bank failures produced by financial panic among the public, who rushed to their local banks and withdrew all their money. In this country, around 40 percent of the nation's banks had in fact fallen into bankruptcy between 1929 and 1932. So to prevent future financial calamities of this sort, Congress in 1933 established a program to insure people's bank deposits up to a certain level. Today that limit is $250,000 on most standard bank accounts, and the insurance fund is funded principally by a tax, or required dues, imposed upon the insured banks. The FDIC also has access to a line of credit of $100 billion with the Treasury Department. As a result, old-style "runs" on banks are pretty much a thing of the past. Depositors take confidence from the official FDIC sign posted at the insured banks around the country stating that their deposited funds are "backed by the full faith and credit of the United States Government."

In 2008, the federal government forestalled a financial meltdown precipitated by a threat of default on the part of massive amounts of mortgage-based securities. To do that, Congress authorized up to $700 billion to buy the problematic securities. This use of the full faith and credit of the United States—for far more than the $100 billion line of credit available to the FDIC—was crucial in bringing the financial crisis to an end. When all was said and done, the US Treasury had distributed some $439 billion of the so-called bailout funds. But it had by 2018 received back all of those funds plus a small profit. So, once again, a massive intervention by the government as its ultimate insurer saved our capitalist marketplace from catastrophic implosion. Good thing that laissez-faire ideologues like Grover Norquist had not successfully carried out his wish to "drown the government in a bathtub."

Beyond its necessary role in navigating the dangers and damage created by the boom-bust cycles of a market economy, government has an important role to play in protecting the public from threats posed by actions others take in response to market incentives and competitive pressures. In a competitive industry, for example, producers and service providers may be tempted to lower their costs by cutting corners with regard to product safety or to the safety of their employees. An airplane manufacturer, for example, might cut its costs by designing its planes in ways that are cheaper but that also create potentially fatal operation problems. (As I write, for example, Boeing is having to confront the fact that they opted to save production time and money by putting more fuel-efficient but also heavier engines on a frame that was not designed for engines of that size. That money-saving expedient resulted in creating the danger that the plane might stall shortly after takeoff. And they tried to prevent that potential disaster by installing automatic adjustments that would take over when a single sensor indicated—accurately or not—the imminence of that danger. That device wound up causing two plane crashes with hundreds of fatalities.) Or airlines could outsource their maintenance and repair operations to cheaper providers—perhaps in other countries—whose reliability is potentially in question. Restaurants can save money by compromising good sanitary practices. Food processors and drug manufacturers can save money by adulterating their products. Mining companies can get an edge on their competitors by engaging in practices that endanger the lives of their workers. And so on.

Some laissez-faire advocates have argued that the threat of legal suits for damages in such cases should be sufficient to prevent such abuses. The problems with reliance upon that expedient, however, are several. First, and most obviously, any such corrections come after the fact and provide no consolation to those who died and little consolation to their families or to those who suffered grievous injury. Second, the offending firms can sometimes escape their liability by declaring bankruptcy. And third, the firms that impose serious dangers on their customers or employees may calculate that doing so makes financial sense. In one instance, for example, an American auto manufacturing company knew that the placement of the gas tank in one of its cars heightened the chance of potentially fatal fires or explosions in rear-end collisions. But they went ahead with that design flaw because their calculations suggested that the cost of changing their design would be higher than the damages they likely would have to pay in legal judgments against them.

These considerations suggest that the best way to head off these dangers to the public is through government regulation and inspection. If all firms in a particular industry have to meet certain safety standards, a level playing field among the competing firms can be maintained at the same time as the customers and employees of the various firms are protected. That is why in this country Congress has established agencies such as the Food and Drug Administration, the Federal Aviation Administration, the Occupational Safety and Health Administration, and the Mine Safety and Health Administration. We also could add to this list the Securities and Exchange Commission, which has among its responsibilities the protection of the securities-buying public from dangerous or fraudulent practices on the part of financial companies.

A final example of situations in which free-market forces are sufficiently damaging and destabilizing that some form of compensatory government intervention seems necessary is when important sections of the market are subject to extreme volatility. Two prominent examples are the markets in agriculture and capital. (These examples were previously mentioned back in chapter 1, but I will briefly remind you about them in the current context.) The problem with agricultural markets is that for many food products both the demand and supply are highly inelastic. Farmers have to make decisions on what crops to plant or what livestock to produce long before they can bring these to market. If the industry as a whole has a bumper year for a particular food product, the price of that commodity can easily tumble below cost: consumers are not going to eat corn three meals a day just because there's a lot more for sale. They may change their eating habits somewhat—but for that to happen, usually prices must change very significantly. Farmers who earn less than they have spent in production costs may as a result wind up going out of business. Then, in the years that follow, the drop in supply—especially in bad years for certain crops—may spike and cause real problems for families trying to feed their kids.

There are no easy or perfect solutions to these challenging dynamics. But in many countries, including our own, governments intervene in agricultural markets in order to maintain a steadier relationship between supply and demand—so that farmers won't go out of business and families can afford to buy adequate nourishment. For some products, governments may decide to maintain acceptable supply levels by setting production quotas. Or the Department of Agriculture may establish price supports and purchase the amount of a particular food product necessary to bring supply and demand into the desired equilibrium. Then the government can distribute some of what they bought to public school systems for their lunch programs and/or spend it overseas as part of its foreign aid program. Programs like these definitely have their hazards and can be subject to political pressures. But they are arguably a considerably better option than suffering the market volatility and economic turmoil that otherwise would plague the agricultural sector of the economy.

In extreme cases, governments also may need to act in order to prevent serious damage resulting from sudden volatility in financial markets. The American economy is so large and diversified that sudden and dramatic capital flight usually does not present that great a threat to the nation's fiscal stability. Even here, however, government authorities occasionally are forced to intervene temporarily in the financial markets on those rare occasions when they threaten to spin out of control. Countries with smaller and much less diversified economies, on the other hand, can suffer great damage if big foreign investors decide to pull large amounts of capital out of their country on short notice. So either their government or some international trade authority may need to set some limits of time and/or amount for such transfers. No one can or should impose outright prohibitions on movements of investment capital. But regulations requiring international withdrawals of capital from vulnerable countries to be more gradual can provide them some protection against having the financial rug pulled out from under their economies and allow them a window to make necessary adjustments.

Important Economic and Social Goods That Markets Cannot Provide

Finally, many very important economic and social investments cannot be privately financed. Some of these can be characterized as "positive externalities" in the strict economic sense of that term. Others can be so described in a more general way. These important goods cannot be accomplished by private financing because their benefits are broadly shared rather than something that could be entirely captured by private investors. To put it another way, all of these goods represent parts of the necessary infrastructure of a prosperous economy and of a stable and successful democratic society.

Important infrastructure investments that qualify as positive externalities in a strictly economic sense are many in any advanced economy. These expenditures, in fact, constitute a very large portion of the budget of federal, state, and local governments. The first responsibility of government is to protect the lives, liberties, and property of its citizens against both external and domestic predators. A large portion of our federal budget, therefore, goes toward funding the military. And governments at every level spend significant amounts on police functions to protect the safety of the public. The list of law enforcement agencies at the national level is long: the FBI, the US

Immigration and Customs Enforcement, the US Marshals Service, the Bureau of Alcohol, Tobacco, Firearms, and Explosives, the Department of Homeland Security, the Drug Enforcement Administration, the Secret Service, US Customs and Border Protection, the IRS Criminal Investigation Division, the US Postal Inspection Service, the US Park Police, the US Border Patrol, the Bureau of Diplomatic Security, the Amtrak Police, the Office of Criminal Investigations, and more. The various states all have their own investigative and law enforcement agencies. And local governments have their police and sheriff's departments. Each level of government also has to establish and fund court systems to adjudicate criminal cases and to assign punishment for infractions of the law. In sum, then, a substantial portion of tax-funded public expenditures is devoted to protecting the law-abiding public by preventing, investigating, prosecuting, and punishing criminal actions domestically and by defending against foreign aggression. (Even the most ardent fans of the market recognize the need to protect people's lives and property, of course. But the point here is that all the necessary protective and adjudicative functions cannot be provided by private protective agents—like those who were chasing Butch Cassidy and the Sundance Kid.)

Another obvious and important area that almost unavoidably requires some collective provision is transportation. All societies have to have avenues for their people to move from one place to another for the various purposes of life; and no advanced economy in a large country has any chance of success without the capacity to transport goods, services, and product components to where they are needed in a universally accessible and efficient way. And, for practical reasons, government action and tax-funded public financing will need to play a significant role in the construction and maintenance of the necessary infrastructure for such a transportation system.

An important part of the story of the commercial and industrial development of the American economy, therefore, has been the planning, financing, and construction of canals, roadways, railroads, and air transportation systems. This is a long story whose details could fill volumes, beginning with the 1806 authorization by Congress for the federal government to arrange and finance the construction of the Cumberland Road from the headwaters of the Potomac River in

Maryland to a point on the Ohio River. And it is a complex story involving the interaction of private entrepreneurs, state governments, and the federal government pretty much from beginning to end.[6] Suffice it to say that throughout this history both federal and state government promotion, organization, finance, and construction have played a necessary and important role throughout.

In 1807, the US Senate directed Secretary of the Treasury Albert Gallatin to report on existing and proposed roads and canals in the country. In his report the following year Gallatin recommended that an interconnected system of roads, canals, and river improvements be funded by the federal government. He wrote in support of his recommendation that "the inconveniences, complaints, and perhaps dangers, which may result from a vast extent of territory, can no otherwise be radically removed or prevented than by opening speedy and easy communications through all its parts. . . . No other single operation [than building a good transportation infrastructure] within the power of Government can more effectually tend to strengthen and perpetuate that Union which secures external independence, domestic peace, and internal liberty."[7] Congress did not immediately agree to implement his proposal for both budgetary and sectional interest reasons. But Gallatin was not wrong. He was, as we now well know, just a few years ahead of his time.

Another important form of infrastructure that requires some government financial support falls under the heading of scientific research and development. Even in the middle of the nineteenth century, John Stuart Mill recognized the importance of this kind of public investment. As he wrote in his *Principles of Political Economy*: "There are many scientific researches, of great value to a nation and to mankind, requiring assiduous devotion of time and labor. . . . The cultivation of speculative knowledge, though one of the most useful of all employments, is a service rendered to a community collectively, not individually, and one consequently for which it is reasonable that the community collectively should pay."[8] In today's high-tech societies, Mill's observation is even more pertinent and important. The success of advanced industrial economies depends more and more upon their capacity for technological advancement and innovation. And that in turn depends substantially upon research and discovery in the basic sciences. But no private firm is in a position to finance and organize the basic scientific research that is the necessary foundation for their success and also for the prosperity of society as a whole.

The case for substantial government investment in research and development was succinctly stated in a recent publication of the Information Technology and Innovation Foundation as follows: "Public expenditures in R&D are critical for increasing the total level of research being conducted, because R&D has spillover effects (aka positive externalities) that firms cannot capture, which causes them to invest less than is socially optimal. . . . To maximize societal welfare, firms should continue to expand investments in R&D until the marginal total benefits to society at large equal the cost of capital. But because firms rightly (in terms of economic rationality) don't take into account external benefits, they underinvest from a societal perspective. . . . Further, public investments in research make private investments more lucrative, . . . providing more lines of research that firms can turn into innovative products. Public R&D is also crucial for [a society's] position in the global economy [because] public R&D funding makes it more likely that its firms are the first to leverage new discoveries, giving them advantages over international competitors."[9] It is also worth noting that scientific and technological innovation plays a critical role in a modern nation's defense capabilities. A nation's position within the global balance of power, and therefore its security against attack, are today largely a function of its relative standing in military technology. And each country's standing in that arms race depends very largely upon its investment in the relevant areas of scientific R&D.

Finally, the most important part of a country's infrastructure is the capabilities of its people. To put the case negatively and bluntly: no nation will be very successful if its populace is sickly and ignorant. To put it in positive economic terms: the most critical part of a country's capital infrastructure is its human capital. And the foundation of human capital is what the ancients referred to as *mens sana in corpore sano*—a sound mind in a healthy body. Practically speaking, that means that the social and economic welfare of any country or city or family is highly dependent upon its members having access to good health care and a good education.

Now the private marketplace is quite capable of providing the goods of health care and education to some extent. Health care providers engage in private practice, and both entrepreneurs and non-profit organizations can and do set up schools at all levels and find willing customers. Both health care and good education, however, have for a number or reasons become increasingly expensive in today's economically advanced societies. In medicine, scientific and technological advances have enabled the medical profession to treat and heal or alleviate many health problems that historically were beyond help. It's worth remembering, for example, that the first president of the United States died just two centuries ago with leeches attached to his body—because that was the best treatment the medical profession had to offer at that time for an infection that today could be handled by a couple of rounds of antibiotics. That would today be a cheap fix. But other important medical interventions are quite expensive: think, for example, of open-heart surgery, hip and knee replacements, proton radiation for cancer treatment, heart and kidney transplants, advanced chemotherapy, stem-cell treatment, and so on. All great things to have available for those who need them. But the price tag for providing these complex and sophisticated services is high, thereby raising the cost of needed treatments—or the insurance that would cover them—beyond the reach of many. Similarly, good job prospects in a modern economy depend upon having a higher level of educational attainment than what would have sufficed only a couple of generations ago. Again, as in health care, those in lower-income families struggle to access the necessary level of education—or wind up struggling under heavy burdens of indebtedness from student loans.

Private philanthropy can—and in our society does—help alleviate some of these economic challenges. Think here, for example, of the large endowment funds that some of our leading universities have been able to amass over the years and use in part for need-based scholarships, as a result of the generosity of their alumni and other private donors. But both for the public good, and for reasons of social equity and a commitment to according all democratic citizens a genuine opportunity to achieve a good life by developing their talents, some public investment is necessary to fill the financial gap in these crucial areas of human capital development. This is the logic behind systems of public education with universal access, grants funded by the federal government to enable access to higher education for students from low-income families, and federally insured student loan programs. In health care, this is the logic behind programs such as Medicaid, Medicare, and the Affordable Care Act. Also necessary in the economy of health care are the public finance and organization of programs important to the defense of public health, whose costs cannot be internalized in a way that makes them amenable to private provision. That is why we have the Center for Disease Control, the Public Health Service, the National Institute of Health, and the Surgeon General's Office. (As this book goes to press, the US government is struggling to cope with a coronavirus pandemic in part because of recent cutbacks in these agencies' funding.) It also may be necessary for the government to sponsor drug research in areas that might be very important for public health reasons but that do not provide attractive profit incentives for private companies. Private pharmaceutical companies, for example, benefit financially much more by developing a marginally better drug for a very widespread condition, such as indigestion or erectile dysfunction, than by discovering a drug that could completely eliminate a serious disease with a single application, or a drug that could more cheaply and effectively combat a disease afflicting only those in underdeveloped countries. The same kinds of market incentives seem clearly to have played a role in the apparent dangerously low sense of urgency (relative to the public health threat) of private drug companies when it comes to the development of new drugs to combat the emergence of infections resistant to existing antibiotics.

Public Goods and Democratic Values

Most of the government expenditures and regulations that we have seen here to be important can be justified by fairly straightforward economic considerations. These interventions either compensate for the failure of the real world to provide the necessary conditions for proper market functioning or to prevent market pressures and dynamics from creating economic damage. But liberal democracies are about more than simply maximizing economic performance. They also see their mission as protecting and promoting broader human goods, such as personal autonomy, the rule of law, civic equality, and the opportunity for all their citizens to develop their human capacities and lead good lives. Free markets can and do play a significant role in achieving these democratic goods. But they can't do it on their own. They need assistance from collective action to achieve these goals.

We earlier noted the macroeconomic reasons for an advanced society to provide universal access to health care and a good education. But our commitment to democratic values and aspirations gives added weight to that imperative. This is especially true when it comes to a nation's children. No children can credibly be said to have been given a real opportunity to succeed in life, much less an equal opportunity, if they are denied access to an education that can equip them to earn a decent living and to fulfill their responsibilities as citizens. Nor can the boast about genuinely equal opportunity be credible if some children are allowed to fail because of unattended health conditions.

Relatively affluent democracies also need to fund some form of economic safety net for all their citizens to keep them afloat when job loss or disability costs them their livelihood. Especially when job loss is the result of structural changes in the economy, it is not only prudent in macroeconomic terms but also morally obligatory for the larger body of citizens who benefit from these changes to provide their struggling fellow citizens with job-retraining programs or with relocation subsidies to move to where jobs are available. The issue of the appropriate levels of duration of support for those in need of longer-run assistance is admittedly vexing. Provide too little, and it is insufficient to prevent deprivation. Provide more generously, and worries about perverse incentives become a legitimate fear. We rightly expect all competent adults to assume the primary responsibility for their own sustenance; and the availability of long-term support may encourage the work-averse among us to live off the efforts of others. Moreover, in terms of basic fairness, it clearly seems problematic to ask low-wage workers to work forty-hour weeks for an income no better or barely better than what we make available free to others.

These latter considerations provide grist for the mill of those who argue for Scrooge-like levels of support for the distressed and disabled, in tandem with strong job-seeking mandates for those on the dole. On the other hand, however, the same considerations provide a very good supporting argument on behalf of "making work pay" and "economic dignity."[10] Fairness to those who "answer the bell" each day to work for their living suggest the need for policy steps such as raising the currently quite low level of the federal minimum wage, continuing support for and possibly expanding the Earned Income Tax Credit, and providing widely available job-training programs. It is worth noting, in this context, that a number of states and localities have recently taken some of these steps on their own. And that includes conservative states such as Arkansas and Tennessee—with the latter providing free tuition to community colleges that offer courses that contribute to marketable job skills. Similarly, more government support for child care and pre-K programs like those found in a number of European countries would also facilitate the ability of young parents to enter the job market.

Programs like these give force to one of the central aspirations and commitments of a good democratic society: namely that all citizens can be free and autonomous beings who are equal to each other in their civic status. That is not a meaningful claim if some citizens have to live in circumstances of abject dependency upon others who are wealthier or more powerful. As Rousseau observed, the practical implication of that reality requires "not that the degree of power and riches [need] to be absolutely identical for everybody; but that power shall never be great enough for violence . . . and that, in respect of riches, no citizen shall ever be wealthy enough to buy another and none poor enough to have to sell himself."[11] With that admonition in mind, every economically advanced democratic society that takes its principled aspirations seriously should do its best to conduct its economic affairs in a way that allows every full-time contributor in its workforce sufficient means to cover the basic needs of life.

Another important function of the several jurisdictions of government should be to provide and support public spaces and institutions accessible to all citizens. I have in mind here public parks, public libraries, public recreation areas, public museums, and civic centers. And I want to emphasize the enormous value of these public spaces and institutions to democratic societies for a couple of reasons: first, because we tend not to recognize and appreciate their importance, instead often simply taking them for granted, and second, because those of a libertarian persuasion often denigrate their value.[12] I ask you then to perform a quick thought experiment and ask yourself to imagine what your city, your state, and this country as a whole would look like were all of our public spaces, public facilities, and public events to disappear overnight. If you are like me, you will realize that both our individual lives and our communal life would be immeasurably poorer. And private enterprises and private clubs could not begin to be adequate substitutes.

Consider first the many public parks in this country. According to the Trust for Public Land, there are over twenty-three thousand parks in our one hundred largest cities alone. Among these are many amazing places that play a huge role in the lives of their residents and visitors alike. Imagine New York without its Central Park or the newer High Line, Chicago without its Lincoln Park or Millennium Park, Los Angeles without its Griffith Park, Philadelphia without its Fairmount Park, Detroit without Belle Isle, Boston without its Commons, Minneapolis without the Theodore Wirth Regional Park, San Francisco without its Golden Gate Park and Dolores Park, Saint Louis without Forest Park, Washington, D.C., without the Mall or Rock Creek Park, Austin without its Zilker Park, New Orleans without its City Park, Sioux City without its Falls Park, and many, many others. These are not simply wonderful garden spots. They are also crucial venues for public cultural and recreational activities open to all. As the City of Chicago's website says of Millennium Park, just to take one example, it functions as "a new kind of town square . . . that provides the backdrop for hundreds of free cultural programs including concerts, exhibitions, tours, and family activities."

Public libraries, which double these days as media centers, also provide great benefits to their communities. At the top of the chain are the major libraries in large cities, such as the New York Public Library, which houses extensive research collections and welcomes millions of visitors yearly. But most towns of any size offer their residents access to some form of public library. And these libraries are rarely mere repositories of books for use, instead providing valuable community services such as access to the internet, literacy classes, and programs for children's early education. In my own diverse midsize city, the several branches of the public library offer many such programs of educational value and wind up functioning as community centers. Three recent public subsidized housing projects in Chicago carry this library as a civic center model to another level. The ground-level floors of these projects are stylish branch libraries, with several floors of apartments above them. These projects have revitalized their neighborhoods, "attracting a mix of toddlers, retirees, after-school teens, job seekers, not to mention the traditional readers and borrowers of DVDs." Along with many branch libraries across the country, they "have morphed into indispensable and bustling neighborhood centers and cultural incubators, offering music lessons, employment advice, citizenship training, entrepreneurship classes and language instruction."[13]

The crucial role of these public spaces and facilities is not confined to our cities. The quality of life in small towns all across the country depends to a considerable extent upon their ability to fund and maintain places where all their inhabitants can congregate, recreate, and learn. The town near my own family's longtime summer vacation home is quite small and not particularly affluent. But it has a strong civic culture and is a great place to live or visit. And a big part of that attractiveness is created by its well-maintained and well-used public places and activities, including a large bayside park with picnic shelters, playgrounds and farmers' markets; another park offering basketball and tennis courts, a skateboard course, and playgrounds; a very pleasant and well-run public library and media center with programs for kids and adults alike; a handsome arts center; and very nice public beaches on two lakes. These public spaces and functions make the town a democratic community. Without them, it would be nothing but a few stores and a couple hundred houses.

Last, but certainly not least, is a system of universally accessible elementary and secondary education. We tend to take our public schools for granted because they are ubiquitous and a standard part of the lives of most citizens. But this system that we now take for granted in this country is essentially a product of the nineteenth century. Well-funded and well-run public schools provide several very important benefits for a democratic society and its members. By teaching basic literacy and mathematical skills and giving instruction in literature and the arts, history and government, the natural sciences, and pre-vocational skills, public schools provide their students with the basic knowledge and some of the skills they need to be competent and productive citizens. They also provide a venue and encouragement for cross-cultural understanding in a pluralistic society. Most of them wind up serving as a kind of social center for their students and as a source of common pride and attachment for the community they serve. And because they are open to all, they represent an absolutely crucial resource for lower-income students who otherwise would be denied access to the basic knowledge and skills needed for a genuine opportunity to lead successful lives. In a free society, parents should have the right to seek private education for their children if they wish. But it is essential for a democratic society to provide and fund first-rate public schools so that they do not wind up being inferior institutions of last resort for those whose families cannot afford better.

Final Words

In chapter 4, I conceded up front that definitive answers about the ideal way for a society to achieve prosperity, mitigate the unfairness of life, and respect the constitutive aspirations and ideals of liberal democracy exceed our grasp. Indeed, I did not merely concede that inability but insisted upon it and explained the reasons for it. In this final chapter, however, I hope that I have made the case that both free markets and intelligent government regulations, protections, and investments for the public good have essential roles to play in achieving both prosperity and the genuine opportunity for all citizens of a democratic society to live free and flourishing lives. Reasonable people can and will differ about the best arrangements and levels of funding for public programs on behalf of military defense, public safety, transportation, education, support for the disabled and destitute, public health, and so on. These issues will necessarily and properly be the subjects of public deliberation and decision in democratic politics. What I hope most of us will understand, however, is that extreme positions on either side are problematic and unwise. For democratic societies to be successful, they need to have both well-functioning free markets and also adroit government programs. They need to have both protected private spaces for people to pursue their diverse conceptions of happiness and also vibrant public venues and institutions for their citizens to pursue their common needs and purposes.

I also would argue that a "mixed economy"—strong markets, strong government—provides the best institutional framework for appropriating and synthesizing the best parts of the several democratic traditions that have shaped contemporary democratic liberalism—the traditions discussed in chapter 3. Each of these traditions has important strong points we need to recognize and incorporate into our contemporary democratic societies—and also, taken alone, potential downsides we need to avoid.

The great strength and value of the civic republican tradition is its devotion to the common good, its dedication to civic equality, and its recognition of the importance of civic virtue. Taken alone as a comprehensive model of democracy, however, it threatens to coerce its citizens into a kind of self-abnegating conformity while neglecting or intruding into the private spaces and opportunities they need in order to develop their distinctive talents and pursue their personal passions. As a comprehensive model of a democratic society, it threatens to turn life into membership in an army. That may facilitate effective common action. But it is not an entirely attractive conception of human flourishing.

Classical "minimal-state" liberalism, in direct contrast, excels in its advocacy and institutional protection of the private spaces and distinctive individual pursuits of its citizens. It also requires tolerance of others from its citizens. And it offers through its protection and celebration of free enterprise and individual rights a socially constructive outlet for the potentially disruptive passions of concupiscence and self-seeking. On the downside, it threatens at the extreme to disarticulate a democratic society into an archipelago of greedy hermits, an aggregation of people largely devoid of public spirit with no support system for those who fall between the cracks. If a civic repub-lican society threatens to become an obedient corporate army, the danger of the minimal state is that it turns into what Tocqueville de-picted as a destructive form of individualism. As he limned this threat, this kind of individualism "disposes each member of the community to sever himself from the mass of his fellows, and to draw apart with his family and friends. . . . Individualism proceeds from erroneous judgement more than from depraved feelings; it originates as much in deficiencies of mind as in perversity of heart. Selfishness blights the germ of all virtue: individualism, at first, only saps the virtues of public life, but in the long run it attacks and destroys all others and is at length absorbed in downright selfishness."[14]

The great strength of the "democratic perfectionism" championed by John Stuart Mill and Walt Whitman is its insistence that the ulti-mate mission and purpose of democracy is to provide the institutional basis for all citizens to be able to develop their human capacities and lead flourishing lives. The danger of this conception of democratic purposes is that it may tempt some to claim special knowledge of what human perfection consists in and to try to force it upon their fellow citizens.

The great strengths of Enlightenment liberalism are first, its aspi-ration to create a democratic society that encompasses the multiple goods of liberty, equality, and civic friendship; and second, its in-sistence upon dedication to the advancement of scientific and civic knowledge as an essential resource for realizing that noble aspiration. The downside of the Enlightenment vision of democracy is its some-what naive optimism about the lack of some tension among the several constitutive goods and values it hoped to achieve. And it also overestimated the political efficacy of scientific knowledge, in part because of its overly sanguine account of human nature.

It would be foolish to fall into the Enlightenment dream that all the various hopes and values of the liberal democratic project are ca-pable of simultaneous and complete achievement. The inherent con-straints and moral tragedies of the human condition do not permit that. Utopia is not a possibility. What is possible, however, is to ar-range our political and economic institutions in a way that provides a place for the individual freedoms of liberalism, the common goods and civic virtues of republicanism, the Enlightenment hopes for the multiple goods of liberty, civic equality, and fraternity, and the democratic perfectionist aspiration for an aristocracy of everyone—a society in which all can lead flourishing lives.

Constitutionally, the best way to strive for this kind of creative synthesis of the several democratic traditions is to establish strong protection for individual freedoms and rights—as in the Bill of Rights—while empowering the popular majority to act on behalf of the general welfare. Most contemporary democracies have in place constitutional provisions of that sort. When it comes to political economy, the best way to strive for this kind of creative synthesis is not to heed the admonitions of those on the extremes who venerate one democratic ideal—whether it be liberty or equality or prosperity or a particular conception of justice—while ignoring other important democratic goods and aspirations. The best political economy in the service of a society dedicated to the multiple important democratic ideals is neither to "drown the government in a bathtub," as some would have it, nor to put the government directly in charge of vast portions of the economy, as others advocate. Both logic and the evidence of the past century strongly indicate that our best hope to achieve the kind of creative synthesis of democratic goals described above is to improve and perfect the "both/and" mixed economy that we—and every other industrialized democratic country—have in place.

As Milton Friedman has pointed out, when democratic governments attempt to impose economic arrangements that would significantly constrain their citizens' ability to make their own decisions about their economic options, those governments are forced to abandon their plans because of popular resistance. On the other hand, as Lawrence Brown and Lawrence Jacobs have pointed out, when minimal-state-oriented administrations in this country have tried to privatize sectors of the economy that impinge on important public goods such as health, education, and transportation, the electorate protests and rejects those plans.[15]

Our democratic debates in the area of political economy, therefore, need to center on what the improvement and perfection of the mixed economy look like in concrete terms. I have my own views about things I would like to see done under this heading. Some of these would involve more of a government role. Some might involve less. Other reasonable people may have different ideas. But these are the kind of focused debates we need to be having these days. What we should not waste our time or attention on are sweeping ideological claims that markets should do everything and governments nothing other than protecting private property, or equally sweeping claims to the contrary that the state needs to run nearly everything on behalf of a particular conception of justice or the public good. To maximize our hopes of achieving a prosperous democratic society with liberty, justice, civic equality, and genuine opportunity for all its responsible citizens to enjoy good lives, we need both strong markets and strong and competent government. We just need to assign them the tasks they are best suited to do and then continually to identify and make the adjustments and improvements necessary to enable them to do their jobs well. Easy to say, but a continuing challenge to do.

A Postscript about Social Justice

The attentive reader may have noticed that I have said very little about social justice in this concluding chapter—something that I myself realized only in retrospect. This seeming omission was not merely an oversight on my part, however. Instead, my reticence to invoke social justice as an independent major basis for the judgments and recommendations I have offered here is a product of my belief that what I described in chapter 4 as the moral tragedy of the world makes it impossible for anyone to claim convincingly that some specific distribution of resources would be entirely fair and just. The main causes of the unattainability of some allegedly perfect scheme of distributive justice are twofold. The first is the intractability of the profound unfairness visited upon us by the circumstances and deep inequities of life itself. Some of these natural inequities are beyond human power to rectify to any significant extent. And measures to mitigate or compensate for them almost inevitably impose undeserved costs or burdens upon the less afflicted among us. The second problem is the one visited upon us by the mysteries of causal determination and human freedom and personal responsibility. If you believe that every event or outcome in human life is entirely the product of external causal forces, then you logically might endorse an entirely egalitarian standard of distributive justice: to each as equally as is possible without making everyone worse off. If, at the opposite extreme, you believe that every event or outcome in anyone's life is entirely caused by that person's own free choices and actions, you logically might be inclined to endorse an entirely proportional standard of justice: people basically deserve precisely what they wind up having. Clearly, neither of these views is really tenable. The vast force of outside circumstances and random individual endowments upon the distribution of economic and social resources in any society is patently obvious. And the belief that human beings have no control whatsoever over their choices and actions would—besides clashing with our own sense of ourselves and our free agency—undermine the basis of our commitment to human dignity and personal responsibility. But if we more reasonably believe that people's share of wealth results from the combined force of outside circumstances and their freely willed choices and actions, we have little ability to determine the relative force of each—which we also realize will differ in different cases.

The resulting intractability of attempts to arrive at a definitive standard for social justice—and the consequent unresolvable persistence of competing arguments about it—need not, I believe, lead to either a counsel of despair or to a lack of concern about unfairness. This is so for at least three reasons. The first of these is that, even if we as a society cannot for good reasons reach agreement upon some specific standard of perfect justice, our innate sense of *in*justice, which is fortunately nearly ubiquitous, should and will come into play in specific cases. We provide free or subsidized school lunches to students from impoverished families, for example, in large part because we recognize how profoundly unfair it would be for them to go hungry while their classmates were eating. PTAs and other donors step up to cover the travel expenses for members of school bands from families who lack the resources to do so when their band has been chosen to participate in a major parade somewhere, because they know that it would be grossly unfair to leave them behind. Judges will take into account the effect of economic deprivation or disastrous parental neglect or abuse when they are deciding what justice requires when they are determining the fate of those whose wrongdoing was partly a con-sequence of these outside circumstances. And so on.

The second reason that we need not rely on some elusive consen-sus about social justice in order to succeed in putting into place poli-cies that mitigate the unfairnesses of life and social forces is that many policies and government programs put into place principally for the purpose of achieving prosperity and social comity happily work on behalf of social justice as well. At least that is so if we make the entirely reasonable assumption that those most disadvantaged by circum-stances of life beyond their control will disproportionally wind up to-ward the bottom of the economic ladder. A summary review of some of the policies and programs that can be found in most of today's eco-nomically advanced democracies should make that clear.

Consider, for example, the distributive consequences, benign from the standpoint of justice, of the following: universal provision of access to good health care, universal access to good education, free or readily available job retraining programs, government provision for a universally accessible transportation infrastructure, universally acces-sible public parks and libraries, minimum-wage and maximum-hours laws, child labor protections, unemployment insurance, antidiscrimi-nation laws, food stamp and school lunch programs, provision of free legal counsel to indigents standing trial, social security retirement programs with distributive criteria that assist lower-income partici-pants, government subsidies for affordable housing, social security disability payments, state subsidies to public universities and commu-nity colleges, federal Pell Grants to lower-income college students, and a progressive income tax structure that imposes higher rates on higher incomes. Some of these programs may well need improvement or ex-pansion. But even as they stand, they clearly go a long way to buffer the vast inequalities produced by the free-market system, to improve the lot of the least advantaged members of society, and to provide op-portunities for economic advancement to children in lower-income families.

Finally, it is important to recognize and take advantage of the fact that the willingness of many people to make sacrifices of time, energy, or money on behalf of their less well-off fellow citizens is not always, and does not have to be, motivated entirely or even primarily by their convictions about social justice. For at least four other moral motivations or dispositions of will inspire people to act beneficently.

The first of these is what Rousseau called "natural pity," or what we would more likely call human compassion. Some people are more compassionate than others, to be sure. But most people are pained by seeing other human beings suffer. (Or by seeing other sentient beings suffer, for that matter. That's why we have organizations like the Society for the Prevention of Cruelty to Animals, animal rescue groups, and the like.) And they are motivated for that reason to act on behalf on alleviating this kind of distress. Second, those of us brought up within the most prominent religious traditions in this country have been taught that the supreme social virtue is "caritas," the disposition to care about and actively care for our neighbors, whom we are admonished "to love as ourselves." So it is both heartening and fairly common to see church-sponsored groups and other civic organizations set up food kitchens or pack tools into trucks and head off to areas hit by floods, hurricanes, or other natural disasters. Third, as we saw in chapter 3, several of the democratic traditions that have shaped our democratic norms and ideals embrace and champion the civic virtue of fraternity—or civic friendship: the disposition and commitment to bond with and serve our fellow citizens and our country, even at times at our own risk or sacrifice. All the many who aspire to perform some kind of public service, to join the military, or to staff philanthropic nonprofits for less remuneration than they could have received in the private sector are motivated to some extent by this kind of ethic. And finally, there is the somewhat less elevated but socially benign motivation of "enlightened self-interest," which motivates us at times to do things in order to improve the lot of our fellow citizens because we recognize that our own lives are likely to go better if those around us are reasonably well off—as opposed to their being so disadvantaged that they become disaffected and desperate.

Without gainsaying the importance of legitimate moral concerns on behalf of social justice, then, in the face of the unresolvable and inevitable disagreements about what justice and fairness demand of us with respect to the distribution of income in our society (one public opinion survey I saw shortly before writing these words showed that 75 percent of registered Republicans agreed with the claim that the wealth distributions of the markets are basically fair, compared with only 25 percent of registered Democrats who did so), it is well and good that these other moral, practical, and humane dispositions are more powerful and important than we often appreciate in motivating people's behavior. These benign dispositions may not suffice to motivate others to pursue exactly what you consider to be social justice. But they certainly push us toward greater civic equality and support for the more disadvantaged members of society that most of us would consider to be important parts of social justice in a democratic society.

NOTES

Introduction

1. John F. Kennedy, "Commencement Address at Yale University, June 11, 1962," John F. Kennedy Presidential Library and Museum, Archives, www.jfklibrary.org/archives/other-resources/john-f-kennedy-speeches /yale-university-19620611.

2. Cited by Russell Jacoby in *The End of Utopia: Politics and Culture in an Age of Apathy* (New York: Basic Books, 1999), chap. 1.

3. Adams reported this incident in his diary. See John Howe Jr., *The Changing Political Thought of John Adams* (Princeton, NJ: Princeton University Press, 1966), 11.

4. See his argument in the chapter of *Democracy in America* entitled "Why Democratic Nations Show a More Ardent and Enduring Love of Equality Than of Liberty" (vol. 2, pt. 2, chap. 1), trans. George Lawrence (New York: Harper and Row, 1966).

5. See David Brooks's column "Thurston Howell Romney," *New York Times*, September 17, 2012, citing a study by Nicholas Eberstadt of the American Enterprise Institute.

6. Quoted in Jacob Hacker and Paul Pierson, "What Krugman and Stiglitz Can Tell Us," review of *End This Depression Now!*, by Paul Krugman, and *The Price of Inequality: How Today's Divided Society Endangers Our Future*, by Joseph E. Stiglitz, *New York Review of Books*, September 27, 2012.

7. James Buchanan and Gordon Tullock, *The Calculus of Consent: Logical Foundations of Constitutional Democracy* (Ann Arbor: University of Michigan Press, 1962).

8. See Julius Kovesi, *Moral Notions* (London: Routledge and Kegan Paul, 1967).

9. The recent appreciative interest in Hayek's thought within respectable scholarly circles, it should be noted, involves attending more to his broader theoretical publications and less to his *The Road to Serfdom*, which was written for a more popular audience.

ONE.   The Political Economy Debate

1. Marie Jean Antoine Nicholas Caritat de Condorcet, *Sketch for a Historical Picture of the Progress of the Human Mind*, trans. June Barraclough (London: Weidenfeld and Nicolson, 1955), 130–31.

2. Adam Smith, *The Wealth of Nations* 1.2, ed. and abr. Richard Teichgreiber III (New York: Random House, 1985), 15.

3. It is worth noting here that the term *most good* in this sentence and in the conceptual universe of economics does not invoke or depend upon any "objective" standard of good and bad, right and wrong. It means "the highest aggregate preference satisfaction of the parties involved."

4. The longevity and public support of the TVA—a New Deal creation that most embodies the classic socialist model of government control of the means of production—is replete with political oddities and ideological inconsistencies. The state of Tennessee is largely dominated today by politicians who continually excoriate "socialism" and "big government," but the same public that responds to such rhetoric and elects them is quite supportive of the TVA, which provides them with reliable electricity and good service at a reasonable cost. More ideologically consistent free-market conservatives, like Barry Goldwater in 1964, have come to grief by failing to live with this paradox. And Ronald Reagan got into serious trouble with General Electric, for whom he served as a major pitchman, for criticizing the TVA, because the TVA was a major buyer of General Electric turbines. Moreover, it was President Obama whose 2013–14 budget mentioned "the possible divestiture of TVA" and said that "reducing or eliminating the federal government's role in programs such as the TVA, which have achieved their original objectives and no longer require federal participation, can help put the nation on a sustainable fiscal path." For that suggestion, Obama officials were roundly criticized by the same Tennessee politicians who routinely denounced his policies as socialist. As the *Economist* noted wryly: "Elected officials in the TVA area are either frosty or outright hostile to Mr. Obama's proposal. Most are Republicans, who might be expected to applaud a plan to shrink government. But power does strange things to politicians" ("The Tennessee Valley

Authority: Dammed if You Don't," *Economist*, April 27, 2013). Power, perhaps, but also a remarkable degree of ideological hypocrisy.

5. Milton Friedman, *Capitalism and Freedom* (Chicago: University of Chicago Press, 1962), 28.

6. Michael Walzer, *Spheres of Justice* (New York: Basic Books, 1983), 68.

7. Thomas Hobbes, *Leviathan* 2.18 (London, 1651), Project Gutenberg, www.gutenberg.org/files/3207/3207-h/3207-h.htm.

8. For a useful overview, see Frank Easterbrook and Daniel Fischel, "Limited Liability and the Corporation," *University of Chicago Law Review* 52, no. 1 (1985): 89–117.

9. Friedman, *Capitalism and Freedom*, 28.

10. For an example of the issues and battles that can arise in this area, see Eric Dexheimer and Jeremy Schwartz, "Growth of Large Private Water Companies Brings Higher Water Rates, Little Recourse for Consumers," *Austin (Texas) Statesman*, December 18, 2011.

11. Friedman, *Capitalism and Freedom*, 28.

12. See, for example, EURODAD, CRBM, WEED, and Bretton Woods Project, "Addressing Development's Black Hole: Regulating Capital Flight," report, May 2008.

13. Friedman, *Capitalism and Freedom*, 102–4.

14. Ibid., 104.

15. See, inter alia, Grant McConnell, *Private Power and American Democracy* (New York: Alfred Knopf, 1967), and Theodore Lowi, *The End of Liberalism* (New York: W. W. Norton, 1969).

16. A. C. Pigou, *The Economics of Welfare* (London: Macmillan, 1932), 332.

17. Laissez-faire and reform liberal scholars largely agree about the structure and causal dynamics of regulatory capture. Thus the neoclassical economist George Stigler writes that "as a rule, regulation is acquired by the industry and is designed and operated primarily for its benefits." Liberal reformers Mark Green and Ralph Nader write that "in short, the regulated industries are often in clear control of the regulatory process." And both critics are dismayed by what they, in common, see. But the source of their dismay—and therefore their preferred reforms—are different. Stigler is unhappy because regulatory capture thwarts the competition and creative destruction of the marketplace, whereas Green and Nader are unhappy because it "blurs what should be a sharp line between regulator and regulatee." So what Green and Nader would like to see is effective "independent regulatory judgement," whereas Stigler would rather let control over the industries in question come from the discipline of market competition instead of from a

government agency. See George Stigler, "The Theory of Economic Regulation," *Bell Journal of Economics and Management Science* 2, no. 1 (1971): 3–21; and Mark Green and Ralph Nader, "Economic Regulation vs. Competition: Uncle Sam the Monopoly Man," *Yale Law Journal* 82, no. 5 (1973): 876.

18. See chap. 3, "The Control of Money," in Friedman, *Capitalism and Freedom*.

19. Friedrich Engels, "Socialism: Utopian and Scientific," in *Marx and Engels: Basic Writings on Politics and Philosophy*, ed. Lewis Feuer (Garden City, NY: Doubleday Anchor Books, 1959), 100.

20. Another significant factor in this picture of capitalism as unsustainable was the claim that each sharp economic contraction threw marginal producers into the ranks of unpropertied laborers and concentrated the capital stock of the country in fewer and fewer hands.

21. Arthur Koestler, *The God That Failed*, ed. Richard Crossman (New York: Harper and Brothers, 1952), 13.

22. See Conrad Black, "Capitalism's Savior," *Wall Street Journal*, October 29, 2003.

23. See John Maynard Keynes, *The General Theory of Employment, Interest and Money* (London: Macmillan, 1936). For an accessible secondary account, see Nicholas Wapshott, *Keynes Hayek: The Clash That Defined Modern Economics* (New York: W. W. Norton, 2011).

TWO. The Moral Philosophy Debate

1. John Locke, *Second Treatise of Civil Government* 5.34, in *Of Civil Government: Two Treatises* (1924; repr., London: J. M. Dent and Sons, 1955).

2. William Graham Sumner, *What Social Classes Owe to Each Other* (New York: Harper and Brothers, 1883), excerpted in Michael Levy, *Political Thought in America: An Anthology* (Chicago: Dorsey Press, 1988), 325–29.

3. Russell Conwell, *Acres of Diamonds* (New York: Harper and Row, 1915), excerpted in Levy, *Political Thought in America*, 337–38.

4. Edmond Cahn, *The Sense of Injustice* (Bloomington: Indiana University Press, 1964), 13, 14, 16, 26.

5. Milton Friedman argues, for example, that laws forbidding racial or gender discrimination in hiring or other economic transactions are unnecessary because the market not only is itself "color blind," as it were, but also will punish economic actors who by discriminating are damaging their own economic success. See chap. 7, "Capitalism and Discrimination," in *Capitalism and Freedom* (Chicago: University of Chicago Press, 1962).

6. It should be noted here that free-market advocate Milton Friedman endorses the public provision of primary and secondary education. He does so, however, not as a requisite of treating disadvantaged children fairly, but as a way to deal with the profound "neighborhood effects" (market externalities) of equipping children to become competent and economically productive members of society. This public subsidy of education, he argues, should take the form of providing students with educational "vouchers"— grants that could be used to pay for education at schools of their choosing. See Friedman, *Capitalism and Freedom*, chap. 6.

7. See ibid., chap. 7.

8. John Rawls, *A Theory of Justice* (Cambridge, MA: Harvard University Press, 1971), 104, 74.

9. Ibid., 83.

10. Ibid., 104.

11. Robert Nozick, *Anarchy, State, and Utopia* (New York: Basic Books, 1974), 214.

12. Rawls, *Theory of Justice*, 315.

13. For a more extended treatment of these issues, see my *Getting the Left Right: The Transformation, Decline, and Reformation of American Liberalism* (Lawrence: University Press of Kansas, 2009), chap. 4.

14. William Galston, *Liberal Purposes* (Cambridge: Cambridge University Press, 1991), 159–60.

15. Friedman, *Capitalism and Freedom*, 198.

16. There is, however, in current law something of a loophole for unrealized—and hence not previously taxed—capital gains in an estate. Those capital gains are not subjected to the capital gains tax when passed on except on the part of an estate that exceeds the current exemption from taxation of $5 million per person or $10 million per couple.

17. Rawls, *Theory of Justice*, 3–4.

18. Ibid., 4–5.

19. David Hume, "Of Justice," sec. 3 of "Enquiry Concerning the Principles of Morals," in *Hume's Moral and Political Philosophy*, ed. Henry Aiken (New York: Hafner Press, 1948), 185, 187, 196.

20. Ludwig von Mises, *Liberalism in the Classical Tradition*, trans. Ralph Raico (San Francisco: Cobden Press, 1985), 7.

21. Ibid., 30.

22. Friedman, *Capitalism and Freedom*, 161–62, 164–65, 170.

23. See Erin Brodwin, "The Happiest Countries in the World, According to Neuroscientists, Statisticians, and Economists," *Business Insider*, April 23, 2015, www.businessinsider.com/new-world-happiness-report-2015 -2015-4.

24. Kimberley Yam, "These Are the Happiest Countries in the World," *Huffington Post*, April 24, 2015.

25. Murray Rothbard, *For a New Liberty*, rev. ed. (New York: Libertarian Review Foundation, 1978), 26–27.

26. Ibid., 27.

27. Nozick, *Anarchy, State, and Utopia*, ix.

28. Rothbard, *For a New Liberty*, 29.

29. Ibid., 39.

30. In this country, many would not be reluctant to give Locke's answer. I have certainly read numerous letters to the editor that insisted upon the writer's "God-given" right to any number of things—including the right to own guns. I equally certainly have never found any basis in the scriptures for such claims. But surely part of what prompts such assertions is a conflation of items in our Bill of Rights with Jefferson's rhetorical flourish at the outset of the Declaration of Independence asserting that "all men" not only are "born equal" but also are "endowed by their Creator with certain inalienable rights." (It is also relevant to observe in this context that Jefferson did *not* include property in his specific examples of these rights, citing "life, liberty, and the pursuit of happiness" rather than Locke's references to "life, liberty, and estate.")

31. Rothbard, *For a New Liberty*, 28.

32. Nozick, *Anarchy, State, and Utopia*, 9, 30.

33. Nozick argues that the only real difference between being forced to work as a slave to an individual master and being required by laws passed by a duly elected democratic legislature to pay taxes for "redistributive" purposes is that in the latter case I have more masters. Ibid., 290–92.

34. Walt Whitman, "Democratic Vistas" (1871), in *Whitman: Poetry and Prose* (New York: Library of America, 1996), 971–72.

35. Samuel Fleischacker, *A Short History of Distributive Justice* (Cambridge, MA: Harvard University Press, 2004).

36. Quoted in ibid., 28–29.

37. Quoted in ibid., 26–27.

38. Quoted in ibid., 72–73.

THREE.   **The Democratic Ideals Debate**

1. Walt Whitman, "Democratic Vistas" (1871), in *Whitman: Poetry and Prose*, ed. Justin Kaplan (New York: Library of America, 1996), 970.

2. Benjamin Constant, "The Liberty of Ancients Compared with That of the Moderns," speech delivered in Paris, 1816, oll.libertyfund.org/titles /2251.

3. Edmund Burke, *Reflections on the Revolution in France* (Garden City, NY: Doubleday Anchor Books, 1973), 110.

4. J. G. A. Pocock, *The Machiavellian Moment: Florentine Political Thought and the Atlantic Republican Tradition* (Princeton, NJ: Princeton University Press, 1975).

5. Jean Jacques Rousseau, *The Social Contract and Discourses* (New York: E. P. Dutton, 1950), 153.

6. Louis Hartz, *The Liberal Tradition in America* (New York: Harcourt, Brace, and World, 1955), 11.

7. Bernard Bailyn, *The Ideological Origins of the American Revolution*, enl. ed. (Cambridge, MA: Harvard University Press, 1992); Pocock, *Machiavellian Moment*.

8. Some of the relevant works on this topic are Jeffrey Isaac, "Republicanism versus Liberalism: A Reconsideration," *History of Political Thought* 9, no. 2 (1988): 349–77; Andreas Kalyvas and Ira Katznelson, *Liberal Beginnings: Making a Republic for the Moderns* (Cambridge, MA: Harvard University Press, 1992); Steve Pincus, "Neither Machiavellian Moment nor Possessive Individualism: Commercial Society and the Defenders of the English Commonwealth," *American Historical Review* 103, no. 3 (1998): 705–36.

9. See Herbert Storing, *What the Anti-Federalists Were For* (Chicago: University of Chicago Press, 1981), 20–22, 73, 75.

10. In her examination of Madison's later essays, Colleen Sheehan reports that Madison displayed there the conviction that "to advance the conditions that form the character and spirit of the citizenry is the first duty of republican statesmen." *The Mind of James Madison: The Legacy of Classical Republicanism* (New York: Cambridge University Press, 2015), 113.

11. "What gripped their minds," writes Bailyn of the colonists, "was the political history of Rome from the conquests in the east and the civil wars in the early first century B.C. to the establishment of the empire on the ruins of the republic at the end of the second century A.D." The colonists drew in particular on writers such as Cicero, Sallust, and Tacitus, who "had hated and feared the trends of their own time, and in their writing had contrasted the present with a better past. . . . The earlier age had been full of virtue: simplicity, patriotism, integrity, a love of justice and of liberty; the present was venal, cynical, and oppressive. For the colonists . . . the analogies to their own times were compelling. They saw their own provincial virtues—rustic and old-fashioned, sturdy and effective—challenged by the corruption at the center

of power, by the threat of tyranny, and by a constitution gone wrong." Bailyn, *Ideological Origins*, 32.

12. Alexis de Tocqueville, *Democracy in America*, trans. George Lawrence, ed. J. P. Mayer (Garden City, NY: Doubleday, 1969), 39, 44.

13. Thomas Jefferson to John Adams, October 28, 1813: "On Aristocracy, Natural and Artificial."

14. Milton Friedman, *Capitalism and Freedom* (Chicago: University of Chicago Press, 1962), 5.

15. See William Galston, *Liberal Pluralism* (New York: Cambridge University Press, 2002).

16. John Locke, *Second Treatise of Civil Government* 2.4, in *Of Civil Government: Two Treatises* (1924; repr., London: J. M. Dent and Sons, 1955). Subsequent citations are to this edition by chapter and section numbers and are given parenthetically in the text.

17. Locke is here citing and endorsing words of the Anglican divine Richard Hooker, in his *Laws of Ecclesiastical Polity*.

18. These are, Locke writes, quoting Richard Hooker once more, "rules and canons, natural reason both drawn for direction of life [of which] no man is ignorant" (2.5).

19. Carl Becker, *The Heavenly City of the Eighteenth Century Philosophers* (New Haven, CT: Yale University Press, 1932); Marquis de Condorcet, *Sketch for a Historical Picture of the Progress of the Human Mind*, trans. June Barraclough (London: Weidenfeld and Nicolson, 1955).

20. Priestley, in his *Essay on the First Principles of Government*, quoted in Becker, *Heavenly City*, 145.

21. Condorcet, *Sketch*, 201. Subsequent citations to this work are given parenthetically by page number in the text.

22. Bruce Ackerman and Ann Alstott, *The Stakeholder Society* (New Haven, CT: Yale University Press, 2000), 4.

23. John Stuart Mill, *On Liberty*, ed. Currin V. Shields (1859; repr., Indianapolis: Bobbs-Merrill, 1966), 14.

24. John Stuart Mill, *Considerations on Representative Government* (1861; repr., Chicago: Henry Regnery, 1962), 50–52.

25. Ibid., 47.

26. Ibid., 46.

27. Ibid., 59–60.

28. Mill did, however, make some qualifications to full universal suffrage. He endorsed a literacy requirement. He thought all who voted needed to pay some tax. And he once even toyed with the idea of giving the more highly educated a greater say, perhaps by giving them several votes—although

he recognized that the dangers and problems with such a scheme rendered it impractical.

29. Mill, *Considerations*, 166, 168.

30. Mill, *On Liberty*, ed. Shields, 71, 77.

31. Ibid., 16.

32. Ibid., 13. Given Mill's talk about what is rightful here, it is worth noting that he is not offering what philosophers would call a "deontological" argument—that is, an argument grounded in claims about rights and justice. Mill explicitly disavows that. "It is proper to state that I forego any advantage which could be derived to my argument from the idea of abstract right as a thing independent of utility . . . in the largest sense, grounded on the permanent interests of man as a progressive being." So, given that disclaimer, his ultimate justification for the harm principle would seem to be that members of a human society "are greater gainers by suffering each other to live [and think and speak and associate] as seems good to themselves than by compelling each to live as seems good to the rest" (14, 17).

33. Whitman, "Democratic Vistas," 953.

34. Ibid., 971–72, 976.

35. Ibid., 971–73.

36. Benjamin Barber, *An Aristocracy of Everyone* (New York: Ballantine Books, 1992).

37. As Kant explains, "It does not require that we know how to attain the moral improvement of men but only that we should know the mechanism of nature to use it on men," and "Thus it is only a question of a good organization of the state (which does lie in man's power), whereby the powers of each selfish inclination are so arranged in opposition that one moderates or destroys the ruinous effect of the other." From the First Supplement, "Of the Guarantee for Perpetual Peace," in *Immanuel Kant on History*, ed. and trans. Lewis White Beck (Upper Saddle River, NJ: Prentice Hall, 1964).

38. Milton Friedman, *Capitalism and Freedom* (Chicago: University of Chicago Press, 1962), 1–2.

39. Regarding Smith, I once had a very capable and conservatively inclined student who wanted to write an honors thesis on the relationship between markets and morals. The plan was for him to read some of the relevant works of Adam Smith, Milton Friedman, Irving Kristol, and Daniel Bell over the summer as background for the thesis. Came the fall, and he appeared at my office, sat down, and looked at me with a mixture of dismay and confusion. I said to him, "You look a bit distressed, Mark. What's the problem?" He paused for a while, and then said in a pained voice: "Adam Smith and Milton Friedman are not at all alike." I laughed and responded, "That just

shows that you have done your reading well." For academic accounts of some of the ways in which Smith—however acute he was in touting the vast superiority of free trade and free markets to protectionism and mercantilism—was not an uncritical advocate of either laissez-faire economics or the minimal state, see Jerry Z. Muller, *Adam Smith in His Time and Ours* (New York: Free Press, 1993), and A. K. Sen, "Capitalism beyond the Crisis," *New York Review of Books*, March 26, 2009.

40. Robert Nozick, *Anarchy, State and Utopia* (New York: Basic Books, 1974), 331–32.

41. Henry Maine, *Ancient Law*, chap. 5 (Cambridge: Cambridge University Press, 1861); William Graham Sumner, "What Social Classes Give to Each Other," in *Political Thought in America*, 2nd ed., ed. Michael Levy (Chicago: Dorsey Press, 1988), 327.

42. Ayn Rand, *Atlas Shrugged* (New York: Penguin Books, 1957), 940.

43. Tyler Cowen, "The United States of Texas: Why the Lone Star State Is America's Future," *Time* magazine, October 28, 2013, 30–37.

44. *Reflections on the Revolution in France* (1793; repr., New York: Doubleday Anchor Books, 1973), 110.

45. Alexis de Tocqueville, *Democracy in America* 2.2.2, trans. Henry Reeve, ed. Richard Heffner (New York: Mentor Books, 1956), 192–93.

46. Charles Murray, *In Pursuit of Happiness and Good Government* (New York: Simon and Schuster, 1988).

47. Tocqueville, *Democracy in America* 1.2.2, trans. Reeve, ed. Heffner, 95.

48. Alexander Hamilton, *Federalist Papers*, no. 15 (New York: Signet, 2014).

49. See chap. 10, "A Framework for Utopia," in Nozick's *Anarchy, State, and Utopia*, and also Murray's conclusion to *In Pursuit of Happiness*, where he writes that Jefferson's model of government centered on county-size "wards" is "a vision suitable not only for a struggling agricultural nation at the outset of the nineteenth century but also for a wealthy postindustrial nation at the close of the twentieth" (303).

50. Barry Shain, *The Myth of American Individualism: The Protestant Origins of American Political Thought* (Princeton, NJ: Princeton University Press, 1994), 32. Shain also argues that this was clearly the dominant view of Revolutionary-era Americans, who "believed that the needs and good of the public must be awarded priority over those of the individual" (23). In part, Shain observes, that is because this civic republican view cohered with the regnant Protestant moral philosophy of the time.

51. www.johnlocke.org.

52. Locke, *Second Treatise* 9.123, 124, 138.

53. Locke, *Second Treatise* 5.27, 2.6.

54. Locke, *Second Treatise* 11.140.

55. Whitman, "Democratic Vistas," 971–72; John Stuart Mill, *Considerations on Representative Government* (Chicago: Henry Regnery, 1962), 32.

56. Mill, *On Liberty*, chap. 5, ed. Shields, 140.

57. Tocqueville, *Democracy in America* 2.4.6, trans. Lawrence, ed. Mayer, 692.

58. Mill, *On Liberty*, chap. 5, ed. Shields, 115.

59. Ibid.

60. Mill, *Principles of Political Economy* 5.11.11, ed. Jonathan Riley (New York: Oxford University Press, 1998), 349.

61. Mill, *On Liberty*, chap. 5, ed. Shields, 128–29.

62. Mill, *Principles of Political Economy* 5.11.13, ed. Riley, 356. Mill cautions his readers there, however, that "there are few things for which it is more mischievous that people should rely on the habitual aid of others, than for the means of subsistence, and unhappily there is no lesson which they more easily learn." For practical reasons, therefore, "the condition of those who are supported by legal charity" should "be kept considerably less desirable than the condition of those who find support for themselves" (5.11.13, ed. Riley, 354–55).

63. Mill, *On Liberty*, chap. 5, ed. Shields, 140.

64. Mill, *Principles of Political Economy* 5.11.9, ed. Riley, 343.

65. Mill, *On Liberty*, chap. 5, ed. Shields, 116.

66. Mill, *Principles of Political Economy* 5.11.12., ed. Riley, 349–51.

67. Mill, *Principles of Political Economy* 5.11.15, ed. Riley, 363–66.

FOUR.   Why No Slam-Dunk Answers

1. Richard Posner, *A Failure of Capitalism: The Crisis of '08 and the Descent into Depression* (Cambridge, MA: Harvard University Press, 2009).

2. A reader seeking an example of the kind of judgments and arguments that I have in mind could do much worse than turn to the book I cited just above, Richard Posner's *Failure of Capitalism*, which seeks to explain the causes of the recession of 2008–9. Some readers might disagree with some of his judgments about the relative significance of the contributory actions, forces, and events that produced the outcome in question. But no one can argue that this is anything other than an exemplary case of the kind of careful and informed explanatory arguments necessary and proper in this area.

3. Edmond Cahn, *The Sense of Injustice* (Bloomington: Indiana University Press, 1949), 13–16.

4. As Paul Ryan's favorite author, Ayn Rand, has written: "The man who creates a new invention receives but a small percentage of his value in terms of material payment, no matter what fortune he makes. . . . But the man who works as a janitor in the factory producing that invention receives an enormous payment in proportion to the mental effort that his job requires of him. . . . The man at the top of the intellectual pyramid contributes the most to all those below him. . . . The man at the bottom who, left to himself, would starve in his hopeless ineptitude, contributes nothing to those above him, but receives the bonus of all their brains." Ayn Rand, *Atlas Shrugged* (New York: Signet Books, 1957), 979–80.

5. The only exceptions to this rule have come where the person who failed to assist had some special relationship with the one in trouble—a relationship that involved responsibility, as in a parent's responsibility for a child.

6. The principal exception to this fundamental requirement of the criminal law arises in cases of "criminal negligence"—where the party subject to criminal penalty clearly failed to observe obvious requirements of taking care. If I ran my car over someone while trying to drive blindfolded, for example, my lack of specific intent to kill that person would likely keep me from being charged with first-degree murder. But I would certainly be charged with "negligent homicide."

7. For a more extensive look at the challenges and moral dilemmas that disparate family circumstances create for democratic society, see James Fishkin, *Justice, Equal Opportunity, and the Family* (New Haven, CT: Yale University Press, 1984).

8. John Tomasi, *Liberalism beyond Justice* (Princeton, NJ: Princeton University Press, 2001), xvi.

Conclusion

1. Milton Friedman, *Capitalism and Freedom* (Chicago: University of Chicago Press, 1962), 11.

2. This pacifying influence was part of Montesquieu's thesis about "sweet commerce" in his *The Spirit of the Laws*. For useful secondary accounts of this argument by various theorists, see Albert Hirschman, *The Passions and the Interests* (Princeton, NJ: Princeton University Press, 1977); Dennis Rasmussen, *The Problems and Promise of Commercial Society* (University Park: Pennsylvania State University Press, 2008).

3. Adam Smith, *The Wealth of Nations* 1.10.2, ed. Edwin Cannan (London: Methuen, 1904), 130.

4. West Coast Hotel Co. v. Parrish, 300 U.S. 379 (1937).

5. Smith, *Wealth of Nations* 1.8, ed. Cannan, 80.

6. For a useful and accessible overview of the highways portion of this story, see John Williamson, "Federal Aid to Roads and Highways since the 18th Century," Congressional Research Service Publication, January 6, 2012, https://fas.org/sgp/crs/misc/R42140.pdf.

7. Ibid., 1–2.

8. John Stuart Mill, *Principles of Political Economy* 5.11, ed. Jonathan Riley (Oxford: Oxford University Press, 1994), 364.

9. Chad Foote and Robert Atkinson, "Dwindling Support for R&D Is a Recipe for Economic and Strategic Decline," Information Technology and Innovation Foundation newsletter, December 14, 2018.

10. For a recent argument on behalf of "economic dignity," see the recent essay by Gene Sperling, who served as national economic adviser and director of the National Economic Council for both President Obama and President Clinton: "Economic Dignity," *Democracy Journal*, no. 52 (Spring 2019).

11. Rousseau, *The Social Contract* 2.11, trans. G. D. H. Cole (New York: E. P. Dutton, 1950), 50.

12. Milton Friedman, for example, writes that he cannot conjure up any neighborhood effects or important monopoly effects that would justify governmental activity in the area of national parks. *Capitalism and Freedom*, 31. And the libertarian humorist P. I. O'Rourke has invited us to take poorly kept public toilets as the paradigm of public facilities.

13. Michael Kimmelman, "Chicago Finds a Way to Improve Public Housing; Libraries," *New York Times*, May 15, 2019.

14. Alexis de Tocqueville, *Democracy in America* 2.2.2, trans. Henry Reeve, ed. Richard Heffner (New York: Mentor Books, 1956), 192–93.

15. Friedman, *Capitalism and Freedom*, 11; Lawrence Brown and Lawrence Jacobs, *The Private Abuse of the Public Interest* (Chicago: University of Chicago Press, 2008), chap. 4.

INDEX

financial institutions, regulations of, 40–41

fiscal policy, 63–64, 65, 210, 211

Fleischacker, Samuel, 97, 99

Food and Drug Administration, 46, 55, 205, 214

food supply market, 45–46, 213–14

forced labor, 193, 240n33

Ford, Ernie, 76

Freddie Mac, 169

freedom: in American political culture, 4–5; economic, 127–28; personal, 198–99

free marketplace: arrangement and procedures in, 150–51; charac-teristics of, 20–21; controversies of, 11, 207–16; debates about fair outcome of, 171; demo-cratic society and, 10–11, 190, 191, 199–200, 203; distributive criterion of, 70–71, 91–92, 102, 195; economic actors of, 150; economic outcomes of, 10, 66, 195–98, 202; effectiveness of, 64, 69, 203; establishment of prices in, 196–97, 204; explana-tions of lagging growth of, 64–65; good society and, 104–5; government interference into, 23–24, 202–5; incentives of, 19; innovations and, 197–98; international order and, 201; investments in, 64; justice and, 102–3, 201–2; limitations of, 216–21; Marxist view of, 191; moral criteria of, 56, 70, 90–92, 102; nondiscriminatory force of, 82, 83; norms and institu-tions of, 150; occupational choice in, 198–99; personal freedoms and, 198–99, 202; political benefits of, 198–203; "poor man" and, 91; private property and, 91; productive labor in, 193–94; promotion of, 4, 7–8; prosperity and, 102, 163, 171; protection of consumers, 204, 205; protection of private sphere, 199; public interest and, 57; real-world deviations from optimal performance of, 203–7; recessions and, 61; self-regulation of, 14–15, 20–21, 151; social benefits of, 191, 200–201, 202; vs. socialism, 3–4; volun-tary exchange in, 14; vs. welfare state, 8–10

Friedman, Milton: advocacy of laissez-faire economy, 59; *Capitalism and Freedom*, 141; comparison to Adam Smith, 243n39; on distribution of economic resources, 28, 93; economic advisory role of, 119; on economic externalities, 51; on free-market distribution, 91–92; on government interfer-ence in the economy, 94, 149, 229; on investment in human capital, 52, 53; on laws against racial or gender discrimi-nation, 238n5; on moral admonitions, 141; on neighbor-hood effects, 22, 148–49, 247n11; proposal of income tax, 87; on public education, 149, 239n6; on regulation of monopolies, 43, 44; on special pleading, 26

Fukuyama, Francis: *The End of History,* 4

Gallatin, Albert, 218
Galston, William, 86, 87, 120
Gates, Bill, 197
General Electric company, 236n4
General Motors, 38, 39
General Will, concept of, 114
Germany, and labor policy, 50
Glorious Revolution, 114
GNP (Gross National Product), 164
God That Failed, The (Koestler), 61
Goldwater, Barry, 119, 236n4
good society, 104–5, 183, 184, 186, 190
Gore, Al, 6
government intervention in the economy: compensatory interventions, 214–15, 221; costs of, 56–58; countercyclical effects of, 61–62, 207–8; critique of, 57–58; fiscal policy, 210–11, 215–16; forms of, 206, 210; goal of, 55–56; legitimate causes of, 204–6; monetary policy, 210–11; moral arrogance and, 26–27; motivations for, 23, 24–25; persistence in, 25–26; priming the pump approach, 65–66; protection of members of the public, 206–7, 213–14; regulation of contract agreements, 205–6; self-seeking interest groups and, 26; social insurance programs, 210, 211–12; technical monopoly and, 23–24
government investments: in agriculture, 215; in education, 220–21, 223; in health care,

220; in human capital, 219–20, 222–23; in infrastructure, 216; in law enforcement agencies, 216–17; in public spaces, 223–25; in scientific research and development, 219; in transportation, 217–18
government oversight agencies, 46
government programs, 6, 50
Great Britain: Act of Toleration, 125, 153; Bill of Rights, 125, 153; colonial rule, 116; National Insurance Act, 211; right to vote, 132; Stamp Tax, 123–24; taxation, 132; Third Reform Act, 132
Great Depression of the 1930s, 29, 61, 62, 65, 168, 209, 212
greater good, 89, 90
Great Recession of 2008–9, 168–70, 209, 213
Greece, and economic crisis, 49, 51
Green, Mark, 237n17
Grotius, Hugo, 98

Hamilton, Alexander, 148
happiness: conception of, 133; highest-ranked countries, 93; income level and, 92–93, 195
hard labor, 76
harm principle, 136
Harrington, James, 113
Hartz, Louis, 114
Hayek, Friedrich von, 4, 8, 59, 142, 146
health care market, 45, 220–21, 232. *See also* public health
Henry, Patrick, 6
Heritage Foundation, 7
Hobbes, Thomas, 36, 184

Medicaid, 6, 28, 221
Medicare, 6, 9, 28, 30, 221
Mill, John Stuart: account of repre-
    sentative government, 134–36,
    138, 157, 159; on capitalism-
    democracy relationships,
    158–59; on charity, 245n62;
    conception of happiness, 133;
    democratic theory of, 120,
    134–36, 156, 157; on govern-
    ment enterprises, 160; on harm
    principle, 136, 243n32; on
    legitimate government activity,
    157–58; *On Liberty*, 91, 132, 133,
    137; on market performance,
    158–59; on practical monopoly,
    159; on principle of individual
    liberty, 160; *Principles of
    Political Economy*, 218; on
    protection of employees, 160;
    on provision of economic
    resources, 159–60; on public
    investments, 218; on purpose
    of democracy, 157, 228; on
    right to vote, 135, 242n28; on
    self-governance, 135; on trade,
    158; utilitarianism of, 132–33;
    works of, 132
Mine Safety and Health Adminis-
    tration, 214
minimum-wage laws, 2, 3, 28,
    206–7, 232
mixed economy, 227
monetary policy, 61–62
money, 18–19
monopoly, 41–42, 43–44, 159, 203–4
Montesquieu, Charles-Louis de
    Secondat, Baron de, 113
moral imperatives of duties and
    rights, 100

moral philosophy debate, 10, 69–71;
    individual rights arguments,
    93–96; justice-based arguments
    for market allocations, 71–75;
    justice-based arguments for
    "welfare state" distribution,
    75–88; non-justice-based moral
    arguments, 88–96; welfare state
    rights arguments, 96–102
moral pluralism, 183, 184, 185, 186
moral tradition, 97, 98
mortgage market, 169
Murray, Charles, 146

Nader, Ralph, 237n17
National Institute of Health, 221
National Labor Relations Act
    (1935), 207
National Public Radio, 27
natural inequities, 230
natural rights, 95, 97, 103
natural sciences, 126–27, 128–29
negative externalities, 204
neighborhood effects, 22, 50–51,
    148–49
New Deal liberalism, 2, 9, 29, 30,
    36, 56
New England Puritanism, 117
New Left, 3
Newton, Isaac, 127
Nixon, Richard, 2–3
nondiscrimination, principle of,
    81–82, 83
Norquist, Grover, 143, 144
Nozick, Robert, 85, 86, 94, 95–96,
    143, 240n33

Obama, Barack, 29, 79, 236n4
Occupational Safety and Health
    Administration, 214

THOMAS A. SPRAGENS, JR., is professor emeritus of political science
at Duke University. He is the author of numerous books, including the
prizewinning *Civic Liberalism: Reflections on Our Democratic Ideals*.

CPSIA information can be obtained
at www.ICGtesting.com
Printed in the USA
LVHW041458041221
705284LV00015B/848

9 780268 200145